FAITH COMMUNITIES AND THE FIGHT
FOR RACIAL JUSTICE

Faith Communities and the Fight for Racial Justice

WHAT HAS WORKED, WHAT HASN'T, AND LESSONS WE CAN LEARN

ROBERT WUTHNOW

PRINCETON UNIVERSITY PRESS

PRINCETON & OXFORD

Published by Princeton University Press
41 William Street, Princeton, New Jersey 08540
99 Banbury Road, Oxford OX2 6JX

press.princeton.edu

All Rights Reserved

Library of Congress Cataloging-in-Publication Data

Names: Wuthnow, Robert, author.
Title: Faith communities and the fight for racial justice: what has worked,
    what hasn't, and lessons we can learn / Robert Wuthnow.
Description: Princeton: Princeton University Press, 2023 | Includes bibliographical
    references and index.
Identifiers: LCCN 2022051020 (print) | LCCN 2022051021 (ebook) |
    ISBN 9780691250830 (hardback) | ISBN 9780691250885 (ebook)
Subjects: LCSH: Civil rights—Religious aspects—United States. |
    Racial justice—United States. | Religious leaders—United States. |
    Civil rights leaders—United States. | BISAC: SOCIAL SCIENCE /
    Sociology of Religion | POLITICAL SCIENCE / Civics & Citizenship
Classification: LCC BL65.C58 W884 2023 (print) | LCC BL65.C58 (ebook) |
    DDC 201/.723—dc23/eng20230422
LC record available at https://lccn.loc.gov/2022051020
LC ebook record available at https://lccn.loc.gov/2022051021

British Library Cataloging-in-Publication Data is available

Editorial: Fred Appel and James Collier
Production Editorial: Theresa Liu
Jacket/Cover Design: Heather Hansen
Production: Erin Suydam
Publicity: Kate Hensley and Kathryn Stevens
Copyeditor: Jennifer Harris

Jacket image: Orkhan Farmanli / Unsplash

This book has been composed in Arno (Classic)

Printed on acid-free paper. ∞

Printed in the United States of America

10 9 8 7 6 5 4 3 2 1

CONTENTS

FAITH COMMUNITIES AND THE FIGHT FOR RACIAL JUSTICE

Introduction

THIS BOOK traces the history of Black and White faith leaders' fight for racial justice since the end of the civil rights movement. It is the story of what they did, how they did it, and what happened as a result. The story is rich in instances of courageous leaders working in small ways to combat discrimination. There is much to be learned about what worked and what can work again.

This is also the story of why these efforts so often failed—how faith communities' advocacy ran into barriers posed by the social, cultural, and political realities of the times, and indeed by the very institutions in which they worked.

The tragic deaths of Trayvon Martin, Michael Brown, Freddie Gray, George Floyd, Breonna Taylor and so many others in recent years have pricked the conscience of faith leaders far and wide. Much is being written and many discussions are being held. This is a teaching moment, many say. They hope it is. They want it to be.

Teaching moments are hard. They require frank discussions of why good intentions so often falter—why a troubled conscience is not enough, why it is difficult to turn beliefs into actions. Therefore, it helps to look at what has been tried—to examine what has been effective and what hasn't.

Faith communities' advocacy for racial justice has been neglected in the recent history of American religion. These efforts have been overshadowed by the Religious Right. Vast collections have been filled with writings about the likes of Jerry Falwell and Pat Robertson and others at the conservative end of the political spectrum. Much less is known about the Black pastors and White pastors who joined forces to create affordable housing, speak against hate crimes, combat segregation, and advocate for voting rights. Even less is known about quiet congregational exchanges, after-school programs, and police review committees. Yet, all of these initiatives were happening, often in quiet ways that garnered little public attention.

How did these initiatives get started? What did leaders who were inspired by the civil rights movement keep doing long after the headlines shifted to other topics? Where did the funding come from to launch anti-racism programs? To issue policy statements? To bring lawsuits? How did coalitions get formed? Why did some initiatives succeed while others failed?

These are the questions this book tries to answer. They are big questions that must be tackled by looking at the specific issues with which racial justice advocacy has been concerned in recent decades. The most important of these have been fair housing, community development, busing, affirmative action, hate crimes, and criminal justice. There have also been considerable efforts to bring about racial reckonings within congregations. And to mobilize protests, political action, and voter registration.

I've combed every source I could think of to learn how progressive faith communities have tried to work on these issues. The story starts in the early 1970s and extends to the present, developing in fits and starts, focusing on different issues at different times, and engaging Black and White faith leaders who sometimes worked cooperatively and more often tackled problems in complementary ways. The materials through which their work can be told are from denominational deliberations, ethnographic studies, quantitative data, government reports, court cases, and vast numbers of on-the-scene accounts written by local observers. Many of the scholars on whose work I draw are ones I have been privileged to know and to learn from over the years. I stitch together the chronology of events in which faith leaders participated, describe the organizations and networks they worked with, and locate what they did within the context of major policy initiatives.

A popular view holds that religious communities have done next to nothing to advance racial justice in recent decades. Whatever faith leaders may have done earlier, this idea tells us, their endeavors died with the civil rights movement. White churches and Black churches alike turned their back on racial reckoning. But that view is wrong.

Little-known faith leaders did what they could to push for racial justice. Faith communities mobilized the leadership and resources to create fair and affordable housing, contribute to community development, support school desegregation, advocate for affirmative action, protest racial profiling, demonstrate against police violence, and mobilize voter registration. These were efforts that need to be remembered. They hold lessons relevant today.

The barriers that religious groups faced are equally important. The barriers were rooted in more than indifference and ill-informed attitudes. The barriers were power structures—social arrangements that often had no ill-will in their intent. They were entrenchments that resisted transformation. These barriers hold lessons too.

The leaders I write about would mostly call themselves progressives. They would mean to say they supported racial equality, were interested in bridging the divide between Blacks and Whites, and were eager to assist in advancing racial justice in the churches and society. Being progressive in this way did not mean they agreed with one another on theology, doctrine, or styles of worship. Often, they did not. Nor did it mean that they represented large constituencies who believed as they did. There were critics within their congregations and denominations as well as supporters.[1]

The advocacy groups, leaders, and congregations in this story were affiliated with majority-White Protestant denominations, Black denominations, Roman Catholic groups, and Jewish organizations. Many of the Protestants were African Methodist Episcopal, Baptist, Lutheran, Methodist, Presbyterian, or United Church of Christ. Some were

Brethren, Disciples of Christ, Mennonites, Moravians, or Quakers. Many of the groups were coalitions of faith-based and nonsectarian organizations.

Much of their advocacy work was performed through church agencies and local congregations, usually by clergy, staff, and lay people acting under the formal auspices of their denominations. The advocacy in which they participated was often spearheaded by Black clergy and in many instances was coordinated by interracial coalitions of Black churches and White churches. It was conducted locally, regionally, and nationally through interfaith cooperation involving Roman Catholic, evangelical Protestant, Black Protestant, Orthodox, Jewish, and Muslim organizations.

I begin the story in 1974, the year of Watergate and Richard Nixon's resignation—the year the nation manifestly hoped to be turning the corner toward a more placid future, putting the turbulent 1960s in the past. Before that, many religious leaders—White as well as Black—had of course been involved in the civil rights movement, or, if not personally active, had been influenced by the movement's ideas. For that reason, many discussions of racial advocacy call readers' attention to the civil rights era as a period to be remembered and to be inspired by. But in so doing, these discussions fail to benefit from the important lessons that can be learned from faith communities' less visible roles in the intervening decades.[2]

By the mid-1970s, the struggle for racial justice was less often talked about but it was far from over. Discrimination and inequality in educational attainment, jobs, affordable housing, healthcare, criminal justice, and voting rights were still the realities that defined American race relations. Nixon's resignation left in place many of the policies that impeded fair housing and effective school desegregation. Many civil rights leaders anticipated that the battle to address racial injustice would now be fought less often in the streets and more significantly in legislative chambers, the courts, city councils, and board rooms. Whether those efforts would receive much support from the public was doubtful. The national mood after Watergate was one of exhaustion with the turmoil of campus unrest, the Vietnam War, and revelations of government misconduct. Across the political spectrum, the focus of national policy shifted to the inflation-plagued economy and Middle East foreign policy.

The priorities defining religion were shifting as well. Jimmy Carter's election in 1976 brought White evangelical "born again" Protestantism to public attention. By the end of the decade, Jerry Falwell's Moral Majority was mobilizing conservative Christians concerned about abortion and homosexuality. For their part, progressive religious groups were focused on ecumenism, gender equality, and nuclear disarmament. It was unclear if many of the progressive faith communities— White or Black—would continue the work for racial justice that Dr. Martin Luther King Jr. had begun. Yet that work did continue— usually in quieter ways but often with significant results.

One of the little known and generally forgotten endeavors I write about occurred near Ferguson, Missouri, four decades before Michael Brown was killed there in 2014. The leader in the story was a young White seminary graduate who organized a housing desegregation project that sparked controversy in the White House and resulted in what became known as the doctrine of disparate impact liability. I describe the key roles that several local churches played in this episode and locate it in the larger context of federal fair and affordable housing programs.

Another largely neglected episode is the story of a Black Presbyterian minister who initiated the nation's first city-wide busing program in Charlotte, North Carolina. This endeavor included dozens of Charlotte's churches, some of which supported the plan and others of which founded private segregation academies rather than participate. The Charlotte program was also crucial to the traumatic cross-town busing initiative in Boston where faith leaders were active both locally and in the state department of education.

Among the other endeavors I write about is the Wilmington Ten case that captured national and international attention—a case that started at a church in Wilmington and was led by a Black high school chemistry teacher who earned a divinity school degree while in prison and became one of his denomination's leading spokespersons for racial justice. He was succeeded in that role by Reverend Traci Blackmon, currently the faith leader who has done more than anyone else to forge ties with Black Lives Matter.

Much of what faith leaders working for racial justice did was strategically local. It happened in response to local events, took place in neighborhoods and towns and school districts, was led by local clergy, and drew on local networks. One of these episodes took place in a small community on the outskirts of Detroit when White supremacists decided to use the community as a staging ground for their meetings and cross burnings. Under the inspiring leadership of an elderly Black parishioner and her White Methodist minister, the community's churches organized an effective plan of resistance to the supremacists.

Advocacy in local communities has continued through the decades. It was the Los Angeles Council of Religious Leaders that organized churches' response to Rodney King's brutal beating in 1991, the Black Ministers Council of New Jersey that played a leading role in drawing public attention to racial profiling in 1998, a little-known Black pastor named Leah Daughtry who led the Democratic party's faith outreach program during the Obama campaign in 2008, and an offshoot of the Sisters of Mercy that the Obama administration enlisted to manage the Neighborhood Stabilization Program in Chicago from 2009 to 2013.

Progressive advocacy for racial justice rarely mobilizes massive participation among rank-and-file churchgoers. The best scholarship on progressive advocacy has shown that less attention should be paid to religion's role in national elections, important as national elections are, and instead should pay greater attention to the strategic local organizing that emerges through the work of a few dedicated leaders. In their landmark study of African American religion, C. Eric Lincoln and Lawrence Mamiya, for example, argued that community organizing and community building arranged in cooperation with other churches and civil rights groups, rather than only electoral politics, are central to Black churches' public engagement. Richard Wood, Mark Warren, Jeffrey Stout, Ruth Braunstein, and many other students of progressive faith-based advocacy emphasize interfaith cooperation as well. These writers urge focusing on the *local* roots of advocacy rather than viewing it as a top-down endeavor. Although ecumenical bodies such as the National Council of Churches and the national offices of major Protestant denominations and the Roman Catholic Church issue statements and offer financial support, these organizations' critics are usually correct in pointing out that the leaders at the top of these groups do not speak for the millions of members the leaders claim to represent. The progressive advocacy that has been most engaged in social justice has been more specialized, local, and directly engaged in grassroots endeavors. Yet it has never been strictly local but has broadened its scope to take account of metropolitan, regional, and national policies.[3]

In her path-breaking research on congregations' organizational networks, Nancy Tatom Ammerman observed that "almost all congregational political and economic activism is channeled through larger outside coalitions and agencies."[4] That has certainly been true of progressive advocacy for racial justice, much of which has been organized through *coalitions*—through people working together across congregations or denominations and among faiths.

The ingredients making these cooperative ventures possible include the following. First, to be interfaith across traditions as diverse as Christianity, Judaism, and Islam—or even to be ecumenical among diverse Protestant denominations—requires a willingness to embrace other traditions as strategic partners. The partners need not share the same theological tenets or adhere to the same styles of worship (usually they do not), but they must see the advantage of working together, and they are more likely to see that advantage if they do acknowledge that groups other than their own have access to the sacred. Second, to be a cooperative venture implies investing time away from the demands of running one's own congregation toward the staffing and maintenance of the coalition. This is an investment that seems reasonable because the coalition brings together expertise and differing perspectives, represents different constituencies, and in combination is more than the sum of its parts. Progressive faith-based coalitions in many instances include among their participants—or work with—organizations that are not faith-oriented, such as labor unions, nonprofit community development corporations, and civil rights groups. And third, faith-based cooperative projects imply an understanding of the value of organized teamwork, meaning that they have committee deliberations, elected boards, and leading contributors rather than being devoted to the "cult of personality" that develops around a single charismatic figure.[5]

Studies show that progressive faith-based communities attract participants who value personal *spiritual practice*. They care deeply about their faith but are also convinced that spiritual practice should contribute to the common good through activities that focus not only on individuals' private lives but also on institutions. Their understanding of spiritual practice emphasizes personal conviction but is equally oriented toward acts that reach into the community. In this regard, progressive faith-based communities differ from ministries that focus almost exclusively on prayer, scripture study, and worship done in the interest of achieving personal fulfillment and eternal salvation. Progressive groups are like many conservative advocacy groups, whose participants also want to reform social institutions. The difference of course is in the kinds of reform desired and the activities through which those reforms are promoted. Examples of these divergent issues and activities in recent decades are not hard to find, often being identified with one or the other of the two political parties and differing about understandings of sexuality, gender, and social welfare.[6]

Perhaps the best, but least appreciated, reason to be interested in religious groups' racial justice advocacy is to understand the hindrances they have confronted. Some discussions treat these hindrances as if they result simply from individuals in the past making racist decisions. That may be true, but the study of racial inequality goes further and means something more when it stresses that racism is *systemic*. Scholars agree that racism persists not only in prejudice and discrimination but also in institutions. An abundance of evidence demonstrates that racism persists through patterns of behavior that are taken for granted and, without anyone having to think about it or necessarily having ill intent, these structures perpetuate unequal access to jobs, educational opportunities, healthcare, housing, criminal justice, and political influence. To say that racism is systemic therefore is not to suggest that it is vague, abstract, or incomprehensible but that racial inequality is perpetuated through decisions in particular institutional settings that reflect the ways in which power is structured in those settings. Systemic racism results from the history of enslavement, segregation, and voter suppression that subjugated the lives of Black Americans throughout the nation's past and have continued to do so today. Systemic racism therefore requires understanding how institutions work, how they become power structures, and how they impede the efforts even of well-intentioned people who want to bring about change.[7]

Systemic racism expresses itself as White privilege in ways as small as not having to worry about being stopped by the police and as large as not being killed if one is stopped by the police. White privilege is also systemic. Whiteness is the invisible default to which behavior is expected to conform, whether on the highway or in the classroom. Whiteness is an expectation about how to speak when answering the phone, greeting a neighbor, or making an appointment. "Acting White," as Monica McDermott persuasively argues in *Whiteness in America*, is not something a person usually has to think about unless that person is not White.[8] White privilege means taking for granted that one's advantages in life are entirely owing to one's own efforts, while failing to understand or care much about the disadvantages that others have faced in pursuing their aspirations.[9]

But popular discussions of Whiteness, including discussions in well-intentioned faith communities, recent studies suggest, too often focus on the tacit norms—mannerisms, modes of speaking, inflections of voice—that govern everyday life, treating these norms as if they can be corrected by White people becoming more conscious of them. White privilege must also be understood as the way in which large-scale social institutions have been—and continue to be—structured to perpetuate both racial inequality and racially differentiated responses to inequality. White privilege in this understanding is less about attitudes—even prejudicial attitudes—than about the institutional arrangements through which asymmetries of power are kept in place. For example, as Stuart Buck shows in *Acting White: The Ironic Legacy of Desegregation,* perceptions of Whiteness and what it means to be White or not White are profoundly influenced by the manner in which school desegregation was attempted and is still being addressed within the constraints of the fundamental disparities of residential segregation.[10]

Many faith communities attempt to confront racial injustice by focusing on attitudes, interpersonal relations, microaggressions, and conversations within families and among neighbors. Discussion groups usefully prompt participants to examine their hearts and minds. But racial justice activists argue that attacking systemic racism as if it were only a matter of hearts and minds can be problematic, encouraging participants to think that they have done all they can merely by behaving kindlier toward their neighbors. Faith leaders therefore have recognized the value of organizing strategic initiatives, focusing on particular modes of intervention, and challenging racial inequality in its institutional manifestations.

In chapter 1, I trace the history of religious leaders' involvement in the fight for fair and affordable housing, emphasizing the policies set in motion in the 1970s and early 1980s that shaped much of what has been possible to accomplish thereafter. Housing has of course been one of the most significant ways in which racial differences and racial inequality have been preserved. Whether through explicit patterns of discrimination or such implicit practices as the pricing of housing developments, the fact that Black families and White families generally live in different neighborhoods clearly reduces the chances of interacting with one another in ways that would facilitate mutual understanding. Separated by residence means that Black children and White children are less likely to be friends—even if they attend the same schools. Living in different neighborhoods makes it less likely that Black families and White families belong to the same community associations and attend the same churches. As far as churches are concerned, geographic separation adds to the difficulty of predominantly Black and predominantly White congregations forming alliances with one another. When the fact that residential separation is compounded by differences in housing prices and household incomes, the differences in where people live also contribute to differences in quality of schools and infrastructure, the availability of jobs, and the chances of being treated fairly or unjustly by law enforcement officers.

The de facto reality of racial segregation in housing has been such an important condition affecting religious practices in the United States that religious leaders who cared about advocating for racial justice have had to take account of it. At present, the preferred way of taking account of this racially separated residential terrain is through the occasional alliances, financial support, and information flows that connect mostly White middle-class suburban congregations with mostly Black inner-city congregations. These connections serve as reminders to the White congregants that they enjoy privileges because of where they live and have a responsibility because of their faith to love their neighbors beyond the immediate neighbors they know best. But there have been times in the past when White religious groups tried to engage the differences in residential patterns more directly. In the 1950s and early 1960s, White religious leaders were involved in some of the protests that resulted in the Fair Housing Act of 1968, which banned explicit forms of discrimination in housing decisions. During the 1970s, activism on behalf of fair housing shifted to programs oriented toward providing affordable housing and locating it in racially integrated middle-class suburban neighborhoods. Those efforts enjoyed some success and proved that religious groups could continue to play a valuable role. But they were also quite limited and after a decade were largely considered to have been a failure or to have accomplished all they could.

In the 1980s, under the Reagan administration, advocacy for fair and affordable housing had to accommodate to the scarcity of federal funding by focusing on community development. Community development focused on rehabilitation and construction projects within Black neighborhoods instead of funding meant to facilitate residential integration by supporting dispersed low-income housing in suburban neighborhoods. Community development necessitated vastly complex financing arrangements that included federal, state, and local contributions and depended on buy-in from banks and real estate companies. For religious groups to play a role at all, they had to work out strategic arrangements with all of these agencies and participants. The religious leaders who succeeded in doing so created nonprofit management organizations of their own or negotiated partnerships with multisectoral nonprofit firms. Size and location were key to these organizations' success. Interracial and White organizations were often poised to benefit from large-scale financing arrangements, while Black organizations were often in the best position to work with residents. What religious groups did and why they were unable to do more is an important part of the story that must be understood if we are to make sense of how religious advocacy for community development has evolved in recent decades. Community development is the focus of chapter 2.

While housing and community development were an ongoing focus of racial justice advocacy, the issue that most directly affected equal opportunity—starting in the late 1970s and continuing in many communities for years—was busing. Whereas affordable housing and community development projects occasionally met resistance from local communities, school desegregation nearly always did. Faith communities' roles were thus quite different than they were in advocating for fair housing. These roles varied depending on the severity of the resistance from White parents, ranging from engaging in overt violence to initiating all-White private schools. Black clergy and Black churches intervened, sometimes with support from White churches, by monitoring buses and busing routes, counseling parents concerned about safety, organizing off-site school programs, initiating lawsuits, and serving on school boards. From the late 1970s onward, equal opportunity in colleges and universities was also a major issue and was most often pursued through affirmative action policies. Like busing, affirmative action has been so contentious that faith communities could hardly remain uninvolved if they cared about racial justice. What they did was usually a matter of improvisation and thus holds important lessons in how to work out practical measures of racial advocacy on the fly. Busing and affirmative action are the focus of chapter 3.

Advocating for fair housing and for workable busing and affirmative action programs put faith leaders in the unenviable position of lacking the authority to accomplish what they wanted to accomplish. The constraints that racial justice advocates faced in their own congregations were more manageable. It was much easier (in theory) to make changes within congregations than it was to work with real estate developers, housing authorities, banks, school boards, judges, and lawyers. Thus, it made sense for faith leaders to turn their attention toward what they could do within their own congregations—which they increasingly did by the last years of the twentieth century. But how that was done and how effective it was depended in large measure on the racial composition of congregations and the neighborhoods in which they were located. Two communities—one in Michigan and one in Florida—provide instructive illustrations of how much the neighborhoods mattered, in addition to showing how the clergy in one setting worked to overcome the community's White racist reputation and in the other effectively kept working for racial justice despite a significant loss of White members. In recent years, racial reckoning has importantly focused on interracial congregations, in addition to which pulpit exchanges and sibling relationships among congregations have also played an important role. On the surface, these activities seem like excellent ways for congregations to facilitate racial reckoning. But a growing number of studies identify pitfalls that must be avoided if these programs are to be effective. These studies also reveal the shortcomings of programs guided by colorblind ideas and dominated by interpersonal etiquette concerns. Racial reckoning is the focus of chapter 4.

Racial inequality in the administration of criminal justice has been a major concern during the entire period under consideration. Combating racial inequality in the criminal justice system has taken shape principally in mobilizing against hate crimes, advocating for police reform, protesting against racial profiling, and addressing the effects of mass incarceration. A series of high-profile cases from the 1970s through the end of the century played a highly significant role in bringing public attention to each of these issues and prompting local and federal legislation. These cases included the Wilmington Ten convictions and sentencing in the 1970s and the protests that developed in Los Angeles in response to the police beating of Rodney King. Just as they were in school desegregation efforts, Black churches were extensively involved in these cases and White religious leaders played important supporting roles—however, these cases left much unanswered about policing and violence. Why that was the case despite the protests that took place and the progress achieved in many communities are the focus of chapter 5.

Faith communities' advocacy for racial justice has always necessitated political action, but Barack Obama's campaign and presidency provided a unique opportunity for progressive religious leaders to play a role in electoral politics and policymaking. The opportunity was shaped not only by Obama being Black but also by his membership in the United Church of Christ and by the fact that progressive religious groups had quietly mobilized to play a greater role in electoral politics after failing to do so during the 2004 presidential election. Understanding the frustration that some social activists felt by the end of Obama's second term in office requires looking, first, at how expectations were generated during the campaign, and second, at how the key issues that the Obama administration faced necessitated faith leaders' pivoting their own activities toward those issues. Among the most important of these issues were economic recovery, healthcare reform, and voting rights. Faith leaders who pundits assumed were satisfied simply to have helped Obama win office now entered new terrain and played new roles in surprising ways. How religious groups aided—and criticized—the administration's policies in these areas are the focus of chapter 6.

The rise of the Black Lives Matter movement following the death of Michael Brown in Ferguson, Missouri, toward the end of Obama's second term in office posed an opportunity—but also a challenge—for faith communities. The opportunity was the heightened public attention the movement brought to racial injustice. The challenge was that Black Lives Matter activists held differing ideas from many church leaders—Black and White—about how best to protest against racial injustice. Movement leaders and faith leaders were at first critical of each other's strategies, but gradually developed a relationship that reflected a division of labor and at times resulted in cooperation. The heightened public attention to racial injustice also prompted new discussions within White churches about White privilege and generated anti-racism initiatives in many progressive denominations. Faith leaders who had not thought much about racial justice for a while found themselves searching for ideas about what to do next. They often talked about White privilege as if it could be corrected through better attitudes but found it difficult to grasp the meaning of systemic racism. How these developments unfolded and the challenges they have faced are the focus of chapter 7.

The paths taken by progressive faith communities in advocating for racial justice over the past half century reveal several striking misconceptions. One of these misconceptions is that progressive faith communities were pretty much synonymous with the White mainline Protestant denominations that were declining—and that because of their decline they did next to nothing of importance for racial justice, even though they had played a role during the civil rights movement. Membership in these denominations did decline, but the decline was not from disgruntled progressives decamping (although there was some of that). It was mostly from middle-class mainline members having fewer children and being older when they had children. The further misconception is that declining membership meant declining advocacy. While there is of course a relationship between membership and advocacy in that members provide financial resources, advocacy within mostly White progressive denominations has always been conducted by dedicated leaders whose work was as often criticized as it was supported. Moreover, progressive advocacy was conducted not only by White mainline Protestant denominations but also by coalitions that included African American churches, groups composed of Roman Catholics or Jews, and in a few instances with faith leaders who defined themselves as theological conservatives.[11]

A second misconception is that American religion in recent decades has remained so fundamentally segregated that understanding advocacy for racial justice is best done by looking only at Black churches or, alternatively, by investigating White churches to see how they embrace White privilege. This misconception reflects the reality that most Black churchgoers do attend predominantly Black churches and most White churchgoers attend predominantly White churches. The fallacy is basing observations on rank-and-file attendance patterns rather than considering the many ways in which faith leaders have worked for racial justice that do not reflect their grassroots memberships. In many instances, residential segregation has meant that Black religious groups addressed racial injustice in different ways from White religious groups. However, the opportunities for cross-racial cooperative and complementary action were many, ranging from joint congregation-based programs and mutual denominational affiliations to Black clergy serving in or being supported by mostly White denominations, to Black and White clergy participating in city-wide coalitions, to forming multiracial congregations. Many of these efforts were difficult to sustain and they were often frustrating in what they were able to achieve, but they should be acknowledged for what they did attempt to accomplish.

A third misconception is that progressive religious groups—whether mostly Black or mostly White—did not cooperate with secular (non-religious) progressive advocacy organizations and, indeed, were usually viewed skeptically by the leaders of those organizations. This misconception has surfaced in various forms, at times in an accurate perception that some progressive faith communities were not on board with gay rights and at other times in an inaccurate perception that faith communities were reluctant to work on issues that might compromise separation of church and state. The reality was that progressive religious groups partnered extensively with secular nonprofit organizations and with national networks that made it possible to be more effective than if they worked alone.[12]

A fourth misconception—a view that, unfortunately, appears to be shared in many well-meaning faith communities—is that the best thing for churches to do is to advance a postracial "colorblind" style of thinking. This way of thinking seems, on the surface, to be a theologically sound idea based on the conviction that we are all God's children. Carried to its logical extreme, it argues that good Christians (and good citizens) should be colorblind; that they should act as if racial injustice is no longer a reality. It is an outlook that fits comfortably with the way many churches have accommodated to the intense therapeutic individualism of American culture: focus everything on individuals' relationship to God, emphasize how God can help individuals feel better about themselves, talk about how to be nice to one's neighbors, encourage people to come to the church where they can feel like a community, and try hard to avoid anything that might seem "divisive." This is a recipe for ignoring the hard facts of racial inequality.

There is one conception of progressive faith communities that tracing the recent history of their advocacy for racial justice confirms. The faith communities that have worked most effectively for racial justice have understood themselves to be integrally connected with other institutions—with neighborhoods, school districts, zoning boards, the police, businesses, and legal systems. They have not retreated into private spaces where the mark of an ideal believer is showing up for worship and serving on a church committee. They have understood themselves to be in service to a God who cares about justice and mercy in the conduct of the courts, the functioning of schools and businesses, the distribution of wealth, and the equity of public affairs.

For faith leaders today who seek to engage in the work of racial justice, the lessons to be learned from the past half century are clear. The share of America's tens of thousands of congregations that have done much to address racial injustice has been small and is likely to remain small. For much of anything to have been done, therefore, faith leaders have had to take risks, seek other like-minded leaders, form coalitions, and draw inventively from the resources of their denominational offices. They have been most effective when they did not address racial injustice as an abstraction or as an interpersonal problem but when they seized on a particular aspect of racial injustice in their communities' institutions—the schools, courts, law enforcement agencies, boards of elected officials, neighborhood groups, and businesses in which significant decisions were being made. Effective faith leaders have had to be strategic in discerning what needed to be done and how they could contribute, choosing at different times and in different places to direct their efforts to topics that ranged from housing, community development, and equity in schools, to affirmative action, hate crimes, criminal justice, voting rights, and related issues.

Faith communities clearly are not a force that somehow shapes (or can shape) public policies on their own. What faith communities have been able to accomplish for racial justice has happened by taking account of the institutions that govern what most of us do most of the time. In these instances, faith communities' contributions have been small—a small share of the affordable housing that has been constructed, a small part in furthering desegregation, a small measure in combating the effects of mass incarceration. Were one to ask what might matter most in effecting change in these realms, one would look to public policies over which religious organizations have little or no control. But to do so would mean failing to appreciate the efforts faith groups and leaders have made—because trying and accomplishing a little is better than not trying at all.

1

Fair and Affordable Housing

A SHORTAGE OF FAIR and affordable housing has plagued the United States for decades. An adequate supply of fair housing has been obstructed by racial discrimination, redlining, predatory loans, and prejudice. Were these barriers to disappear, the lack of housing at prices that low-income renters or homeowners can afford stands in the way of many minority families. Addressing these concerns has been a topic to which civil rights organizations, government agencies, and community groups have directed their attention over the years—never to the complete satisfaction of anyone, but often with small incremental gains. Religious leaders have frequently played an important role in these efforts.

Reverend Gerald W. "Jerry" Hopkins was a newly ordained Presbyterian minister in the early 1970s with a dream of contributing to the fight for social justice. Hopkins was White, lived in a White neighborhood, and served a White congregation in the Northern Virginia suburbs outside Washington, DC. He wanted to secure support to build fair and affordable housing for the community's low-income families and thus to assist in this way with racial integration. Housing was in short supply, especially for Black families who still faced significant racial discrimination despite the recent passage of the Fair Housing Act.

Government funding for subsidized housing was available through the Federal Housing Administration, but Hopkins doubted much could be done to bring racial integration to suburban communities unless there was local support. To that end, he formed an ecumenical coalition

called the Community Ministry of Fairfax County and launched the
Coalition for Housing Action, through which he hoped to pressure the
county's zoning board to require builders to include affordable housing
in the county's rapidly expanding new construction. Hopkins achieved
some success even while incurring opposition from the community. But
like dozens of similar efforts by churches, nonprofit organizations, and
government agencies, the impact on racial patterns in suburban housing
was disappointing. In 1950, 10 percent of Fairfax County's population
was Black; in 1980, only 5.8 percent was Black.[1]

This example poses important questions for us to consider these
many years later. Why did progressive religious leaders think that they
could address racial injustice by getting involved in affordable housing
projects? What barriers did they encounter? How did those barriers
represent White privilege? And why is affordable housing and racial
diversity still so uncommon in suburban communities like Fairfax
County, Virginia?

There were of course many factors contributing to the persistence of
racial segregation and the prevailing shortage of affordable housing.
Faith communities were hardly able to contribute except in small ways
to addressing these problems. But if we are to understand an important
chapter in progressive faith communities' advocacy for racial justice, we
must examine how Black churches, White churches, ecumenical groups,
and interfaith coalitions became active supporters of racially inclusive
urban renewal projects in the late 1960s, how the frustrations they
experienced in those endeavors shifted attention increasingly toward
suburban housing, and how the relatively weak results of those efforts
have had a lasting influence on the racial patterning of suburban religious groups.

As plans like Hopkins's were being initiated in the early 1970s, it was
evident that suburbanization was the key population trend affecting
housing needs and opportunities. In 1950, 41 million Americans lived in
suburbs, a number that grew to 75 million in 1970 and was expected to
reach 100 million by the end of the decade. Yet only 4.8 percent of the
suburban population in 1970 was Black, which meant that achieving
residential desegregation had to include a focus on the suburbs. The

barriers standing in the way of that happening included overt racial prejudice, patterns of settlement and housing preferences, and above all economic disparities that prevented Black families from purchasing or renting homes in expensive suburban housing developments.

One way to address the problem was to provide affordable rental housing. In 1974, there were approximately 1.3 million low-rent public housing units in the United States, more than twice as many as in 1960. Of these units' residents, 43 percent were Black, even though Blacks constituted only about 13 percent of the US population. During the 1960s, the Department of Housing and Urban Development (HUD) had spent hundreds of millions on housing construction and rehabilitation in neighborhoods designated for urban renewal, but HUD now shifted a growing portion of its funding toward housing in suburban communities.[2]

Progressive religious groups had been interested in advocating for fair and affordable housing during the 1950s and 1960s. Much of this advocacy consisted of endorsing plans for government investment in public housing. The Episcopal Diocese of Maryland in 1950, for example, issued a statement calling on local communities to establish public housing authorities, provide funding for low-income housing, eradicate the "evils and dangers" of slum living, and in these ways ensure that thousands of families could "live decently in this great nation in accordance with the will of Christ." Similarly, the Protestant Council of the City of New York, representing White and Black congregations and joined by the American Jewish Congress, proposed an increase in public housing and called for federal laws to be changed to keep housing from becoming segregated.

In Detroit, a coalition of Protestant, Catholic, and Jewish leaders joined the NAACP in demanding an end to the segregation practiced by the housing authority. In Boston, Catholic and Protestant leaders addressed the fact that more public housing was needed but that even more urgently needed were remedies against slumlords exploiting the poor.[3] Through the rest of the decade and into the 1960s, religious groups in Baltimore, Chicago, Cleveland, Detroit, Los Angeles, New York, Philadelphia, and numerous other locations advocated against segregation and for increases in public housing. But by the early 1970s, the politics of public housing were changing and religious groups' responses were also having to adapt.

In this chapter, I discuss progressive religious leaders' involvement in fair and affordable housing efforts during the critical years that shaped the residential patterns and policies that prevailed in subsequent decades: the focus on federally subsidized suburban housing in the early 1970s, the evolution of the doctrine of disparate impact liability, and the reduction of federal support in the early 1980s. In chapter 2, I discuss faith communities' participation in collaborative housing endeavors under tax-credit programs in the late 1980s and 1990s, the George W. Bush administration's faith-based and community development programs, and the "furthering fair housing" proposals initiated by the Obama administration. During each of these periods, religious groups played a small but significant role in bringing faith perspectives on racial justice to bear on housing policies.

The part that religious groups played has largely been overlooked or forgotten—replaced by the idea that congregations' help happens in small acts of civic kindness. But the efforts that progressive religious groups initiated in the 1970s and 1980s followed a different path, attempting to address racial injustice by direct involvement in building and rehabilitating affordable housing. And these efforts did not end when housing policies changed. The lessons learned in those forward-thinking initiatives have been advanced in significant ways, producing remarkable success in some instances, and in many others demonstrating the systemic barriers that prevent further equity in housing from being achieved.

Federally Subsidized Suburban Housing

A few days after President Nixon's scandal-ridden resignation, President Ford signed into law the Housing and Community Development Act of 1974. The legislation authorized $11.9 billion over three years, much of it in block grants to local communities to spend on urban renewal projects that were required to comply with civil rights laws as well as meeting community standards. House and Senate versions of the bill had been pending during the heat of the Watergate investigation and were still being negotiated with the White House in the final days before Nixon resigned. Impetus for the legislation had begun in January 1973, when the Nixon administration terminated new construction under the federal assistance housing programs that had been responsible for building several hundred thousand subsidized homes and apartments a year as well as providing rent and mortgage assistance to low-income families.

These longstanding housing programs had been initiated as part of the New Deal under the National Housing Act of 1934, reauthorized under the Housing Act of 1949, and greatly expanded during the 1950s and 1960s. Located in or near predominantly Black inner-city neighborhoods where the demand for low-income housing was increasing because of slum clearance as well as from population growth, the public housing units were occupied by a high percentage of Black families. Nixon argued that the programs were too expensive and not meeting the intended families' needs. Civil rights groups, public interest groups, and state housing authorities sued but failed to win in the courts, which left any hope for affordable housing assistance in the hands of Congress. A key feature of the resulting legislation was the Section 8 Housing Program, which provided subsidies to private organizations to build and manage affordable homes and thereby opened the possibilities for federally supported low-income housing to be constructed as garden-style apartments rather than as high-rise towers and for the units to be in suburbs rather than in central cities.[4]

Church groups' engagement in affordable housing efforts had grown in the years prior to the 1974 legislation. These efforts reflected continuities with church groups' involvement during the nineteenth and early twentieth centuries in "poor farms," "workhouses," "homes for the aged," orphanages, and institutions for the blind, handicapped, and mentally ill. In the 1950s, churches, synagogues, and other nonprofit groups responded to the need for low-income housing for the elderly by constructing apartment complexes subsidized by the Federal Housing Administration (FHA). Congregations in decaying inner-city neighborhoods also turned increasingly toward affordable housing in conjunction with ministries among the urban poor.

By the late 1960s, the racial composition of many of these urban neighborhoods was shifting toward larger proportions of Blacks and smaller proportions of Whites. One of the ways in which churches responded was by convening meetings about open housing. In 1967, the US Catholic Bishops at a meeting in Washington, DC, declared open housing essential to communities' well-being.[5] Soon after, the National Council of Churches and many of its member denominations expressed support for the 1968 Fair Housing Act. Over the next five years, meetings at churches in Atlanta, Chicago, Dallas, Los Angeles, and dozens of other cities challenged participants to address affordable housing needs in their communities.

The members of a United Methodist congregation in an all-White Chicago suburb—responding to Nixon's moratorium on affordable housing construction in 1973—took the unusual step of publicly confessing its own complicity: "We confess," the congregation said, "that Blacks, Browns, and nonaffluent Whites are barred from our county because of the affluent price structure in housing and our political decisions." Some of the congregation followed up with cards to the county supervisors. On the cards was the familiar Bible verse: "Behold I stand at the door and knock; if anyone hears my voice and opens it, I will come to him."[6]

An act of confession like this linked the church to other groups in the county that were pressing for affordable housing, including the League of Women Voters, a housing rights task force, and a county-wide coalition of congregations. In other communities, clergy councils launched open housing covenant campaigns in which realtors and homeowners were asked to pledge explicitly that they would not discriminate based on race, creed, or national origin when selling or renting property. Many of the meetings aimed to bring Black clergy and White clergy together. Reverend J. Randolph Taylor, a White Presbyterian minister who led the effort in Atlanta, for example, recalled his growing conviction that: "The 'we' has got to include Blacks as well as Whites, and that's true for the Black community as well as the White community. Each community can fool itself that it can do this alone, but it can't," he said, but "Together we can really move in terms of the structures and systems."[7]

Another response from religious organizations was to initiate investigations to ascertain—and thereby draw attention to—the extent of segregation and housing discrimination. Presbyterian leaders in Chicago, for example, conducted a survey of thirty-seven previously all-White neighborhoods and found that the number of Black families now living in these neighborhoods increased from 46 in 1964 to 75 in 1965. Yet another response was to lobby against local and state legislation concerned with limiting fair housing. For example, when Proposition 14, an anti-fair-housing referendum, was put to voters in California in 1964, a third of liberal Protestant clergy in a study conducted in northern California said that they had organized a group in their congregation opposing the measure, approximately half joined an anti-Proposition 14 campaign committee, and upward of three-fourths said that they had issued a statement opposing the proposition.[8]

In addition to these ways of responding, church groups became directly active during the 1960s and early 1970s in constructing and managing housing projects, usually with loans from the FHA under the 1961 Housing Act, which provided for financing of 40-year loans if the housing was built on a nonprofit basis. Building affordable housing was something faith communities could do collectively and concretely as civically engaged organizations, rather than only hosting discussions about racial justice or mobilizing individuals to make contributions— important as those discussions and contributions were. Usually, it took a denominational agency or an interfaith coalition to do the planning, raise the funds, and secure the cooperation from municipal authorities to complete these initiatives.

The United Church of Christ's Board of Homeland Ministries, for example, launched a program in 1965 to construct subsidized, low-income, racially integrated rental housing in an urban renewal area in Detroit that it hoped would encourage similar projects in other cities. In 1967, the Greater Baltimore Interfaith Housing Council, composed of Roman Catholic, Black Protestant, and White Protestant churches, announced a plan to build low-income apartments and townhouses in

Baltimore, and in 1969 the group launched a 300-unit project in nearby Columbia, Maryland. Also in 1969, the Chambers Memorial Baptist Church, the Metropolitan Methodist Church, and the United Moravian Church launched housing rehabilitation projects for low-income working families in Harlem. Other low-income urban renewal housing projects were initiated by church groups in Washington, DC, Philadelphia, Hartford, Wilmington, Pittsburgh, Boston, Chicago, Dallas, and New York City. A study conducted in 1971 by the Council of Churches of the City of New York found that in the city alone, more than 150 churches and synagogues were involved in various housing construction, repair, and mortgage assistance projects.[9]

With funding from the FHA, which encouraged churches and other nonprofit organizations to apply for loans, some of the projects were immense. For example, in 1970 a White United Church of Christ congregation in suburban Maryland working with a Black church in Washington, DC, completed a 128-unit apartment building in DC at a cost of more than $2 million. Concurrently, work commenced in Chicago on a massive $10 million urban renewal housing development consisting of 450 units in twelve buildings all constructed with prefabricated materials. The project was sponsored by the Chicago Presbytery, the Sixth Grace Presbyterian Church, and the Chicago Conference of African Methodist Episcopal Churches. Another Chicago project was even larger, providing 563 cooperative units and 348 rental units at a cost of $15 million. Sponsored by the Antioch Missionary Baptist Church, it was the largest development of its kind under sponsorship and management of an all-Black organization.[10]

The advantage that housing initiatives launched by interfaith coalitions enjoyed was usually to draw more widely on financial resources and to represent more diverse interests. However, interfaith coalitions had weaknesses that kept them from doing more. One weakness was that conservative Protestant denominations typically refused to participate in ecumenical endeavors. A second was that White leaders were often prone to adopt paternalistic attitudes toward Black leaders. There were also tensions among coalition participants over priorities and financial commitments. The Chicago Conference on Religion and Race, for example, was largely successful in bringing together representatives of the Chicago Archdiocese, the Protestant Church Federation of Greater Chicago, and the Chicago Board of Rabbis. Yet the coalition's leaders struggled to work out thorny disagreements among its leaders concerning programmatic strategies and funding arrangements to move forward effectively with housing projects.[11]

While the projects that religious groups initiated provided affordable housing in predominantly Black urban neighborhoods, many of the housing projects that these groups sponsored had other purposes, especially providing low-income rental units for retirees. For example, in 1970 three high-rise apartment buildings totaling more than five hundred units were constructed in Orlando, Florida, under the sponsorship of the Central Nazarene Church of Orlando, First Baptist Church of Orlando, and the Central Florida Jewish Community Council. The units were open to residents of any religion and were intended to meet the needs of the growing numbers of elderly people retiring in Florida. A similar project was initiated by the Chicago Area Council of Liberal Churches, which included 182 units for elderly residents in a fifteen-story high-rise. With 40-year loans at 3 percent interest from the Federal Housing Administration, religious groups saw projects like these not only as ways to serve their members and communities but also as good investments. One estimate of the scale of work being conducted was that in 1971 the Interreligious Coalition for Housing—composed principally of American Baptist, Lutheran, Presbyterian, and United Church of Christ congregations—was involved in more than two hundred housing projects totaling $587 million.[12]

Over the next few years, church-sponsored construction of affordable housing continued but faced growing opposition. For example, the Interchurch Housing Corporation in Hartford, Connecticut, proposed a 160-unit housing complex, but residents argued that the complex would bring newcomers who would add to the town's burden for schools, crime prevention, and sanitation services while failing to contribute their share in property taxes. White residents in Cleveland argued that a small public housing project proposed by a local Orthodox Church to assist low-income Black families should not proceed because

Black families would not want to live there anyway. In Chicago, the pastor who initiated the $15 million project ran into enough opposition when he tried to start another project that he vowed never to engage in housing development again. In other communities, opponents argued against new affordable housing on grounds that existing projects were struggling.[13]

As congressional hearings began in response to Nixon's moratorium on federally subsidized housing, religious leaders were among those who testified about the importance of continuing the work that had been accomplished. The leaders who testified represented Black Protestant denominations, White Protestant denominations, the Roman Catholic Church, and Jewish organizations. Presbyterian minister Reverend Robert E. Johnson spoke for the Interreligious Coalition for Housing, a coalition representing eleven mainline Protestant denominations, the National Conference of Catholic Charities, and the Union of American Hebrew Congregations. Working with private contractors, lawyers, and banks, mortgage companies, and the Federal Housing Administration, the coalition's partners had built or rehabilitated more than 25,000 housing units for families, couples, and singles. More than 92,000 volunteer hours had been donated, he said, an equivalent of nearly $1 million, all of which was now in jeopardy because of the moratorium. "Where are our national priorities leading us," he asked, "when in a peacetime economy, our defense budget goes up and our expenditures for helping our needy people to help themselves goes down tremendously?"[14]

Reverend Johnson acknowledged that somewhere between 2 and 5 percent of all the FHA subsidized housing projects were in default. He said that there had been management difficulties and unanticipated costs, but he thought that the legislators should consider subsidized housing overall a success. The other religious leaders agreed. Said one: "A kind of 'strict liability' has become the housing policy of the day"—a policy, he thought, that made sense for aircraft but not when meeting national housing goals. Still, it was the failures that seemed to be attracting the public's attention.[15]

Baber Village was one of the affordable housing developments that was struggling. Located in the nearly 90 percent Black neighborhood of Seat Pleasant in Prince George's County, Maryland, Baber Village was a 200-unit, three-story, garden-style apartment complex. Opened in 1969 at a cost of almost $3 million, it was named for prominent African Methodist Episcopal (AME) Bishop George W. Baber and was sponsored and managed by the Washington Conference of the AME Church. Like similar housing projects in the DC metropolitan area organized by the United Church of Christ, Presbyterians Incorporated, Bible Way Church, and Mt. Airy Baptist Church, Baber Village was subsidized by loans from the Federal Housing Administration. In addition, qualified residents were eligible to receive FHA rental supplements, which meant paying as little as $45 a month for a two-bedroom apartment compared with $150 on the open market. The complex was widely hailed as a highly preferrable option to public housing for distressed families and as a fine example of churches' engagement in good deeds for the community.[16]

A year after it opened, Baber Village's reputation was quite different. Residents complained of shoddy construction, eroded courtyards, broken windows, and an accumulation of trash. Neighboring middle-class residents said that the village was becoming a slum. An investigation showed that much of problem was the company that had been hired to manage the property. The management company, which was run by a friend of the builder who was also a friend of Vice President Spiro Agnew, claimed that the residents themselves were at fault and accused the FHA of imposing unreasonable regulations of what could be done to act against the residents.

By the following summer, Baber Village had become Exhibit One in cautionary tales about why affordable housing for low-income Black families was a bad idea. The Department of Housing and Urban Development had been forced to assume the mortgage, the Prudential Insurance company that provided the loan pulled back from funding other projects, and critics laid blame to everything from Lyndon Johnson's overly ambitious Great Society program, to the FHA and greedy developers, to the churches' naivete in thinking that they could handle a housing project, to poor families not taking care of their homes and having too many children. Critics predicted—correctly, as it turned out—that the project would probably wind up being demolished.[17]

Technically, Baber Village was a suburban housing development, located as it was about six miles east of the US Capitol. By the late 1960s, population trends were making it evident that any strategy to provide racially inclusive affordable housing needed to take account of possibilities in the suburbs as well as projects focusing on urban renewal in the cities. Among these possibilities were purchasing land at affordable prices in exurban locations, repurposing land owned by religious organizations, and working with real estate developers in suburbs to ensure that affordable housing was constructed.

At a meeting in suburban Chicago in 1971, representatives of Catholic and mainstream Protestant denominations debated the possibilities involving church-owned land, which was sometimes only the lot across the street from an inner-city church but in other cases consisted of farm acreage and suburban property acquired through bequests or purchased for future expansion. Using the land for low-income housing would be the socially responsible thing to do, they agreed, but were they prepared for pushback from homeowners and local officials and, for that matter, would urban Black families have enough money or be interested in relocating to mostly White communities? An Episcopal church with land donated by a parishioner in Maryland wondered the same thing: even to supply subsidized housing for the elderly, would suburban communities approve or object?[18]

In late 1973, in preparation for the congressional hearings, the Department of Housing and Urban Development under the direction of Secretary James T. Lynn completed a comprehensive review of national housing policy. The report documented the huge increase in federally subsidized housing starts that had taken place over the past decade, rising from fewer than 50,000 in 1963 to nearly 430,000 in 1970, or, as a proportion of all US housing starts, an increase from less than 3 percent to nearly 30 percent. The report revealed that Blacks had higher shares of subsidized units than Whites, taking into account differences in levels of income, and that subsidized housing was a factor in low-income families moving from central-city neighborhoods to suburbs. While there was some evidence that subsidized housing was contributing to residential integration, the report acknowledged that this contribution was small.

The report also documented several impediments to achieving the programs' goals and indeed argued that the overall investment should be reduced. Among the impediments were the rising costs of construction and rental subsidies, administrative problems with eligibility criteria and infrastructure, and public perceptions of scandal and excessive architectural fees. In anticipation of local municipalities being given greater control over decisions about subsidized housing, the report also identified numerous means through which federally assisted projects were being blocked. These included exclusionary zoning rules that placed limits on growth because of inadequate schools and roads, building and sewer moratoria, environmental regulations, austere building codes and inspection requirements, and rent controls.[19]

The Housing and Community Development Act that President Ford signed in 1974 had several primary goals. These included addressing the rising overall demand for housing, reducing the concentration of low-income families in central cities, remediating the deterioration of housing in impoverished inner-city neighborhoods, and stimulating the housing market in an effective response to the current crisis in inflation and high energy costs. These goals were to be achieved through federal programs that would facilitate state and local government efforts and private investment. The legislation also sought to address racial injustice in three ways. It prohibited discrimination in housing assistance programs based on race, color, national origin, disability, age, religion, and sex. It was expected to disproportionately benefit Black families because they were more likely than White families to qualify for housing assistance. And housing assistance was to be made available not only in cities but also in suburbs, thus promoting racial integration in suburban neighborhoods.

Implementing the goals concerning racial justice was therefore contingent on a complex of considerations involving the White as well as the Black population, economic differences, the interests of various stakeholders in the housing industry, and perceptions of the problems facing urban neighborhoods. While housing was the specific focus of the legislation, the fact that community development was an explicit goal added further complexity, including how terms such as "slums," "blight," "deterioration," "spatial isolation," "diversity," "vitality," "aesthetic," and "value" were interpreted—all of which characterized the qualities of communities that were to be embraced or avoided. Arguments about budgets, costs and benefits, and return on investment were key, but community development necessitated addressing questions about where housing should be built, who had a say in the decisions, and what the criteria should be for making the decisions.

The 1974 housing act continued the opportunities that previous measures had provided for religious groups to play a role in providing housing assistance. In keeping with separation of church and state, no government funding was available to churches for religious purposes. But churches could establish religious organizations that qualified for funding like other nonprofit organizations. The legislation specifically included assistance to neighborhood-based nonprofit organizations, local development corporations, and other nonprofit organizations serving the development needs of communities. These organizations could receive funding for the purpose of neighborhood revitalization and development and for helping residents reduce their costs of housing. Programs meeting these objectives included new construction, rehabilitation or demolition of existing construction, and rental assistance. Much of the language emphasized the spatial deconcentrating of low-income families from the "blighting influences" of deteriorating urban neighborhoods.[20]

Responses to the legislation from affordable housing policy experts were mixed because persons likely to benefit most were middle-class home buyers and home builders owing to a substantial increase in the ceiling on mortgages backed by the federal mortgage association. Moreover, of the total $11.9 billion authorized to cover three years of funding, the amount budgeted for subsidized housing was only $1.16 billion in 1974 and $1.32 billion in 1975. And while suburban counties were now eligible for funds, local communities were given more power to approve or disapprove proposals.[21]

Concerned about suburban communities' enlarged role, the US Commission on Civil Rights issued a report titled *Equal Opportunity in Suburbia* calling for desegregation to be made an explicit aim of supplementary legislation and for local veto power over rent supplement programs to be abolished. Documenting that subsidized housing obtained by Black families had mostly been in "blighted" areas, while the majority of housing obtained by White families was outside "blighted" areas, the report revealed that a large share of all the subsidized housing was in areas totally segregated by race. With information collected from dozens of renters, prospective home buyers, and real estate agents, the report also detailed the numerous ways in which segregation was being maintained.

The mechanisms with which de facto discrimination was practiced included all-White zoning boards, transportation committees, and planning boards; realtors quoting different prices for Black and White families and offering different advice about financing; lax enforcement of anti-discrimination statutes; and costly or time-consuming litigation about land use and building codes. The report singled out Fairfax County, Virginia, where Reverend Hopkins was now having modest success as a member of the housing board in achieving low-income housing by working directly with developers. Fairfax had passed an ordinance requiring that site plans in specified townhouse and apartment zones allocate 6 percent of the planned units to low-income housing and 15 percent to moderate-income housing. However, the ordinance applied only to projects of fifty units or more and included several loopholes that builders were exploiting to their advantage.[22]

Disparate Impact Liability

Simultaneous with these civil rights concerns, a church-based affordable housing proposal in St. Louis County, Missouri—where, decades later, demonstrators protesting the killing of Michael Brown would turn "Black Lives Matter" into a national movement—played an important role in litigation that led to the doctrine known as disparate impact liability. This interpretation of civil rights law was a significant development even though its effects were often ambiguous. Disparate impact basically challenged the idea that racism could be proven only if explicit racist intentions were openly expressed. Instead, racial justice as far as affordable housing was concerned was recast in terms of the equity or inequity in how racial minorities were affected. This recasting was a way to pose questions about racial inequality that were otherwise being suppressed under the cover of arguments about the poor, neighborhoods, and housing values in which the parties involved took the position that race was not a factor at all because nobody was making explicitly racist statements. The St. Louis case was resolved through the input of many organizations, but the religious groups that played a role illustrate how a positive contribution can sometimes be made even when a group fails to achieve its main objective.

What became known as the Park View Heights affordable housing project is best credited to the person who played a central role in its planning: Jack Quigley. Quigley was a 1963 graduate of Amherst College who then enrolled at Union Theological Seminary in New York City and subsequently earned a doctorate in ministry from Eden Theological Seminary in Webster Groves, Missouri. Prior to his arrival in St. Louis, Quigley had worked with a Black sharecroppers' cooperative in Georgia and after leaving St. Louis would do pastoral counseling, work as a psychotherapist at Veterans' Administrations hospitals, and be the bookkeeper for the United Farm Workers' Union in California. During his first year at Union Theological Seminary, Quigley had been injured in a swimming accident. He was paralyzed from the neck down.[23]

Undeterred by the physical challenges he faced, Quigley formed the Inter-Religious Center for Urban Affairs in St. Louis in 1967. With meager financial resources, the center's goal was to develop a low-income housing plan, craft a program for emergency relief, protest discriminatory police activities, and, above all, prick the consciences of churchgoing people about racial and economic injustice. To that end, the center sponsored lectures and seminars, set up a hotline, and found ways to publicize its activities in the newspapers and on radio. Quigley gave lectures and networked with prominent congregations and powerful clergy groups such as the Mid-City Community Congress and the Metropolitan Church Federation of Greater St. Louis. By 1969, Quigley and the Inter-Religious Center for Urban Affairs, which included Catholic, Jewish, and Protestant representatives, were well-known. The center's plan was to establish an ecumenical housing fund to which applicants could submit plans for support to construct an affordable housing complex.[24]

The money for the ecumenical housing fund came from several philanthropic foundations, churches, and small donations from individuals. The largest sum was a $200,000 interest-free loan from the Second Presbyterian Church in St. Louis. The church's decision to underwrite affordable housing in this way reflected the convergence of three developments. First, the church's pastor, Reverend W. Sherman Skinner, had chaired his denomination's committee to study and make recommendations about its positions on race, war, and poverty, and Skinner was known in St. Louis for sermons and televised appearances in which he spoke about race, poverty, and the need for fresh thinking in the churches about social issues. Second, in April 1969, Student Nonviolent Coordinating Committee (SNCC) leader James Forman at a conference in Detroit had called on the nation's White churches and synagogues to pay $500 million in reparations to Black people and announced that sit-ins at churches would begin the following week— sit-ins that in fact happened the following week, including one at Presbyterian headquarters in New York City, and were accompanied by Forman speaking to the Presbyterians' General Assembly meeting. And third, a few weeks later, the Sunday service at Second Presbyterian Church in St. Louis was interrupted by a group of local Black leaders demanding reparations.[25]

The interest-free loan from Second Presbyterian gave Quigley's board the funding it needed to solicit applications from organizations interested in launching an affordable housing project. The winning submission was from St. Mark's United Methodist Church of Florissant, a church of only sixty members that would work through the United Methodists' Metro Ministry social welfare agency to initiate a project and secure the major portion of its funding under Section 236 of the 1968 Housing and Urban Development Act. The project was to be a 210-unit garden-style apartment complex on twelve acres of land about six miles from the church. It was called Park View Heights.

Opposition from the community where the complex was to be located emerged as soon as the plan was announced. A neighborhood "improvement association" mailed flyers to more than four thousand residents in the area, sent letters to HUD and the White House, and organized meetings to air concerned citizens' opposition. The opponents' spokespersons called the project an "abscess" on their community, accused the church's activists of being incapable of maintaining such a project, and complained that the government was using the hard-earned tax money of middle-class wage-earners to subsidize low-income families. The opponents denied that race was an issue, saying only that they had moved to the area to escape crime and substandard schools. One said that she would be afraid to walk out of her home if the affordable housing units were approved because of the Black faces she would see.[26]

As controversy grew, the *St. Louis Post-Dispatch* wrote about the US Department of Justice stepping up its efforts to enforce fair housing laws but framed the coverage in a way that gave readers reasons to think affordable housing in their middle-class neighborhoods might be a bad idea. Certainly, it was reasonable to fear the prospect of low-income housing creating a "high-rise slum," the paper editorialized, and, for that matter, "facilitating a population transfer to the suburbs, regardless of benefits, would make the cities' problems worse."[27]

Taking the other side, the Inter-Church Association of Metropolitan St. Louis issued a strong statement endorsing the Park View project. "Few churches, such as St. Mark's, and few denominational boards, such as the Metro Ministry, have directly sought to find a solution to the economic and social stratification of contemporary American society," the statement declared. "You now find focused on yourselves an enmity between men which is itself a cause of an unreconciled society. Few church groups have been willing to risk so much, and few must bear the burden of opposition which you now bear. We wish to share your burden."[28]

Signed by more than a dozen heads of Methodist, Presbyterian, African Methodist Episcopal, Episcopal, and United Church of Christ organizations, the statement asserted, "We want you to know that many of us personally participated in the decision made over two years ago to utilize the resources of the church in meeting the need for decent housing in metropolitan St. Louis. Through the Ecumenical Housing Fund, you and other neighborhood and church groups have begun to alleviate this problem." The project was consistent with their denominations' principles, they said. "We take exception to the people now alleging that you are kooks and rabble-rousers and that your plan is a foolish attempt to get the church involved in an activity in which it should not be involved."

The difficulty the opposition faced was that the area in which the project was to be located was unincorporated, which meant the county had jurisdiction and the county's zoning permitted the area to include multiple-family buildings. To circumvent that difficulty, the opposition worked quickly and successfully to incorporate the area—the new community was called Black Jack—and rezoned the tract in question to allow only single-family housing. In response, HUD's regional office recommended to the Department of Justice that it take legal action to prevent the new municipality from blocking the project. Quigley, the Inter-Religious Center for Urban Affairs, and an organization called the National Committee Against Discrimination in Housing said that they would participate if a lawsuit was filed.[29]

Park View Heights was now the focus of a debate in Washington. HUD secretary and former Michigan governor George Romney, who had been arguing for stronger civil rights support, called Black Jack's action a "blatant violation of the Constitution and the law" and asked for legal proceedings to begin. But Attorney General John Mitchell, who would become a household name during the Watergate scandal, opposed the Department of Justice intervening. Nixon, without referring specifically to the case, issued a remark against "forced integration of the suburbs" that Park View's opponents interpreted as taking their side.[30] Privately, Nixon described the Black Jack case as a "can of worms." In June 1971, after further haggling among the president's advisors, the

White House put out a policy statement that defended acting "in appropriate circumstances" to prosecute a community that excluded subsidized housing for racial reasons.[31]

Following Nixon's June 1971 statement, the Justice Department filed a lawsuit against the city of Black Jack, charging it with instituting restrictive zoning to keep out Blacks and the poor. In 1974, the US District Court for the Eastern District of Missouri ruled in Black Jack's favor, stating that municipalities had a right to decide how land was zoned. But on appeal in 1975, the court reversed the earlier decision, arguing that Black Jack had in fact engaged in discrimination. Five more years elapsed before Black Jack lost its final appeal in 1980 and agreed to pay the Park View Heights group $450,000 in damages incurred by having to abandon the project.[32]

The 1975 ruling provided grounds on which subsequent claims about disparate impact liability could be made. Although the US Supreme Court did not take a definitive stand on the matter until 2015, the doctrine that emerged between 1975 and 1980 from Black Jack and similar cases involving housing and employment prohibited practices and policies that had disproportionate negative effects on racial minorities and other protected groups under the Fair Housing Act of 1968, even if the practice and policy was not on its face discriminatory or meant to be discriminatory. In short, the basis on which discrimination could be deemed illegal shifted from intent to impact. On these grounds, the appeals court ruled that Black Jack's action to incorporate itself and to rezone the tract in question to prevent affordable housing from being built was discriminatory to the disproportionate number of Black families who would have benefited from the housing complex, even though Black Jack's leaders may not have explicitly said that was their intention.

However, the Black Jack ruling left several openings for communities to use when they wanted to keep out affordable housing. First, the Park View Heights' attorneys had gone to considerable effort collecting statistics to demonstrate that Blacks likely would have moved into the complex—statistics that in other cases could be interpreted differently because *anticipated* occupancy is harder to prove than after-the-fact occupancy. The attorneys also had to demonstrate that other affordable housing options were lacking—which would not be as easy to prove in other communities. Second, the court acknowledged, as in other civil rights cases and in freedom of speech and assembly cases, that the community might have a compelling interest that superseded claims about affordable housing. And third, disparate impact liability was relevant only if lawsuits were filed and only if the courts, HUD, and the Department of Justice were willing to see the doctrine enforced. The number of cases involving housing discrimination declined so dramatically, in fact, that observers accused the Department of Justice of being lax in enforcing disparate impact liability.[33]

2

Community Development

IN ONE OF HIS FIRST CAMPAIGN appearances after winning the 1980 GOP presidential nomination, Ronald Reagan visited a Black and Hispanic neighborhood in the South Bronx where President Carter had promised federal support for a redevelopment program that failed to materialize. Earlier in the day, Reagan told a meeting of Black leaders that he supported civil rights and wanted their votes. He said that he would address low-income housing problems by restraining the growth of federal spending, lowering income taxes, initiating enterprise zones, giving state and local governments greater discretion in using federal funds, and creating an urban homesteading program that would allow low-income families to purchase and renovate abandoned housing units. The South Bronx visit did not go well. When Reagan tried to describe his plans, the unreceptive crowd shouted him down.[1]

Housing cuts were among the most severe of the Reagan administration's reductions in spending for domestic social programs. The overall authorization for federal housing programs fell from a proposed budget under the Carter administration of $32 billion in 1981 to roughly $20 billion in 1982, a further reduction to $10.6 billion for 1983, and only $4.1 billion for 1984. Besides contributing to Reagan's goal of reducing the federal budget, the cuts that dealt specifically with affordable housing were meant to address the rising costs of rehabilitating units owned by the government and the continuing costs of government assistance to private landlords through low-interest mortgages. Additionally, the reductions were motivated by concerns that subsidies were being used to rehabilitate inner-city housing rather than assisting with the geographic dispersion of low-income housing. There was some evidence as well that real estate developers were being disincentivized to play an active role in providing affordable housing. An estimated $3.3 billion was to be saved by halting or drastically reducing construction of new public housing units, limiting subsidies for the operating costs of private low-income housing, and instituting a voucher program through which low-income families would receive coupons to be used to assist in paying rent for housing they might be able to find on the open market.[2]

In contrast to previous housing policies that assumed that there was an insufficient stock of affordable housing and thus that more needed to be built, Reagan's strategy took for granted that there was an ample amount of housing and that low-income families would be able to take advantage of it if they simply had some assistance in covering the cost of rental payments or mortgages. This strategy was estimated to cut federal expenditures on low-income housing by approximately half that of public housing. The strategy was based on field experiments with housing allowances conducted by the Rand Corporation in Green Bay, Wisconsin, and South Bend, Indiana, involving assistance to approximately twenty thousand households. The allowances required tenants themselves to correct health or safety hazards that were in violation of housing codes, such as defective electrical switches and broken windows. The assumption therefore was that tenants and homeowners could readily figure out how to make these improvements or persuade friendly neighbors and landlords to help make them, and in the process put in sweat equity that would leave them feeling better about themselves.[3]

The voucher program was initiated on a trial basis in 1983 under the Housing Urban and Rural Recovery Act. The program became permanent in 1987, was modified in 1998, and by 2010, HUD was assisting the renters of more than 2 million units under the program. Supporters of the changes argued that the housing programs of the 1960s and 1970s had either focused on monster high-rise public housing buildings that were now in disrepair or on scattered garden-style apartments that were unpopular in suburban communities and subject to local corruption. Supporters also argued that a voucher program could be tailored more effectively to the varying needs of individual families and could give them greater freedom in deciding where to live. Opponents argued that the voucher program required low-income families to cover more of their own housing costs and did nothing to address the shortage of available affordable housing. Those shortages were more acute in some markets than in others but were generally of greatest concern where rising rental costs were pushing families to spend increasing shares of their income on housing and where fewer low-income apartments were available because of buildings being converted to condominiums.[4]

Adapting to Reduced Federal Support

At meetings to discuss housing, religious leaders increasingly focused on unmet needs more than on plans that might be in the offing to build housing, even though some new construction projects were under consideration. At a meeting in Seattle, for example, representatives of the clergy council addressed the fact that hundreds of low-income residential buildings in the downtown area were being torn down or renovated into high-priced office space, leaving approximately three thousand people homeless and in need of emergency assistance. A report in Washington, DC, found 134,000 families in the region needing housing assistance and another 33,000 families on waiting lists. Over the past decade, the number on waiting lists had risen more than 80 percent in the District of Columbia; in Fairfax County, more than 700 percent. A clergy-led Social Action Committee described a similar problem in Connecticut. Pastors were having to place women and children in homeless shelters. The committee hoped the churches could pool their efforts and pay the rent for a few of the families.[5]

Several of the denominational groups and interfaith coalitions that had formed in the 1960s and 1970s to construct affordable housing lobbied with state and local governments to make up the gap created by the federal government's reduced investment. One of the groups that had been founded in the late 1960s with National Council of Churches support was the Presbyterian Joint Strategy and Action Committee. Another was the Metropolitan Interfaith Council on Affordable Housing

(MICAH), which by the late 1980s represented fifty mostly suburban Protestant congregations, Catholic parishes, and Jewish organizations. In St. Louis, the earlier faith-based affordable housing efforts were continuing through the Ecumenical Housing Production Corporation, and in the Baltimore area, under the direction of the Interfaith Housing Alliance.

The reduction in federal support for the construction of new affordable housing necessitated a shift in focus among religious groups away from attempting to sponsor and manage such projects toward devising alternative strategies. These strategies developed along four principal lines: urban redevelopment housing plans in predominantly Black neighborhoods under the auspices of Black churches and interreligious councils, the increasing role of nonsectarian nonprofit organizations in developing new or newly renovated affordable housing, the continuing and increasingly complex struggle to create affordable housing opportunities in predominantly White suburban neighborhoods, and a renewed emphasis on congregation-based charitable assistance programs for low-income and homeless individuals and families.

Urban redevelopment housing programs in predominantly Black neighborhoods continued in the 1980s largely on the model of the ones initiated in the late 1960s and 1970s but less frequently and focusing more often on rehabilitation than on new construction. One of the most ambitious of the new construction programs was the Nehemiah Plan in an East Brooklyn neighborhood where 82 percent of the population was Black, 15 percent was Latino, 3 percent was White, and 36 percent was on public assistance. Initiated in 1981, the Nehemiah Plan was a $12 million project sponsored by an interdenominational, interracial coalition of Black churches and White religious organizations called East Brooklyn Congregations. Using cost-cutting construction methods and with local input and tight control over management and funding, the coalition anticipated being able to buck the upward trend in the city's housing prices.

By 1985, the Nehemiah organization had built 320 low-income homes, had 300 more under construction, and by the end of the decade accounted for 38 percent of the net increase in East Brooklyn's housing stock and 77 percent of the increase in single-family homes. Although several denominational groups turned down its requests for support, the group's success depended on contributions from St. Paul Community Baptist Church, the Episcopal Diocese of Long Island, Lutheran Church Missouri Synod, the Roman Catholic Diocese of Brooklyn, and other sponsoring churches as well as a no-interest loan from the city and advice about fundraising and community mobilization from the Industrial Areas Foundation. Residents also benefited from subsidies provided by the city for land acquisition and local improvements and the state's low-interest mortgage agency.[6] By the early 1990s, interfaith groups had implemented similar Nehemiah affordable housing projects in Los Angeles and Philadelphia. These Nehemiah projects succeeded largely through the work of ecumenical coalitions of religious organizations, whose role included moral suasion and networking with public officials as well as financial support, and by securing enough input from local and state agencies to make up for the lack of federal funding.

A different approach was to formulate a plan that could succeed on a smaller scale through private funding. This was the model that Church of the Saviour gained national attention for implementing. Church of the Saviour was an interracial, interdenominational church located about two miles from the White House in Adams-Morgan, where gentrification was pushing up housing values and driving out low-income tenants. Since its inception in 1947, the church had led progressive efforts to welcome and minister to the inner-city poor. The best opportunity that the church had to help preserve affordable housing for low-income families in the early 1970s was to renovate existing buildings. Under a separate nonprofit organization called the Jubilee Housing Corporation, a plan was drawn up in 1973, and by 1977 two decaying 1920s-era buildings had been rehabilitated.

To keep expenses down, the church relied on volunteers, who were estimated to have put in more than 50,000 hours. The project also secured a $200,000 grant from the Lilly Endowment, an Indianapolis-based foundation that prioritized funding for ministerial and congregational assistance. Besides the housing assistance it provided, the church tried to cultivate trust among the tenants through responsive management practices, job placement, emergency financial assistance, and personal relationships. It was this model that the church hoped to implement in other small projects in the 1980s.[7]

Church of the Saviour's Jubilee Housing Corporation enlisted real estate developer James W. Rouse to serve on its board. Rouse was responsible for some of the region's most notable developments, including the planned community at Columbia, Maryland, was a member at Church of the Saviour, and was interested in affordable housing. In 1981, Rouse formed the Enterprise Development Corporation, adopting some of the ideas that had proven successful in the Jubilee project, and including the pastor at Church of the Saviour on its board.

Enterprise became a model that would be used increasingly by religious groups for affordable housing. Instead of working only through religious networks, they would participate in nonsectarian nonprofit organizations that could operate on a larger scale, bring together people with relevant knowledge from the worlds of real estate development and finance, and work more effectively to raise money and navigate relationships with public officials. These nonprofit organizations had the further advantage for developers of initiating projects that would benefit the developers' for-profit interests, such as determining where affordable housing should be located in relation to commercial development and persuading local planning boards to modify housing density restrictions. Between 1981 and 1994, the Enterprise Development Corporation built more than 40,000 low-income housing units, working with faith-based coalitions and other community-based nonprofit organizations.[8]

Community-based development organizations benefited from knowing local customs and needs, enlisting volunteers, and drawing help from churches, and in many instances they were able to forge alliances across racial lines. Unlike churches, these independent nonprofit development organizations were better positioned to focus specifically and exclusively on housing and thus to secure foundation grants, philanthropic gifts, and corporate support, as well as low-interest loans and tax incentives from government. These nonprofit organizations were well-positioned to launch new projects and to operate on a large enough scale to influence public policies.[9]

Yonkers Interfaith Education and Leadership Development (YIELD) was one of the best examples of a nonprofit community development organization expanding its operations to accommodate changing housing needs and policies. YIELD was a coalition of Catholic, Jewish, and Protestant congregations supported by several tenants' associations and the Longshoremen's local union. It originated with the Yonkers Area Conference of Catholic Clergy, which gave it a strong base in the churches and Catholic neighborhoods. Composed of Black, Hispanic, and White leaders, more than two hundred pastors, priests, congregants, and community representatives were involved. The coalition's leaders shared a strong commitment to social justice.

With more than 17,000 housing units in Yonkers converted to condominiums and virtually no new affordable housing constructed, YIELD's leaders opted to focus on clarifying the area's overall housing needs and plans. The coalition's efforts began by educating a few of its leaders in housing policies and then expanded its training program to include clergy and lay leaders who were willing to become involved in local politics. Subsequent activities included meeting with tenants who were being threatened with eviction, securing passage of a law requiring owners of buildings to establish a reserve fund for capital repairs, and working with police to provide better patrolling of public housing units. YIELD also compiled and published a handbook for tenants, owners, and city officials and established a low-interest loan fund for tenants. One of its major challenges was mediating between citizens' groups with differing interests and representing these interests with the city's and state's housing authorities. As the city proceeded with plans to make approximately two hundred low-income units available at seven locations, YIELD's role shifted toward providing information to prospective tenants, monitoring instances of discrimination, and communicating with public officials.[10]

New construction of affordable housing in predominantly White suburbs included the occasional program sponsored by religious groups, but these programs were increasingly the result of nonsectarian nonprofit organizations. Religion was often present in these organizations through individuals and groups being included on boards and committees, but religious groups were less often the primary organizers and the activities in which these organizations participated shifted from one thing to another according to the opportunities that became available and the challenges they faced locally. Pushback from White middle-class neighbors was often a problem, as were the balancing acts required to address local needs while attempting to achieve social justice objectives.

The North Shore Interfaith Housing Council, located in the upscale 95 percent White suburb of Wilmette, Illinois, was an example that illustrated the challenges and adaptations that faith communities faced in advocating for affordable housing in neighborhoods of this kind. The council—a coalition of Christian and Jewish organizations—formed in 1972 at the time when federal subsidies for affordable housing were still possible. A survey conducted by the First Congregational Church of Wilmette found that elderly residents were moving away because housing in the area was becoming too expensive for them to stay. The council succeeded in putting together a plan to secure public as well as private funding and opened a 51-unit complex for elderly residents in 1977.

As federal funding diminished, the North Shore group shifted its focus toward lobbying city and county government on zoning and development plans, advocating about housing with local employers and private developers, and staffing a center to help low-income and minority families locate available housing. Much of the center's work focused on the elderly, recently divorced mothers, and evicted families who needed short-term assistance. The council also tried to persuade congregations to purchase and rehabilitate apartments or houses.

By 1982, the council's sponsoring membership had grown to forty congregations and seventeen nonsectarian community groups representing ten North Shore suburbs. A study that year showed that nearly a third of the subsidized housing units in suburban Cook County was in middle- and upper-income census tracts, which meant that one of the contributions the council could make was helping low-income families who were living in these units, and in some cases mediating disputes with middle- and upper-income neighbors. The council found that racial tensions were more often the result of White and Black families avoiding one another and privately harboring prejudices than it was of overt discrimination. "People don't stand outside a house to harass their neighbors," the council's director said in a 1984 interview. "But they might ignore the neighbors or not take over the coffeecake they would normally bring."[11]

In other predominantly White suburban communities, opposition from residents was often successful in delaying and effectively killing affordable housing projects despite religious groups supporting them. On Long Island, for example, the Suffolk Interreligious Coalition on Housing worked in collaboration with the local NAACP for three years to garner favorable public opinion by hosting meetings at churches, holding seminars about affordable housing, conducting tours, and appearing at municipal hearings, but when the final vote was taken more than a thousand opponents showed up and the plan was rejected. In addition to community opposition, the county faced the realization that federal funding was drying up and that floating a bond issue to raise local funding was impossible at a time when the lack of federal aid for mortgages was straining middle-income families' budgets.[12]

The problems were similar in New Jersey, where the state's landmark 1975 Mount Laurel decision requiring towns to provide realistic opportunities for low- and moderate-income housing had been so poorly enforced that the New Jersey Supreme Court handed down a stinging 270-page decision in 1983 declaring that exclusionary ordinances and noncompliance would no longer be tolerated. The ruling gave the state greater leverage in forcing town planning committees to design and implement affordable housing programs.

However, the state's leverage was weakened by local decisions being left in the hands of local officials whose interests also reflected the conflicting pressures of real estate developers, banks, open land advocates, for-profit employers, and taxpayers. The complexities were evident in one of the New Jersey towns in which the committee responding to an affordable housing lawsuit was composed of two lawyers, a builder, two business leaders specializing in real estate loans, and the founder of a neighborhood ecumenical church organization who also happened to be a partner in a major energy management company. Among the issues the committee debated were where low-income housing should be located, was it necessary, and did the court have the right to usurp local control of planning.[13]

The way religious groups circumvented the complexities and resistance that so often accompanied housing projects was generally to keep them on a modest scale. This had been Church of the Saviour's strategy in renovating only two buildings at the start. Other churches sometimes turned a former sanctuary, rectory, or manse into low-income apartments when the congregation relocated farther into the suburbs. Others were able to construct an apartment building on a vacant lot adjacent to the church instead of using it for parking or purchase and renovate a nearby building. These projects were easy to win support for as long as they were small, relatively inexpensive, and served families who were part of the congregation. Still, there were hidden expenses, legal hurdles, inspections, and zoning rules that took up more time and energy than many churches could provide. Forming a nonprofit corporation independent of the church was usually the first step, followed by consultations with other nonprofits, interfaith agencies, and government offices to learn the ropes.

The uncertainties and resistance involved in major affordable housing initiatives, compounded by the scarcity of federal funding, meant that most churches tried to assist with low-income housing—if they tried at all—by organizing volunteer efforts and perhaps contributing financial help to support individual families. For many churches, these kinds of activities fit seamlessly into existing outreach ministries to needy families in their communities and corresponded well with ideas about love of neighbor, good works, and person-to-person care as well as a desire to avoid entanglements with government programs. When Reagan's affordable housing cuts were announced, the evangelical magazine Christianity Today, for example, advised churches to think about providing loans or emergency financial assistance to poor families, designating an apartment or a house that the church might own as temporary rental space for a low-income family, starting a prayer group to pray for the poor, and showing compassion in members' personal lives.[14]

Collaborative Financing

In 1986, the Reagan administration acknowledged that vouchers alone were insufficient to address the demand for affordable housing by creating the Low-Income Housing Tax Credit (LIHTC) program. Administered jointly by HUD and the Internal Revenue Service (IRS), the program required proposals to be submitted and evaluated on a competitive basis. The tax credits were allocated to state housing authorities using a formula based on population and economic considerations. The housing authorities then evaluated the proposals they received from interested parties in relation to housing policy and community development goals. The tax credits enabled private for-profit developers to reduce construction costs and thereby allow the units to be rented at rates below market value. Developers could also use the tax credits to offset the costs of for-profit projects or could sell them to financial institutions. Besides providing incentives for commercially viable projects, the program attracted nonprofit groups and facilitated faith-based construction and rehabilitation efforts. Although investors were initially slow to respond, the program became the largest vehicle for the construction of subsidized housing in the 1990s.[15]

The religious groups that participated in affordable housing plans had always worked across sectoral lines to achieve the input required from the federal government, local jurisdictions, and private building contractors. But for the religious groups that continued to be involved in the 1990s, the arrangements became increasingly complex, requiring coordination with multiple entities to bring an affordable housing plan to fruition.[16] Devolution of authority from federal to local jurisdictions was intended to deflect criticism of HUD by encouraging initiatives from local leaders who "know best how to set community and housing priorities and make them work." Tax credits were the main strategy through which devolution was achieved. However, as one observer remarked, "Tax credits typically form one layer of a much more complex financing package combining subsidies from other sources such as low-interest financing from state or local housing agencies, philanthropic grants, donated land, [and] block grants." These "financial gymnastics," the writer explained, were necessary because tax credits alone were insufficient to "get rents low enough for the lowest-income households."[17]

Typically, the participants involved in successful applications for funding through the LIHTC program included multiple layers of government agencies, developers, and investors. At the federal level, the IRS allocated tax credits and administered the credits on investors' tax forms, and HUD established income thresholds for families' eligibility. State housing agencies set priorities, scored applications, and monitored compliance. County and municipal agencies administered permits and sometimes provided land, subsidized infrastructure, and created additional tax incentives. The developers worked with various local organizations that formed specifically to handle a particular project or collection of projects and collaborated with banks for the capital to initiate the projects. In addition, property managers, attorneys, investment syndicators, and consultants usually played a mediating role.[18]

Nonprofit community development corporations were in a good position to work out the organizational gymnastics involved. Besides these organizations' tax-exempt status reducing their overhead costs, many of them pooled resources and provided managerial experience that a particular applicant would have lacked. For investors, it was often more efficient to work with larger pooled accounts than with smaller accounts. Many nonprofits also had relationships with local neighborhoods, tenants' and homeowners' associations, unions, and churches through which the nonprofits could claim to know which groups were credible investment risks. Organizations such as YIELD, Brooklyn Nehemiah, and Jubilee Housing, for example, could vouch for the member churches, prospective homeowners, and tenants they worked with, and in this way obtain more favorable rates on loans than otherwise would have been possible.[19]

States were required under HUD and IRS regulations to allocate at least 10 percent of their low-income housing tax credits to nonprofit associations, and, by some estimates, nonprofits were involved in as many as a quarter of all tax-credit housing programs in the late 1980s and 1990s.[20] The largest of these organizations, such as the Local Initiatives Support Corporation (LISC) and the Enterprise Foundation, served as intermediaries whose staff provided professional expertise and whose networks linked the relevant participants. Both LISC and Enterprise, for example, were involved with the Abyssinian Development Corporation's extensive mixed-housing projects in Harlem in the early 1990s.[21] Many of the interfaith coalitions also became larger, more professional, and more diverse, even as the scope of the projects on which they worked was often relatively modest. Addressing racial inequality through affordable housing also became increasingly complex, especially as home prices in suburban neighborhoods put homeownership out of reach for growing numbers of low-income families and as attention turned from suburban developments to rehabilitation projects in Black inner-city neighborhoods.

By the late 1980s, more than four thousand nonprofit organizations were involved in building, rehabilitating, or managing rental housing for low-income residents or making housing purchasable for low-income homeowners, and by the end of the century more than five thousand were active.[22] The largest of these nonprofit entities was called Navigate Affordable Housing Partners, an organization founded in 1980 in Birmingham, Alabama, to construct housing for the elderly and disabled, and which then expanded its contract management services to nonprofits in fifteen states. Most of the smaller organizations performed similar activities in particular counties and municipalities or served as legal entities under which specific affordable housing complexes were organized. Of the approximately three hundred nonprofit low-income housing organizations that were identifiably faith-based (using words such as "interfaith," "church," "ecumenical," "Chabad," "Christian," and "Catholic" in their titles), many had grown from local clergy councils initially concerned with ecumenical ministries to the urban poor while others had emerged in response to specific opportunities and needs.

Interfaith nonprofit housing organizations representing large metropolitan areas were functioning by the early 1990s in major cities, including Boston, Dallas, Los Angeles, New York, Philadelphia, Pittsburgh, San Diego, and St. Louis. Similar interfaith housing organizations were present in many smaller cities, such as Easton, Pennsylvania; Lincoln,

Nebraska; New Britain, Connecticut; Richmond, Virginia; and Wooster, Ohio. These were community-wide organizations that churches and synagogues had founded and still participated in as sponsors and through representative on boards, but that functioned mostly as the owners and management companies in charge of multiple housing complexes.

The San Diego Interfaith Housing Foundation typified the process through which many of these municipal organizations developed. Its roots could be traced to the civil rights movement when the San Diego Council of Churches formed the Citizens Interracial Committee to fight discrimination in housing and employment. The committee organized specifically to oppose California Proposition 14, the ballot initiative that would have repealed the state's open housing legislation. The Citizens Interracial Committee's principal leader was John W. Johnson, a Morehouse College graduate and Navy veteran who directed the San Diego Urban League, served on the boards of the interracial Christian Fellowship Congregational Community Church and the San Diego Council of Churches, and went on to become the general field secretary for the National Urban League.

The San Diego Interfaith Housing Foundation emerged out of the Citizens Interracial Committee in 1968, inspired by the fact, as one of the leaders remarked, that the White middle class "at the gut level just isn't aware of the deep frustrations in the Black community." By the end of the century, the foundation had built and managed five hundred affordable rental units. It also spun off more than a dozen smaller interfaith organizations to handle the details of its apartment complexes in specific locations.[23]

The focus and scope of operations among church-based housing organizations varied in ways reflecting their histories and communities. The Reformed Church of Highland Park Affordable Housing Corporation was an example of a project initiated by a single congregation. Located in New Jersey across the Raritan River from Rutgers University, the church's interest in affordable housing started when the congregation supported one of its families in becoming foster parents. During a subsequent renovation project, the church constructed a seven-unit apartment suite in its educational wing to provide temporary housing for homeless families. With municipal, county, and state funding, the congregation's housing organization then assisted churches in half a dozen other communities to rehabilitate housing for low-income tenants.[24]

The variety in faith-based organizations' focus was further evident in the contrast between two low-income housing operations a few miles apart in suburban Maryland. The one, called the Interfaith Housing Alliance, was responsible for fourteen hundred low-income rental units, for which it also provided tenants with financial advising and job training. The other, called the Interfaith Housing Coalition, operated only thirteen rental units but drew several million dollars in support from more than a hundred affiliated congregations as well as government funding to provide temporary housing and emergency financial assistance.

Among the hurdles community development groups faced was gaining the requisite know-how about the legal and financial complexities involved in initiating projects. Faith-based groups were sometimes able to play a constructive role simply by convening information sessions. For example, an interfaith network in Virginia whose focus had broadly been on doing something to help the poor got the ball rolling on affordable housing by hosting a panel discussion about HUD subsidies that brought together real estate managers, apartment complex owners, tenants, a state legislative assistant, and a HUD representative. Besides the information it provided, the meeting gave the participants an opportunity to air differing views about government responsibilities and regulations.[25]

One of the most serious difficulties many of the groups encountered was that different participants worked on different schedules and under different constraints. What was often described as "bureaucracy" and "red tape" was the complexity involved in bringing representatives of many different bureaucracies together, each with its own version of red tape. Opponents of affordable housing projects could induce lengthy, time-consuming delays or prevent them from happening at all by calling for another round of public hearings or by filing a lawsuit. Even when the lawsuit failed, it could lengthen the process to the point that one or more of the funding sources backed out. The federal government's role was another source of uncertainty. In addition to proposals for funding being competitive, programs and requirements were frequently revised or their renewal was in doubt because of administrations' changing priorities.[26]

Faith-based coalitions that could operate on a large scale often had an advantage over smaller ones of being able to draw on more congregations for financial contributions and being in a better position to speak as representatives of the religious leadership of an entire metropolitan area. The Washington Interfaith Network (WIN) gained national attention as one of the most influential of these large faith-based coalitions. Founded by Black pastors and representing more than fifty dues-paying groups including Black churches, mainline White Protestant churches, Catholic parishes, synagogues, and mosques, WIN initiated an ambitious plan in 1996 to build new affordable homes in the District of Columbia's majority Black southeastern quadrant, and, after four years of intensive work, broke ground for a 147-unit project. The project's financing included $3.7 million from the city, which also donated the land, $1 million from the federal government, and $500,000 as an interest-free loan from a local bank.

An initial boost came from WIN's affiliation with the Industrial Areas Foundation, which provided advice about community organizing. Another boost came from first lady Hillary Clinton, who hosted a meeting at the White House between WIN's leaders and major foundation leaders. WIN's efforts were mostly at the grassroots—meeting with clergy, denominational heads, and community leaders, and learning about public safety issues, jobs, and schools—while at the same time dealing with foot-dragging from housing officials and haggling with real estate developers. But to further its work, WIN also became involved in DC politics, distributing 75,000 scorecards, and asking candidates to pledge their support for more affordable housing. Reverend Lionel Edmonds of Mount Lebanon Baptist Church, one of the coalition's principal leaders, credited the organization's success to commitment, discipline, multiracialism, and prayer.[27]

Quite the opposite strategy was to avoid complex government regulations and funding uncertainties as much as possible by relying on private financing. Spathies Construction Corporation, a Chicago firm owned and managed by developer Bill Spathies, was instrumental in an endeavor of this kind. Spathies, a born-again Christian with twenty years of experience building expensive homes, wanted to be of service to low-income families. During the 1990s, Spathies built thirty affordable homes. Rather than applying for government funds, he worked out private financing and entered into joint-venture agreements with local churches. The churches vetted the prospective buyers, selected the ones with good credit ratings, handled the purchasing arrangements, and kept in touch with the new owners. The churches' no-cost involvement helped to lower the overall price of the housing. Equally important was the churches' role in determining who among the many needing affordable housing would be among the few selected.[28]

Habitat for Humanity, which also drew support from theologically conservative churches, adopted a similar strategy to Spathies's but operationalized it on a grander scale. Founded in 1976, Habitat built its first house for a low-income owner in 1979 at Americus, Georgia, subsequently gained national publicity when former president Jimmy Carter became involved in 1984, and by 1991 had constructed ten thousand houses. Habitat relied heavily on donations and volunteer labor but also depended on government funding. A Habitat project to build an affordable house in Fayetteville, New York, in the mid-1990s was typical. The Immaculate Conception Roman Catholic Church spearheaded the project and then enlisted promises of donations and volunteer labor from another Catholic parish, two Methodist congregations, a United Church of Christ congregation, a Lutheran church, and a nondenominational church.

Sociologist Jerome P. Baggett, who wrote a book about Habitat based on research at building sites in the 1990s, concluded that the organization did well at getting volunteers involved in their communities but was less effective at facilitating social interaction between the mostly White middle-class volunteers and the mostly Black or Hispanic homeowner families. Baggett also observed paternalism on the organization's staff and volunteers' part that left homeowners feeling that they were being judged by White middle-class standards.[29] However, Habitat, like other organizations that mobilize large numbers of volunteers, exposed volunteers to needs that could be a motive for becoming involved in broader efforts to address these needs. A middle-class Black volunteer interviewed in the 1990s as part of a study of civic involvement, for example, explained, "I'd work all day and feel good about it and then on the way home I'd be driving through all these bombed out areas. You could fly over that section of the city in a helicopter and you wouldn't even be able to see what Habitat had been doing." He redirected his volunteering into working with an organization called the Black Network for Progress that focused on racism, African American pride, and pushing the federal government to increase its support of affordable housing.[30]

Nearly all of the faith-related affordable housing coalitions were nonprofit organizations, but one stood out as a profit-making company. This was the Revelation Corporation, founded in 1996 in Memphis—a joint venture between a mortgage company and a coalition of five Black Baptist denominations. Revelation generated revenue by partnering with companies to purchase their goods and services at a discount on the promise of churches' pastors and deacons encouraging church members to buy only Revelation-approved products. Thirty percent of the proceeds went to the participating churches for pastors' pensions and expenses. The remaining 70 percent of the proceeds were invested in a national housing fund to make loans deemed too risky for commercial banks. Although Revelation's plan did not achieve success on the scale its founders hoped, it did construct some three hundred homes in Memphis for first-time buyers, helped about 4,000 families secure apartment leases, and assisted about 1,000 families in purchasing homes.[31]

In many communities, faith-based organizations were bit players compared to the outsized roles taken by large nonprofit intermediaries, government agencies, banks, and developers. However, small faith-based organizations were able to contribute in constructive ways. Black clergy, as trusted leaders in their communities, could articulate the needs and interests of their communities. Clergy coalitions could bring Black clergy and White clergy together in expressions of solidarity. By participating in denominational networks, inner-city clergy could challenge suburban colleagues to support affordable housing efforts. Crucially, religious leaders' faith traditions gave them a language in which to speak sincerely about caring for the poor. There were instances, too, when religious leaders spoke frankly about racism, violating when they did the customary euphemisms of "community development."[32]

Less visibly than in the planning and implementation of community development projects, clergy and lay members of congregations also played a role behind the scenes in facilitating the transition of low-income families into rental units and home ownership. A study of Indianapolis, for example, found more than a dozen churches involved in sponsoring home ownership seminars required of prospective residents for home mortgages. The clergy who participated in these seminars not only provided valuable information to prospective residents but also looked out for the residents to help ensure that they were being treated fairly by the banks. The study also suggested that clergy's continuing presence in low-income neighborhoods contributed to the success of affordable housing by serving on crime-watch and law enforcement committees and by teaching at youth centers.[33]

Within their congregations, clergy's role included making the case that affordable housing, if it was to be considered at all, was a topic deserving of members' time and financial support because of its spiritual connections. The pastor of an African Methodist Episcopal Church in Washington, DC, whose members committed themselves to supporting a housing rehabilitation project in their community was probably typical when he described "the enormous challenge I faced in light of the church experiencing over a decade of unsuccessful attempts to solve this problem." Establishing a successful building fund had to be about rebuilding the relationships and self-esteem destroyed by institutional racism, he said. It had to be about rebuilding broken dreams.[34]

Faith-Based Initiatives

The success of organizations like the East Brooklyn Congregations, Jubilee Housing Corporation, and the Washington Interfaith Network demonstrated that faith communities could contribute valuably to affordable housing and, in consequence, gave government officials a reason to argue that such work should be encouraged. To that end, HUD secretary Henry Cisneros in 1993 established the Religious Organizations Initiative to expand awareness of faith groups' role in community development. Cisneros, who had worked with church-based community organizing groups during his tenure as mayor in San Antonio, was interested in furthering the involvement of faith communities as partners in HUD projects. To make that happen, he enlisted Reverend Suzan Johnson Cook, a Union Theological Seminary–trained pastor of a Black Baptist church in New York City, to serve as HUD–church liaison. This was a role she fulfilled by meeting with pastors, attending conferences, and participating in the President's Advisory Board on Race. In 1996, with Johnson Cook's assistance, Cisneros circulated a white paper that cited numerous examples of congregations' participation in housing and social service ministries and argued that faith communities' potential to be even more important in addressing inner-city problems lay in the fact that they were intimately involved in low-income minority neighborhoods, valued community engagement, and could "touch the soul" in ways that other organizations did not.[35]

When Andrew Cuomo (future governor of New York) replaced Cisneros as HUD secretary in 1996, Cuomo established the Center for Community and Interfaith Partnerships to carry on the liaison work that Johnson Cook had done under Cisneros's leadership. Cuomo had worked with religious organizations assisting homeless persons in New York and then as an assistant secretary at HUD and had ties with leaders at Catholic Charities. Through these contacts, Cuomo brought in Reverend Joseph Hacala, a Jesuit leader who had headed the US Catholic Conference Campaign for Human Development, to direct the new center. "Community and faith-based groups are the closest to the poor in terms of understanding their needs and being in the best position to help them," Cuomo said when asked about the center's purpose. "I want the center to take a bottom-up approach, working with the groups, not for them. It's to be a new partnership aimed at empowering and revitalizing communities."[36]

Over the next three years, HUD's efforts to put the idea of partnering with faith communities into practice included educating staff at regional offices to understand better how to work with religious groups, hosting conferences for religious leaders with Reverend Hacala, setting up and funding organizations around the country to provide technical assistance to nonprofit groups interested in applying for grants, and establishing homeownership zones and empowerment zones in which faith groups were expected to play a grassroots organizing role. Although these partnerships sometimes provoked questions about separation of church and state, the increased visibility of faith communities in affordable housing efforts received favorable reactions even from critics who doubted that religion could play a substantial role in alleviating poverty.[37]

Toward the end of his tenure at HUD, Cuomo addressed a conference of community leaders in Los Angeles, praising the role of faith-based organizations in efforts to provide affordable housing, but cautioning against the idea that somehow private efforts could take the place of government funding. He challenged the leaders to draw more intently from their traditions of justice and mercy to focus efforts on racial inequality. "You have nothing to celebrate when you still have basic racial injustice in this nation," he said. "We don't like to talk about it and we don't like to admit it because it shames us and it should, but if you don't stand up and say it, you are condemned to live with it forever."[38]

Cuomo's message resonated with a citywide effort that faith leaders were implementing in Chicago. Called "Congregations Building ComInUNITY," this was an initiative cosponsored by the Leadership Council for Metropolitan Open Communities and the National Conference for Community and Justice. The initiative's aim was to heighten awareness among Chicago's congregations of the city's increasing racial and ethnic diversity and the continuing discrimination facing low-income residents in need of affordable housing. Two hundred of the city's churches pledged to provide information to their members about faith-based initiatives and how to support fair housing and diversity in their communities.[39]

One of George W. Bush's first acts as president in 2001 was forming the White House Office of Faith-Based and Community Initiatives, which, among a wide range of activities, carried on the work at HUD in partnering with faith communities. While continuing the outreach programs already in place, the new office reflected Bush's emphasis on "compassionate conservatism" and the positive impressions he had gained as Texas governor of evangelical Christian prison ministries. Like the previous programs at HUD, the new programs were geared toward facilitating partnerships with faith communities but also sought to focus on congregations that had felt excluded or incapable of participating. A HUD study commissioned to assess the state of faith-based organizations in community development concluded that only a small fraction of congregations were involved in housing efforts but that there was considerable upside potential because of congregations' interest in charitable service activities.[40] "All too often," HUD's new secretary Mel Martinez explained to a gathering of religious leaders in Philadelphia, "the government has inadvertently hampered the efforts of faith-based organizations to assist federal agencies carrying out their missions," adding that federal agencies had been "overzealous" in enforcing separation of church and state. He hoped to remove these barriers and provide stronger incentives for faith-based charitable work.[41]

The Bush administration's faith-based housing initiatives focused on homeownership counseling, funding for church-operated homeless shelters and short-term housing assistance, and overcoming barriers to enable smaller and newer faith-based nonprofit housing organizations to receive government funding. Homeownership counseling was meant to facilitate the administration's larger emphasis on homeownership by training clergy and setting up specialized nonprofit centers to provide qualified first-time buyers with information about how to establish a favorable credit rating, how to obtain a mortgage on equitable terms, and what to do as a responsible homeowner. The hope was that counseling low-income and minority buyers would lower the risk that they were perceived to represent and thus achieve lower mortgage rates from lenders. If the program brought marginally qualified mortgagors into the market, that was also perceived—but eventually with dire consequences—to be of benefit to the subprime lending industry. The funding for homeless shelters and transitional housing was meant to assist congregations involved in emergency relief for food, clothing, and utilities. Located within church buildings, these programs required leniency in how separate the service areas and worship spaces had to be to uphold church–state separation. The funding for smaller and newer faith-based groups was meant to encourage their participation through technical assistance with grant applications and by doing a better job of publicizing opportunities for funding. These efforts also included working with state and municipal officials to overcome biases against faith-based groups.[42]

Some funding was redirected into these programs, but they "weren't really new money," as one faith-based leader in Chicago remarked, "but a reframing."[43] In keeping with its image of being friendly to faith communities of all kinds, the Bush administration emphasized how much faith communities were contributing and how generously they were being supported, even though it was often difficult to substantiate these claims. Only a handful of HUD's Housing Counseling Program grants, for example, went to faith-based organizations. There were also difficulties in quantifying faith-based organizations' involvement.[44] One study—a survey of some 1,300 congregations in Philadelphia—found that although 35 percent were in some way assisting people with low incomes, only 4 percent were involved in housing rehabilitation initiatives, and even fewer (2.6 percent) were involved in new building initiatives.[45] The most credible assessment, a report from Harvard's Hauser Center for Non-Profit Organizations, concluded that the financial risks and complexity of housing development projects prevented most faith-based organizations from playing a more prominent role.[46]

The risks and complexities that the Harvard report described were the barriers that faith-based groups encountered in Minneapolis, Minnesota, for example, as they tried to launch an affordable housing project with financial contributions from churches and volunteer labor. Although the mayor was supportive, the city's budget for grants and loans was subject to pending state budget cuts and there were proposals for housing rehabilitation that competed with proposals for new construction. Months of uncertainties left the churches wondering how and when they should try to contribute. As one leader explained, "We don't think we could convince our congregations we have a need until we're building houses."[47]

Such difficulties notwithstanding, scattered and sometimes significant affordable housing projects did continue under the sponsorship of faith-based organizations during the Bush years, mostly on the models developed in the previous decade, but with some new participants whose interest was inspired by the administration's outreach. In a small mixed-race community up the Hudson River from New York City, for example, a HUD program analyst worked with the county human rights office and the local ministers' alliance to alert the population to predatory lending practices. In Nashville, where the metropolitan housing agency had been funding faith-based groups involved in affordable housing in the 1990s, several new partnerships emerged when HUD announced rule changes that seemed more welcoming to religious groups. Through another initiative, HUD sold foreclosed houses to faith-based groups at a deep discount who then rehabilitated them and made them available to low-income homeowners.[48]

But the Bush administration's focus on faith-based initiatives had another impact that was hard to ignore. That impact was on how faith communities' work was interpreted. Policymakers took the position that faith-based organizations had, on the one hand, been severely limited—even discriminated against—by unreasonable government regulations that kept them from doing good work in their communities and, on the other hand, argued that faith-based organizations had been doing much more than anyone had realized. These were contradictory claims, suggesting that faith-based organizations hadn't been able to do much of anything, yet had done quite a lot. Reconciling these claims was accomplished by highlighting the cases in which faith-based organizations had achieved great success—against the odds, and in ways that fit the administration's arguments.

The National Community Corporation (NCC) was the faith-based community development organization that received attention in nearly every early-twenty-first-century account of what faith-based organizations could achieve. Located in Newark, New Jersey, NCC was responsible for creating an effective infrastructure of technical expertise and managerial skill, constructing more than two thousand affordable housing units, rehabilitating an entire neighborhood, supplying the community with a daycare center and senior citizen housing, and bringing in a profitable supermarket. These achievements made it the largest nonprofit organization in the state and one of the largest in the nation. Compared with many nonprofit housing coalitions, NCC had indeed achieved remarkable success. Starting from a small church-based group in the late 1960s, it had survived Nixon's moratorium on housing subsidies, adapted to Reagan's and Clinton's housing policies, avoided scandals, and made wise investments. The NCC story therefore showcased the major themes of the administration's faith-based initiatives. Grounded in religious faith, NCC had navigated abstruse government regulations and barriers, demonstrated the virtues of private sector initiative, shown compassion, and launched a money-making commercial enterprise—all without ever having had to address racial inequality or discrimination.

But this framing of NCC's story neglected crucial aspects of its development—ones that better illustrated the organization's role in struggling for racial justice. The parish in which NCC originated—Queen of Angels Church—was, as one writer observed, the "formation center for civil rights and community activists" in the 1960s, serving as Newark's Southern Christian Leadership Conference headquarters and ministering in its predominantly Black community even as tens of thousands of Newark's White residents fled to the suburbs.[49] Among other things, the church's priests openly challenged the archdiocese's "white racist attitudes," and in so doing earning strong support from the Black community. For its part, the community's Black leadership argued for an emphasis on empowerment rather than a focus on "White compassion."[50] Moreover, NCC's theological vision was less oriented toward charity than toward justice, racial reckoning, and strengthening disadvantaged groups' God-given dignity.[51]

White compassion's role—generous but ambivalent—was instructive as well. In 1969, NCC launched a fundraising drive that brought in $60,000—a figure that soon grew to $200,000—from donors who purchased $5 "shares" in the corporation. The donations both enabled NCC's purchase of the land on which to build affordable housing and elevated its credibility in securing federal and state funding and the city's cooperation. "These are growing projects which will not change the world but they are seeds of goodness because Black and White people can work together," an NCC newsletter declared.[52] However, most of the donations came from families in predominantly White middle-class suburbs located comfortably some fifteen to twenty-five miles from Newark—donors whose ancestors may have lived in Newark but who now had little or no contact with Newark's Black residents. In one of the few studies of its kind, a journalist talked with White leaders in several of the participating suburban churches. They described their frustration in attempting to combat racial segregation in their own communities. It had been easier, they acknowledged, to host seminars, hold meetings, and send money for the work NCC was doing in Newark than it was to press for integration closer to home.[53]

Furthering Fair Housing

Nearly a half century after the 1968 Fair Housing Act, the various plans under which affordable housing needs had been addressed remained notably deficient in ensuring that racial equity was achieved. After a series of studies documented the seriousness of ongoing discrimination involving implicit redlining and predatory lending, the Obama administration issued a new regulation called Affirmatively Furthering Fair Housing.[54] In calling for meaningful action to combat racial discrimination and residential segregation, the plan aimed to foster access to diverse, inclusive communities. The plan's relevance for churches that cared about racial justice was that here was an intervention by the federal government that they could support, in contrast to the many one-off battles that occurred behind the scenes with developers and county officials. The further relevance for faith communities was that the plan's stated objective was to inspire public discussion of racial issues. Discussion was something religious groups could do.[55]

Progressive religious groups became involved in the ensuing discussions. They did so as interfaith coalitions, as representatives of individual congregations, and in conjunction with nationwide groups such as the National Fair Housing Alliance, the Housing Assistance Council, and the Poverty and Race Research Action Council. In an example hailed as a model of good organization, religious groups were among those represented as part of a large network of private and public organizations that participated in a three-year series of meetings in the Greater Kansas City area to discuss the relationships among affordable housing and residential segregation, access to public transportation, employment, and schools. As a result, the organization decided, among other things, to use affordable housing more strategically to place qualifying Black families in predominantly White middle-class neighborhoods.

For the faith groups represented in the Affirmatively Furthering Fair Housing program, the meetings were an opportunity to learn about the complexities of urban planning, forge networks with community leaders, and, if nothing else, have a seat at the table. Having a seat at the table meant an opportunity to voice concerns and to gain information about citizens' complaints concerning bias based on race, gender, sexuality, and disability. Through their involvement, the participants earned good standing in the community, demonstrated their interest in social justice, and in many cases secured support for food banks and social service ministries. The disadvantage was that the process—especially when concerning an entire metropolitan area—required months and months of meetings, usually dealt with issues beyond the average citizen's expertise, and offered no assurance of accomplishing anything. The plan's detractors considered it, at best, another instance of bureaucratic inefficiency, and, at worst, an intrusion of government into their lives.[56]

While most of the resistance to affordable housing came from neighbors who said that their rights to good schools, marketable home prices, and freedom from crime would be violated by the presence of low-income housing, one of the arguments against affordable housing claimed to champion the rights of low-income occupants themselves. This argument—advanced over the years—gained traction again under the Trump administration. One version said that low-income families who were being placed in federally subsidized apartment complexes were being discriminated against relative to other low-income families who could freely decide where they wanted to live. Another version said that the low-income families who were not receiving subsidized housing were being treated unfairly because they were having to bear some of the increased tax burden. Yet another version implicitly justified existing patterns of segregation by emphasizing racial and ethnic minority families' preference for living among families of similar racial and ethnic composition—staying close to "the gumbo you like," as a participant in a New Orleans discussion put it. This last argument included religion, claiming, as a case in Baltimore did, that Black people clearly preferred to live in Black neighborhoods because they went to Black churches and wanted to be close to their churches.[57]

In 2018, the Trump administration put on hold and proposed to terminate the Affirmatively Furthering Fair Housing rule, claiming its regulations imposed an unreasonable burden on local jurisdictions, and proposed replacing it with a new rule called Preserving Community and Neighborhood Choice that, among other things, would permit jurisdictions to address only one area they might regard as important, such as access for people with disabilities, while ignoring a disparate racial impact. The National Fair Housing Alliance and civil rights organizations roundly condemned this proposal.

Progressive religious groups also condemned it. The Presbyterian Church (USA), for example, passed a resolution at its General Assembly meeting, arguing that the proposal would weaken the effectiveness of fair housing legislation and that race should be specifically monitored as a potential barrier to fair housing, rather than allowing proposals to be approved that only addressed other potential barriers. "Racial discrimination continues to be a barrier to fair housing, resulting from the United States' long history of racist policies like redlining and subprime loans," the resolution stated, adding, "If race continues to be ignored by 'color-blind' housing policies, communities of color will continue to be harmed by racial discrimination in housing."[58] The Evangelical Lutheran Church in America was equally critical, stating that "any form of social, economic, and cultural discrimination is incompatible with God's design of a fair and just world."[59]

Spokespersons for the US Conference of Bishops and Catholic Charities USA also denounced the proposal, stating: "Discriminatory practices such as redlining, disinvestment from communities, discriminatory practices in selling or renting homes, and racial and economic segregation have undermined fair housing for generations and continue to harm communities of color today. HUD's new rule minimizes the affirmative responsibility to promote fair housing by removing clear guidance and effective accountability. Fair housing regulations remain one of the key tools for addressing long standing inequities and historical disadvantages and must be strengthened, not weakened."[60]

Drawing on the Bible, the Religious Action Center of Reform Judaism also objected to the proposal. "Throughout our text and tradition," the group asserted, "we learn that Abraham opens his tent to the road and welcomes others to his community. Inspired by Abraham's proactive effort to build a welcoming and inclusive community, we work to combat segregation and housing discrimination, and support comprehensive efforts to affirmatively further fair housing. Unfortunately, this proposed rule would undo the progress our government has made in pursuit of these fundamental values."[61]

If it had done nothing else, then, the Affirmatively Further Fair Housing discussion—and the Trump administration's attempt to quiet it—brought racial justice back into prominence. After years in which affordable housing policies had mostly been conceived in other terms (such as "community development") that did not explicitly acknowledge racial discrimination, the retrieval of racial justice was one to which progressive religious groups felt that they could make a small contribution. Supporting fair and affordable housing was a way to contribute.

In January 2021, during his first week in office, President Joe Biden issued an executive action called "Redressing Our Nation's and the

Federal Government's History of Discriminatory Housing Practices and Policies," which sought to focus further attention on racial justice in housing. Noting the considerable extent to which segregation was still a barrier to racial minorities having access to good schools, jobs, and healthcare, while also being a factor in disparate exposure to polluted water and air, a spokesperson for the National Fair Housing Alliance responded to the executive action by underscoring its significance: "We are glad that the Biden-Harris Administration understands these structural barriers to housing equity and intends to be a partner in implementing fair housing priorities that ensure everyone has access to decent, affordable housing in healthy, vibrant, well-resourced communities free from discrimination."[62] The need for religious groups to focus on housing, too, could be summarized simply: "Where you live matters because place is inextricably linked to opportunity."

In retrospect, the affordable housing and community development efforts in which faith communities engaged in the 1970s and 1980s established patterns that continued long after the projects they launched were successfully completed or had failed. One of the enduring legacies was the formation of interfaith, interdenominational, and interreligious organizations devoted specifically to the advancement of affordable housing in particular neighborhoods, counties, cities, and regions. By the 1990s, dozens of these organizations were functioning in large metropolitan areas like Chicago, New York, and Philadelphia and in smaller out-of-the-way communities in Kansas, Missouri, Mississippi, Nebraska, and other states. Additionally, many nonsectarian nonprofits concerned with affordable housing and community development included churches and synagogues among their sponsoring members. Many of these organizations had constructed and renovated housing that was still providing homes for low-income families.

Several of the affordable housing organizations that started as local interfaith initiatives grew into national networks. The East Brooklyn Congregations' Nehemiah organization built 4,500 homes in East Brooklyn and through arrangements with Industrial Areas Foundation affiliates and other nonprofits constructed a thousand Nehemiah houses in the South Bronx, another thousand in Baltimore, and several hundred in Philadelphia and Washington, DC. The Enterprise Development Corporation's efforts spread to sixty cities and included millions of dollars in grants and loans as well as thousands of low-income housing units.

East Brooklyn, Enterprise, and many other faith-oriented nonprofits won government funding by working with residents, formulating plans that went against gentrification, securing cooperation from private builders, and facilitating jobs and community safety. Focusing in depth as many of them did on local conditions and needs, these organizations facilitated achievements in affordable housing that also strengthened local empowerment. American studies scholar Dennis Deslippe, who examined the East Brooklyn Congregations' Nehemiah achievements, wrote, "Their legions of trained local organizers and successful actions revealed the significant influence citizens' power organizations brought on centralizing and technocratic forms of power."[63]

For churches and other faith-based organizations, the impetus for affordable housing stemmed from deep convictions about responsibilities to the poor—responsibilities that included housing and shelter as well as food, clothing, jobs, healthcare, and the other necessities of life.[64] Decent housing represented a crucial understanding of the relationship between individuals' spiritual well-being and their social surroundings. Hearts and minds were important enough that teaching, preaching, and training were essential: low-income families were likely to do better if they felt confident about their opportunities and took pride in their accomplishments. At the same time, the surroundings in which people lived had such an important impact on their thoughts and beliefs that better housing could be an important contribution to self-respect as well. An observer of the Jubilee project at Church of the Saviour put it this way: "The common persuasion of the group was that affordable, decent housing was an essential necessity in creating change in the lives of those caught in the desperate pressures of inner-city existence."[65]

Progressive religious groups' contributions to fair and affordable housing required tenacity in the face of changing government policies, uncertain markets, neighborhood resistance, and errors in construction and management. In most cases, it took coalitions among congregations to assemble the crucial funding and expertise. An effective program always required the cooperation of housing authorities, banks, developers, and homeowners or tenants. Nonprofit community development organizations played an essential role in providing faith-based groups with information and advice. When any of these puzzle pieces went missing, the likelihood of failure increased dramatically.

The aim of effecting greater interracial cooperation and residential integration through affordable housing programs was only modestly realized. The cooperation achieved was most notable among the sponsoring organizations, where representatives of Black and White congregations worked together for months and sometimes years. This was an accomplishment in itself, requiring the participants to confront racial differences, even if it did not reach deeply into congregations' memberships.[66] The goal of achieving racial integration in suburban communities was often stymied by resistance from White middle-class neighbors and was compromised by community planning strategies that placed affordable housing below many other priorities. There were instances in which racism was addressed head-on, but more often the issues were couched in arguments about efficiency, housing values, transportation, and schools.

The language motivating faith communities to be involved in fair and affordable housing efforts focused on *affordable* more than it did on *fair*. Advocating for affordable housing by constructing and rehabilitating it, managing apartment complexes for low-income renters, helping first-time buyers purchase homes, and assisting with mortgage negotiations all corresponded well with theological arguments about helping the needy. The housing was also supposed to be provided in fairness according to the civil rights and fair housing legislation of the 1960s. That was the way to do justice. As far as racial justice was concerned, advocating for fair and affordable housing primarily meant assisting Black and White families in ways that benefited both. Secondarily, it implied an expectation—whether realized or not—that Black and White families who happened to live in the same neighborhoods might interact with one another. Doing justice less often meant prioritizing efforts explicitly to achieve residential desegregation. Much of the historic legacy of residential segregation remained as a significant factor influencing every other attempt that was made to advocate for racial justice.

In Northern Virginia, where Reverend Jerry Hopkins hoped in the early 1970s to reduce racial segregation by promoting affordable housing, few of the region's churches had followed his lead. A modest coalition in one community and a private philanthropic-minded developer in another were the most actively engaged. Virginians Organized for Interfaith Community Engagement—a coalition of fifty religious organizations— did what it could to keep faith communities informed of the need for county governments and the state to address the shortages of available housing, but the coalition focused more on supplying information than on construction and renovation. The large faith-based nonprofit organizations that had rehabilitated low-income housing in DC had remained active in the predominantly Black suburbs in Maryland but not in the majority White suburbs in Virginia. "Achieving racial justice in Virginia requires overcoming housing segregation," a task force convened by a private consulting firm concluded, noting that "neighborhoods are more racially segregated today than they were fifty years ago" and adding for emphasis that "housing segregation affects education, job opportunities, family income, health and access to a quality of life."[67]

At the heart of the problem were the histories of discriminatory laws that reinforced current racial inequities in housing. These inequities included racial disparities in home ownership, asset accumulation, and access to the kinds of jobs and incomes on which residence in most of the region's suburban neighborhoods depended. In addition, the regional and municipal planning commissions that considered proposals for affordable housing operated at the vortex of competing interests from developers, employers, homeowners, advocates for open land and sustainable energy, and advocates for economic growth and low taxes. The faith communities and community development organizations that made a dent in the demand for affordable housing were sufficiently motivated to figure out how to work around the complexities of these constraints. It was a daunting endeavor, but one that could sometimes succeed when congregations participated in coalitions with sufficient resources and expertise.

3

Busing and Affirmative Action

REVEREND DARIUS SWANN was in his first year of teaching at Johnson C. Smith College in Charlotte, North Carolina, when he filed a lawsuit
that would dramatically change the trajectory of school desegregation.
Johnson C. Smith College was a historically Black school founded in
1867 by a wealthy Philadelphia widow whose husband had been killed
fighting for the Union Army in 1862. Swann was a graduate of Johnson C. Smith College and its seminary and, after serving for more than
a decade as a missionary in China and India, had earned a master's in
theology from Union Theological Seminary in New York. In their lawsuit, Swann and his wife Vera—also on the faculty at Johnson C. Smith
College—charged the Charlotte-Mecklenburg school system with racial discrimination for assigning their son to a segregated school instead
of an integrated school near their home. In 1971, the US Supreme Court
in *Swann v. Charlotte-Mecklenburg Board of Education* ruled in the
Swanns' favor, affirming a lower court's decision two years earlier. The case
was the landmark decision that opened the way for busing to be used to
achieve school desegregation in cities and towns nationwide.[1]

Busing provoked resistance from White families intent on protecting
the racial integrity of their schools. In Charlotte, the federal judge who
had ruled in the Swanns' case received death threats, his offices were
firebombed, and bombs exploded near his home. The Swanns' lawyer
and a Black minister were threatened, crosses were burned, and Confederate flags were unfurled. The Swanns left the area, moving to New
York and then to Hawaii, where Reverend Swann earned a doctorate,

and subsequently to India. As racial conflict escalated, a biracial clergy group tried to calm the situation. But Charlotte's churches were divided. The Mecklenburg Presbytery supported the busing requirement, urged its churches to "do everything in their power" to make the plan work, and warned against allowing church buildings "to be used for private schools established to circumvent integration." But Charlotte's largest church, Northside Baptist, a rapidly growing fundamentalist congregation of fifteen hundred members, ran an all-White private school, known locally as a "segregation academy," serving 850 pupils.[2]

Compared with the fight for fair and affordable housing, the struggle for school desegregation was in some ways simpler and in many other ways more difficult. Desegregation was simpler than raising millions of dollars, navigating the policy thickets of government bureaucracy, negotiating with resistant neighbors to build affordable housing, and then work for years with management companies and tenants. But desegregation affected families more intimately. It mattered deeply to White and Black families alike where their children attended school and how they were educated.

Desegregation was of course compounded by the same problem that fair and affordable housing had been meant to remediate. Residential segregation was the reality that necessitated something like busing if Black and White children were to attend the same schools. That was the major factor that the school officials in Charlotte faced. Despite school integration having been officially accepted, Charlotte's Black population was concentrated almost entirely in one quadrant of the city, allowing schools in each quadrant to remain largely segregated. When the community's Fair Housing Committee was organized, it was only a voluntary affair staffed by a few interested citizens, and when the city announced rezoning proposals to locate low-income housing in two predominantly White neighborhoods, three thousand protesters showed up in one and ten thousand did in the other. The federal judge in the Swann case stressed this geographic factor, writing, "The quality of public education should not depend on the economic or racial accident of the neighborhoods in which a child's parents have chosen to live—or find they must live—nor on the color of his skin."[3]

The Charlotte case illustrated the difficult questions that faith communities would face in taking sides on desegregation and racial equality for the rest of the twentieth century and beyond. Should religious groups support busing or oppose it? Should they support other means of achieving equal educational opportunities? Should they provide private schools that White parents could use to circumvent integration? If they did provide private schools, when would they come to accept integration? And what should their response be to affirmative action proposals, to questions about separation of church and state, and to complaints about the continuing reality of racial injustice in schools, colleges, and universities?

In this chapter, I sketch the principal ways in which progressive faith communities responded to these questions. The responses changed as the topics of greatest public concern evolved—from the controversies associated with busing in the 1970s, to questions about affirmative action in the 1980s and 1990s, and the continuing uncertainties attached to affirmative action in the twenty-first century. Like the ways in which progressive faith communities advocated for fair and affordable housing, these communities' advocacy for racial justice in education exhibited tenacity, had small but not insignificant effects, and revealed the complexities of the systems in which racial inequality is embedded.

Court-Ordered Busing

It was inevitable that busing would arouse passions on all sides. In the Charlotte case, Chief Justice Warren E. Burger argued that busing was a reasonable solution to achieve school desegregation, noting that nearly 40 percent of pupils nationwide were already being bused. In this view, busing was simply the result of the nation's evolution from the one-room schoolhouse to consolidated school systems. But the ruling acknowledged instances in which objections to busing might be made. These instances included busing involving unreasonable distances and busing being unnecessary for students living in racially mixed neighborhoods. There were also uncertainties about the proportions of Black and White students needing to be bused to achieve truly integrated schools.[4] Thus, there were sufficient possibilities for interpretation that local communities would have to work out the details—and do so amid interest groups taking opposing positions.

Busing's opponents in Charlotte organized themselves as the Concerned Parents' Association and held mass meetings to express their opposition. Their statements to the press advanced three arguments: first, busing to achieve court-ordered racial balance quotas was a costly intervention that would likely lower rather than enhance the quality of public education; second, cross-town busing threatened the neighborhood solidarity that families enjoyed; and third, forced attendance violated the basic freedom of choice that democracy was meant to uphold. Of the three arguments, the one about damage to educational quality ran counter to several studies showing just the opposite. Yet those studies were in quite different communities and were hardly persuasive to White parents who feared for their children's safety. As one of the mothers in Charlotte who regarded court-ordered busing unconstitutional declared, "I, for one, fear going into the black areas of our city. I dare not attend a PTA meeting alone, or let my child remain after school for activities, or drive my child to and from school in these areas. I fear molestation, cuttings and attacks on my car and person."[5]

The argument about preserving neighborhoods received less attention than probably would have been expected, but, as this mother's remark illustrates, blended with the idea that White neighborhoods were preferrable because they were safe. The third argument—about freedom of choice—gained the most traction. To Charlotte's White parents, freedom meant not only the desire to choose but also the hard-earned right to choose. "My husband and I have denied ourselves many things to buy a decent home in a nice neighborhood, convenient to churches, shopping centers, and schools, where our children can grow strong, where we can walk at night unafraid, where our children can walk to school," another Charlotte mother asserted. Now the court says my children "will not be permitted to walk four blocks to school. They must be uprooted from their neighborhood, herded into buses, spend two and a half to three hours a day riding with a teenage driver in downtown rush-hour traffic. I will not allow my children to be used as 'percentages' by a bunch of political idiots who think only in terms of votes and money." [6]

The most articulate spokesperson *against* the "freedom of choice" argument was Reverend Preston Pendergrass, the distinguished Black pastor of Charlotte's Antioch Baptist Church. Neither Blacks nor Whites were truly free, he argued. "Blacks are slaves to a paternalistic system, inferiority complex, fear of economic reprisals, and the constant brainwashing of the news media, and are, therefore, afraid to choose to enroll in previously all white schools." Whites were not as free as they thought, either. "Whites are slaves to the false doctrine of white supremacy, false teaching about blacks, lack of contact with and understanding of blacks, fear of black neighborhoods and ill-equipped black schools, and the same brainwashing of the news media." In short, "both whites and blacks are slaves to a segregated social system, and neither is free to choose." [7]

Proponents of court-ordered busing challenged the policy's opponents on two grounds. One argument asserted that busing should be upheld because it was the law. The other argument defended busing as the means to achieve the morally defensible principle of racial justice. Neither of these arguments had quite the emotional appeal that White parents' arguments about the safety and well-being of their children did. Both depended more on reason than on emotion, which meant that for every argument in favor of busing, there were counterarguments. For example, why should the law be dictated by a judge, critics asked, when there were other laws that had been passed by elected officials? Was not freedom of choice the highest law?

On the surface, the moral argument against segregation and in favor of busing was more compelling than the idea of simply complying with the law. But the public was divided even about the morality involved. A national poll found that 38 percent of White people considered it morally wrong and 42 percent thought it morally right "for most White children to go to White schools and most Black children to go to Black schools." Among Black people, of course, the responses were quite different: only 15 percent said this was morally right. [8]

Obeying the law and embracing morality were the arguments that Charlotte's progressive religious leaders advanced in support of busing. These religious leaders' credibility depended on what they had been doing all along for racial cooperation, not just what they may have said about busing. As was true in most cities, there was an ecumenical association through which the clergy addressed issues of common concern. The Charlotte Ministerial Association had been formed in the 1890s and over the years had met regularly to hear lectures, organize community-wide worship services, and guide the city on such concerns as juvenile delinquency and Sunday closing laws. It was an all-Protestant association with wide participation across the denominational spectrum. Its affiliates included Baptist, Christian, Episcopal, Lutheran, Methodist, Moravian, Presbyterian, and even the more conservative Associate Reformed Presbyterian Church that Billy Graham's parents had been members of earlier in the century. In the 1950s, the association addressed such concerns as teenage drinking, crime, the county's rapidly growing population, and how better to serve the low-income areas of the city. The association had been segregated until 1956, when a merger was effected with the Interdenominational Ministers' Alliance led by Black pastors.

In 1965, five years before busing began in Charlotte, the homes of the state NAACP president who lived in Charlotte, his brother who was a city council representative, and the civil rights attorney who would handle the Swanns' lawsuit were bombed. As the community rallied to denounce the violence, the ministerial association held an interracial worship service and issued a statement announcing the formation of a committee to recommend ways to help end racial discrimination. The association's leaders saw this action as a significant step that surely would prompt further efforts. Other pastors were less confident, noting that most churches and many of the community's civic organizations were segregated. Said one of the Black pastors, "So far as I'm concerned, we haven't done one thing, just made a nice statement."[9]

Busing's opponents in 1970 seized on the fact that the community's clergy had not done more to put their preaching into practice. Had the White clergy sent their own children to Black schools? Had they worked with city officials to find solutions other than busing? Were they saying that White people who opposed busing were immoral? Did they really believe that? Some of Charlotte's Black parents were concerned, too, wondering how Black students in mostly White schools would be treated and where they would find support.

Progressive religious leaders' voice was weak enough that retrospective accounts of the Charlotte busing controversy have attached little significance to their role. Implementing the court's decision fell mostly to the schools' administrators, teachers, and parents. Desegregation required courage and patience. Ultimately, busing's success depended on students slowly learning to get along across racial lines. As one of the high school students recalled, "It was rough here. We were so segregated that many Blacks had never encountered Whites close up." He added, "A fight between two people, if one was White and the other Black, became not just a personal thing, but the start of a race riot."[10]

Compared with the school officials and students directly involved, progressive religious leaders were fringe participants in Charlotte's desegregation achievements. Members of the ministerial association, though, were actively involved. One of the pastors served on the mayor's community relations committee. A second served on the school board. Another organized a committee to support a strike by Black hospital workers that occurred at the height of the busing controversy. Yet another telegrammed Justice Burger urging the Supreme Court to move expeditiously in support of busing. Others organized a telephone counseling service in hopes of providing anxious parents a way to blow off steam. Still others called on the community, whatever its views about busing, to move forward together rather than dwelling on their concerns. As one pastor put it, "It is time for the Christian people in Charlotte to stand up and say that for the sake of the innocent we should curb our wrath and direct our energies in a more positive direction."[11]

The busing struggle also prompted Charlotte's progressive faith leaders to forge new alliances. One alliance was with the North Carolina Human Relations Association, which urged the state's representatives in Congress to vote against a proposed antibusing constitutional amendment. Another alliance was with the Charlotte-Mecklenburg

Community Relations Committee—an endeavor to bridge racial differences beyond the schools. A third alliance was the formation of a new Charlotte Area Clergy Association, which included Catholics and Jews as well as Protestants in the hope of strengthening faith communities' social ministries.

By 1974, Charlotte was reluctantly accommodating to busing. Students gradually adapted to riding the buses each morning and afternoon and to being in different schools, conflict between White and Black students had become less common, and school administrators fielded fewer complaints from parents. As much more of the busing involved Black children than White children, a biracial advisory group formed to work on a plan to even the mix. Some of the White churches organized volunteers to tutor Black children whose needs had become more familiar because of busing. "We have stumbled our way into a kind of acceptance," one of the White ministers mused. "The busing issue was for a very long time an open wound in this community, but I see signs now that it's becoming a scar." One of the court order's vigorous opponents agreed. "Black and White people have got to learn to live together," he said. "The Lord didn't mean for us to be fighting. But it's a hard thing. Black and White is hard."[12]

A small but significant share of White parents decided the best way forward was to opt out of the public schools. About six thousand fewer children were enrolled in Charlotte's public schools in 1974 than in 1969. Enrollment in private schools climbed from fewer than three thousand to more than eight thousand. The rise in enrollment in private schools was driven by middle- and upper-income White families who could afford the tuition and occurred far more often when White children were being bused to predominantly Black schools than when Black children were bused to predominantly White schools.[13]

The differences among Charlotte's faith communities were most evident between the churches that sponsored private schools and the ones that did not. In 1974, there were thirty private schools in Charlotte. Of the 8,000 pupils in these schools, only 585 were Black, and of those, 453 attended all-Black schools, leaving only 132 in the almost-all-White schools. Fifteen of the thirty schools had been founded since the advent of busing. Of the thirty, twelve were all White, two were all Black, and eleven of the other schools had fewer than five Black students. The two Presbyterian schools were sponsored by churches independent of the Southern Presbyterian denomination. The two Baptist schools were also independent, the largest being the one sponsored by the Northside Baptist Church. The only school affiliated with a ministerial association church was a Lutheran school founded in 1942 by a White church that declared segregation morally wrong in 1960, pledged itself to work for integration, hosted seminars about racism, and supported the Fair Housing Association in the late 1960s. This was the only private school that achieved the desired 30 percent Black to 70 percent White deseg-regation goal.[14]

As tensions eased in Charlotte, Boston became the focus of some of the nation's most intense conflict over court-ordered busing. In Septem-ber 1974, after three years of de jure integration that left the schools mostly segregated, Judge Arthur Garrity implemented a busing order that linked the nearly 100 percent White predominantly Irish Catholic South Boston schools with Black schools in Roxbury. Besides the intent of the court order being similar in Boston and Charlotte, there was one other similarity. A person trained in theology played a key role in both. In Charlotte, it was Reverend Darius Swann. In Boston, it was Reverend Charles Glenn.

Glenn was White, a Harvard graduate with five years of postgraduate study in theology at the Church Divinity School of the Pacific in Cali-fornia, the University of Tübingen in Germany, and the Episcopal Theo-logical School in Massachusetts. From 1963 to 1966, Glenn had served as an ordained assistant minister at St. John's Episcopal Church in inner-city Boston and from 1966 to 1968 as the National Episcopal Church's coordinator for anti-poverty programs. According to writer J. Anthony Lukas, Glenn was a veteran of the civil rights movement, having "marched at Selma, been arrested in North Carolina, worked with a Black church in Roxbury, and helped organize Boston's first school boy-cott." Glenn (also like Swann) would earn a PhD and leave full-time ministry—serving for the next four decades as a state educational offi-cial in Massachusetts and as a distinguished scholar, teacher, and researcher at Boston University. In 1974, the task of working out the details of Judge Garrity's desegregation order fell to Glenn, who was directing the state's Equal Education Opportunity office. Glenn's plan set in motion the busing of students between South Boston and Roxbury.[15]

In most other ways, the conflict that erupted in Boston was quite different from the one in Charlotte. Whereas Charlotte's included peaceful mass anti-busing meetings, Boston's turned violent. In his Pulitzer prize–winning account, Lukas described what happened on September 12, 1974: "When buses carrying Black students pulled up at South Boston High School that morning, groups of angry Whites shouted, 'N- go home!' and six hours later, as buses from the high school rolled back down Day Boulevard . . . crowds pelted them with eggs, beer bottles, soda cans, and rocks, shattering windows and injuring nine students."[16] Violence continued through September and October as White youths attacked Blacks and Black students eventually responded by attacking Whites. Off in Charlotte, the community prided itself on having set a better example. In one of the Charlotte high schools, students raised $700 and paid for four students from Boston to come visit in the hope of picking up some constructive ideas.[17]

The faith commitments behind Glenn's interest in racial justice were mostly hidden, as they were for Swann.[18] The public role of faith commitments was performed by Boston's religious leaders. Whereas Charlotte's religious scene was dominated by Presbyterians and Baptists, Boston's was heavily Catholic. The archdiocese's response to the busing crisis was coordinated by Humberto Cardinal Medeiros and Auxiliary Bishop Joseph J. Ruocco. Their plan was to keep a low profile and work quietly behind the scenes. Although Medeiros supported desegregation at a public hearing and declared that Catholic schools were not to become a haven for those fleeing the public schools, the church's preferred form of involvement was to urge calm, rather than advocate for busing or to criticize busing's opponents.

Medeiros and his staff interpreted the White parishioners' response as driven more by fear than by racism. His staff directed the clergy and lay volunteers to alleviate parents' anxiety—for example, by helping mothers' get across town as quickly as possible when a child became sick at school. The clergy also held town meetings and met privately with individual members of their congregations. Some of the priests also participated in mixed-race parents' meetings designed to bridge racial differences.

The church's response satisfied neither the desegregation advocates nor the anti-busing activists. However, the church's statements appeared to be more supportive than critical of the anti-busing constituents. For example, in arguing that their responsibility was to "all the people," church leaders described the court as "those who thrust forced busing upon the mothers and fathers of Boston" and complained about "those who refuse to accept the 'law of God' which is higher than the Constitution." Medieros's manner of addressing racial injustice was also cast in generalities that critics found vaguely disconcerting—for example, declaring in a Lenten message that "human hostility—whether because of race, creed or color of skin—must be destroyed through our absorption into Christ."[19] As in Charlotte, White church leaders in Boston believed the best about the White people in their community. Joined by Protestant clergy, the priests in South Boston published a letter calling for nonviolence in which they said, "[We] do not question the motives of those in our community who have taken positions on either side of this issue. Rather we presume their good faith and lack of prejudice." The letter called only that the "law of the land" be obeyed.[20]

Unlike Catholic leaders whose ministries were directed to predominantly White constituencies, pro-busing leaders' constituencies were predominantly Black. These groups specialized in issues specific to Black neighborhoods, including urban renewal, affordable housing, youth programs, and anti-discrimination policies. By 1974, more than a dozen of these groups were in existence in the Roxbury area. They were the result of struggles in the 1950s and 1960s for racial justice, empowerment, and community development. Churches had played a prominent role in their founding and activities.[21]

Freedom House was one of the earliest and most important of these activist groups. Founded in 1949 by Muriel and Otto Snowden, a Black couple who worked at St. Mark's Episcopal Church Social Center in

Roxbury, Freedom House was the principal organization through which Roxbury's Black families challenged Boston's discriminatory urban renewal and housing relocation programs in the 1950s. Much of Freedom House's work in these years was done in conjunction with the Washington Park Citizens Urban Renewal Committee and the Boston Redevelopment Authority. Freedom House also became the hub of Boston's Black Freedom Movement and developed the education, community parks, and youth welfare programs that led to its involvement in education politics in the 1960s. This involvement continued its relationship with St. Mark's Episcopal Church and forged links between Freedom House and Elliot Congregational Church, American Friends Service Committee, YMCA, Urban League, and agencies of the Boston Public Schools.[22]

In 1963, Freedom House was among the groups participating in the interracial Freedom Stay Out movement that boycotted the Boston public schools in protest of the school administrators' refusal to act against segregation. The stayout movement was led by Reverend James P. Breeden and Noel S. Day. Breeden was curate at St. James Episcopal Church in Roxbury, where he and his wife worked with Black students in an after-school tutoring program. Day had replaced Snowden as director of St. Mark's Social Center. Besides St. James and St. Mark's, the other churches that organized and provided space for the pupils participating in the stayout movement were the Charles Street AME Church, Columbus Avenue AME Church, All Saints Lutheran Church, Blue Hill Protestant Center, St. Cyprian's Episcopal Church, and Tremont Street Methodist Church. In 1963, approximately three thousand students participated in the movement; in 1964, that number grew to twenty thousand. Students in the program studied an extensive curriculum that included African diasporic history among other topics. Several of the participating churches also provided tutorial programs and welfare-rights support for public-assistance recipients.[23]

In 1974, as court-ordered busing began, the groups that had spearheaded the stayout movement had expanded and been joined by new special-purpose groups focusing on quality education, tutoring, and educational policy. Freedom House, which had become the Freedom

House Institute for Schools and Education (FHISE), played the crucial role in coordinating the activities of the various groups pressuring the school system for desegregation and advocating for educational self-determination. These activities focused both on promoting community understanding of desegregation and on protecting the safety of the students directly involved.[24]

The fight over busing would continue in Boston for another three years, during which time Freedom House and the alliances working with it would confront the new challenges of school openings and closings, monitoring violent conflicts between Black and White students, and mobilizing support for neighborhood empowerment. Church leaders became less visible as attention increasingly required the work of teachers, educational specialists, and community activists. However, the role that faith communities played in supporting desegregation was no less important because of having mostly been behind the scenes. The teachings that faith communities were capable of advancing argued that busing was worth supporting, not only because it was court-ordered but also because racial injustice was wrong. Progressive leaders also proposed arguments about the basic compatibility of faith with educational goals that sought to enrich learning through intercultural exchange.

A desegregation plan that provides another example of progressive faith communities' involvement was the one in Seattle. This plan, like those in other cities, was controversial, but contrasted with the court-ordered busing that proved so divisive in Boston. Seattle implemented busing voluntarily in 1978 when community groups and the school system took action to head off a threatened lawsuit. Seattle's religious leadership contrasted with the clergy-led efforts in Charlotte and Boston. In Seattle, the pivotal role was played by a lay leader named Ann Siqueland who had become an advocate for equality and social justice through the Lutheran church in which she and her husband were active. Working with the Church Council of Greater Seattle, Siqueland spearheaded an effort that, among other things, included a program with other church council members to produce a nine-week curriculum about racial inequality that was used widely in area churches. The curriculum instructed church members in the history of segregation, desegregation law, the theological argument for desegregation, and an action guide for implementing desegregation in the Seattle schools. In her book, *Without a Court Order: The Desegregation of Seattle's Schools*, Siqueland chronicled the roles that the church council played in cooperation with the council's Black congregations and White congregations, the American Friends Service Committee, the Seattle chapter of the American Jewish Congress, the Urban League, the ACLU, and the NAACP. In 1979, these organizations mobilized to prevent an anti-busing initiative in the state from being implemented. In 1982, the US Supreme Court declared that the state's anti-busing initiative was unconstitutional.[25]

The patterns of religious involvement in Charlotte, Boston, and Seattle were replicated in Chicago, Dallas, Los Angeles, Minneapolis, Nashville, and numerous other locations, each with distinctive local characteristics. The controversies were rarely as contentious as in Boston, but they took concerted effort to resolve, usually taking several years, and then often facing revisions in later years.[26] Most observers concluded that progressive faith communities could have done more to support desegregation, but critics acknowledged that some religious groups had contributed quite a lot—given the overwhelming unpopularity of court-ordered busing.[27] Local congregations supplied volunteers who set up tutoring programs, monitored busing to protect children's safety, hosted interracial meetings, served on school committees, and distributed information about desegregation even as other congregations hosted meetings of anti-busing groups and sponsored private schools.[28] Additionally, national and regional religious bodies— such as the National Council of Churches, Presbyterian Church (USA), Indiana Interreligious Commission on Human Equality, and others—issued statements supporting school integration and outlining ways for churches to help, and religious leaders gave sermons and wrote essays providing new theological defenses of racial unity. These publications emphasized that whatever the churches did required cooperating across racial lines, gaining the necessary expertise to be effective, and forming alliances with other community groups.[29]

Affirmative Action

As desegregation plans worked their way through school committees and the courts, affirmative action in institutions of higher education became the issue that dominated much of the discussion about racial justice in which religious groups were involved. Although affirmative action in various ways had been practiced before World War II, it was not until the 1960s that the term "affirmative action" came to be used in reference to government policies, and not until the late 1960s that ideas about racial goals, timetables, and quotas came to define the meaning of affirmative action. Having been relatively obscured as a topic by the much more controversial issue of busing during the early 1970s, affirmative action was nevertheless propelled into public attention by legal action against it in the mid- to late 1970s and then by public opposition to it in the 1980s.

As questions about how to implement affirmative action with or without specific numeric goals gained attention, religious groups became involved in discussing, supporting, or opposing various affirmative action programs. The two court cases—*DeFunis* and *Bakke*—that drew national attention elicited strong statements from religious groups and did so in ways that had lasting implications for how to think about discrimination. The cases were preceded by religious groups having already been primed to think about discrimination because of busing, school desegregation, and affordable housing plans. The idea of using certain metrics, quotas, and percentages as goals to be achieved through affirmative action was in fact a logical extension of employing similar metrics as goals for the racial composition of schools and housing developments.

DeFunis v. Odegaard was settled by the US Supreme Court in 1974. The plaintiff, Marco DeFunis Jr., a twenty-two-year-old Sephardic Jew, sued the University of Washington Law School, arguing that he had been unfairly denied admission because the school had admitted minority students with lower scores than his. This policy of preferential treatment for minorities, Defunis's attorneys argued, was discriminatory against nonminorities. The court ruled that the case was moot because

DeFunis, who had won admission through a lower court ruling, was near graduation by the time the case came before the higher court. The case nevertheless attracted wide interest prior to the court's decision because of the arguments the lawyers put forward on each side and because of statements in the Supreme Court's decision about support-ing the elimination of racial barriers. The case also pitted religious groups with differing views of affirmative action against one another.

A few Christian leaders responded to the case. For example, an edito-rial in *Christian Century* described the case while it was pending—but offered no indication of the editors' views—and a meeting in Chicago among Black clergy discussed the broader issue of quotas.[30] Nearly all the commentary, however, was from Jewish leaders who were interested because of DeFunis's religion and in view of the long history of discrimi-nation against Jews in higher education.

The Jewish organizations that filed *amici* briefs supporting DeFunis had all been on the progressive side of cases involving equal rights and discrimination but now argued that it was DeFunis whose equal pro-tection had been violated by being subjected to different criteria for admission. These organizations included the American Jewish Com-mittee, American Jewish Congress, Jewish Rights Council, and Anti-Defamation League of B'nai B'rith. Their briefs conceded that equal protection might be compromised if the state had a clear and compel-ling interest for doing so, but they said the state had not established this condition. Their briefs also argued that the "White majority" included vulnerable groups within it such that it should not be treated as an undifferentiated monolith set against the interests of disadvantaged minorities. This would be an argument with important implications in later cases involving other religious minorities.[31]

The groups that sided in favor of affirmative action in the *DeFunis* case included the Union of American Hebrew Congregations and the National Council of Jewish Women.[32] The briefs that these organ-izations filed argued that policies explicitly acknowledging race, racial inequality, and the persistence of racism were constitutionally permis-sible and indeed necessary even though the policies would entail sacri-fice from other groups. The briefs argued further that universities' "color blind" policies were not in fact colorblind and that "merit" as defined with standardized measures was not the only criterion universities should use in admissions policies. "We believe that the risks of discretionary preferences—though real—are not so large as the risks of endangering all necessary affirmative action programs to bring disadvantaged and minority groups into the mainstream of educational life," the National Council of Jewish Women's brief declared. "As Jews we must continue to fight for all of our rights and causes. However, our long history for social justice demands that we not turn our backs on other minority groups seeking the same advantages so long withheld from them. Eliminating the blot of national racism in our country requires sacrifice and accommodation by all Americans so that future generations will be free of this bitter horror."[33]

Despite the different sides they had taken, within a few months of the *DeFunis* decision the major Jewish organizations came together again in supporting on principle affirmative action programs, seeking guidelines for implementing them, and meeting with Black leaders to strengthen ties. These meetings included representatives of the American Jewish Committee, American Jewish Congress, Anti-Defamation League of B'nai B'rith, and Synagogue Council of America. Black leaders included A. Philip Randolph, Bayard Rustin, and Charles B. Rangel. Issues of common concern focused on economic problems, job layoffs, and discrimination.[34]

The arguments put forward in the *DeFunis* case gained a significantly wider hearing in the Bakke case. On June 26, 1978, the US Supreme Court in *Regents of the University of California v. Bakke* handed down a ruling that effectively allowed affirmative action programs to continue but placed limits on how they were implemented. Bakke had been denied admission to the University of California at Davis medical school, which had reserved 16 percent of its admissions for minority applicants, some of whose grades and test scores were lower than his. Bakke sued, charging that he was the victim of reverse discrimination because of being White. The court in California sided with Bakke. "A White boy or girl from Appalachia without any shoes is just as disadvantaged as a Black kid from the ghetto without any shoes," the judge asserted. "There's a certain aspect of accepted inferiority by minorities," he said. "They say, 'Well, we can't compete on a basis of equality. Therefore, we're going to have to lower standards to take them in.' I'm unwilling to concede they can't compete."[35] The US Supreme Court in a split decision said the university had acted illegally by using quotas to deny Bakke admission but had not acted illegally simply by having an affirmative action policy that recognized race as a factor promoting diversity in admitting students.[36]

Along with civil rights organizations and college administrators, religious groups had been watching the *Bakke* case as it went through the judicial process. Jewish organizations were interested to see if the outcome would be like the *DeFunis* decision. Black religious leaders anticipated the possibility that gains being made through affirmative action would be set back. White Christian groups lined up both in favor of affirmative action and against reverse discrimination. Most of the major religious groups issued statements before or in response to the Supreme Court's decision.

Unlike many of the affordable housing and school desegregation efforts in which progressive faith communities had been involved, the Bakke case necessitated a different kind of advocacy. Because the decision was up to the Supreme Court, the opportunities for advocacy were limited to making public statements about the case. While the case was pending, advocacy groups' options were to issue statements in the hope of either influencing the court or of shaping public opinion about whatever the court decided. When the decision was announced, the options shifted to commenting on the decision or working to influence how other institutions implemented affirmative action. Because the court's decision was ambiguous as to how exactly race could be considered without quotas being used, there was ample opportunity for discussion about how best to move forward.

Progressive religious groups' advocacy fell into three broad categories: arguing for affirmative action while also arguing against quotas, mobilizing sentiment encouraging the court to rule against *Bakke* or for affirmative action using quotas to be implemented in other ways, and emphasizing the importance of addressing racism no matter what the court decided. The first approach was most evident among the *amici* briefs submitted in the case. The American Jewish Committee and the American Jewish Congress, as organizations long committed to protecting the constitutional rights of all Americans, filed a brief in support of *Bakke*. The brief argued that constitutional rights to equal protection under the law are granted to individuals, not to groups, and that racial distinctions used by state agencies were unconstitutional. The brief argued that means other than quotas should be used to take account of "genuine disadvantage," such as special procedures to identify disadvantaged applicants. There was no evidence, the brief asserted, to support the idea that quota-based affirmative action would serve the broader aim of benefiting minority communities. In sum, affirmative action programs were a good idea as a way of recognizing the disadvantages that some segments of the population faced, but hard quotas were unacceptable because they undermined the concept of individual merit and the value of judging people based on their own qualifications.[37]

United Methodist Church leaders issued statements expressing similarly qualified support for assisting disadvantaged minorities without endorsing racial quotas. Like Presbyterian leaders, Methodists had been challenged by James Forman's 1969 demand for reparations, but Methodists' response was even more divided than Presbyterians'—leaving the denomination cautious about how to address racial issues.[38] The Methodist approach was, among other things, to appoint Black pastors to lead the denomination's Board of Church and Society—the agency charged with formulating ideas about social issues without speaking on behalf of the denomination. In 1978, Reverend George Outen, as the second Black pastor to hold this position, issued statements urging support of affirmative action whatever the court was to decide. However, other Methodist officials seemed to distance themselves from Outen's response by arguing that the best way of addressing race was to engage more actively in personal evangelism.[39]

The second approach—mobilizing in the hope of influencing the court and other leaders—was used mostly by Black clergy and other civil rights advocates. Marches, demonstrations, and prayer vigils were held in support of affirmative action. A broad coalition in Cleveland, for example, including the Greater Cleveland Interchurch Council as well as representatives of individual congregations, students' groups, trade unions, and lawyers' associations, pledged its support of affirmative action. In New York, the National Council of Churches through its Interreligious Foundation for Community Organization convened a conference of clergy and attorneys to counter criticisms of affirmative action. In Washington, DC, Black clergy held a prayer vigil near the White House, and in San Francisco churches hosted rallies of students and activists. Other groups, including representatives of the African Methodist Episcopal Church and Black caucuses within the Disciples of Christ and United Church of Christ, sent letters urging President Carter to take a more aggressive role in implementing affirmative action initiatives.[40]

The third approach—using the *Bakke* case to draw attention to the larger issue of racial injustice—was common to all the progressive advocacy groups but was perhaps most notably illustrated by Black community leader Jim Ingram in Detroit. Recognized by *Newsweek* as "Detroit's most respected Black radio personality," Ingram was a commentator on WJLB radio and a columnist for the *Michigan Chronicle*. He was also associated with the Shrine of the Black Madonna, the church founded by prominent United Church of Christ Black Christian Nationalist leader Reverend Albert B. Cleage Jr. Commenting on the *Bakke* case, Ingram devoted a series of columns to framing the argument for affirmative action in terms emphasizing the priority of racial justice for the churches and religious leaders.[41]

Ingram bluntly rejected the argument that affirmative action was unfair to White people. "Now we hear the cry," he wrote, "'Why should I suffer the sins of my father's simply because I am White?' I'd be willing to bet every single one of these folks never once cried: 'Why should I enjoy the benefits of my father's racism, simply because I'm White?'" Equal protection under the law, he argued, was being used perniciously to perpetuate White racial supremacy.[42] In another column, Ingram addressed faith communities' indifference to racial injustice. "To use a term many of our ministers use," he wrote, "it has always been this 'hardness of heart' toward its racial minorities that has revealed America's self-righteous claims of freedom and equality as an empty, demeaning lie." The Black church, Ingram observed, "exists as a result of American religion's historic promulgation of racism, whether through sins of commission, omission or submission to the concept and practice of white supremacy." The leaders of White churches, he charged, "would do well to examine their arrogance and false piety in both the eyes of man and of God."[43]

Ingram further argued that the Bible called believers to move beyond claims about equality. "The Bible doesn't speak of treating the poor and disadvantaged equally, but of treating them specially, of seeking to correct the wrongs that have been done to them." He reminded readers that the Bible speaks much more often about justice than about equality. "The Bible recognized the injustices of the world, reveals that they are embedded in the very structure of things, and demands not equality, but restitution." He called for religious leaders to "enter into a social action thrust that serves notice on all organized religion that the time has come to stop playing games with both God and God's children and end the blatant hypocrisy that has plagued organized religion for centuries."[44]

Progressive advocacy for affirmative action, as Ingram made clear, was up against color-blind arguments that focused entirely on individual merit. Affirmative action advocacy also faced opposition from a new force in religion that political analysts were gradually coming to understand. This was the so-called New Christian Right. Loosely organized in opposition to abortion and homosexuality and in support of school prayer and traditional family values, the New Christian Right was an assemblage of special-interest groups that included the Moral Majority, Religious Roundtable, National Christian Action Coalition, Eagle Forum, and Christian Voters Victory Fund. With assistance from conservative Republican political organizers Richard Viguerie, Paul Weyrich, and Howard Phillips, these organizations shared mailing lists, held rallies, and reached evangelical Protestants and traditional Catholics.

The *Bakke* decision was of interest to conservative-leaning religious leaders who viewed it as having implications for gender roles as well as for race relations. Phyllis Schlafly, the conservative Catholic leader of an organization opposing the Equal Rights Amendment guaranteeing equal rights for women, became an outspoken opponent of interpreting the *Bakke* case in a way that might facilitate affirmative action. A bridge between the legal aspects of the *Bakke* case and its religious implications was also forged by attorney William J. Bennett and journalist Terry Eastland. The two—who would gain prominence as conservative leaders during the Reagan administration—published essays interpreting the *Bakke* decision, co-authored a widely read book attacking reverse discrimination, and argued for conservative faith communities to become more engaged in politics.[45]

Although the Religious Right's attention focused chiefly on abortion and homosexuality, affirmative action evoked resistance from religiously conservative organizations. The leaders of these organizations objected to government policies dictating what they could or could not do in terms of admitting students, hiring faculty, and administering programs. Ironically, this issue gained attention in 1976 when the US Supreme Court ruled that church-related colleges could receive government subsidies for nonreligious activities, such as buildings, student support, and general maintenance. "The Supreme Court," a conservative columnist declared, "pulled down the cross from the top of a church," noting that a Methodist college in Maryland was ridding itself of religious symbols, apparently to ensure its government subsidies.[46] The most publicized case specifically involving race was Bob Jones University, which claimed exemption from having to admit Black students on grounds that doing so violated the university's religious freedom. The US Supreme Court ruled against the university in 1983, but several religious organizations—Baptist, Mennonite, and Presbyterian, among others—filed *amici* briefs in support of upholding religious freedom.[47]

Unlike Bob Jones University, other church-related institutions did not claim exemption from including racial minorities but posed questions about how far government policies could go when religious freedom was at stake. For example, a Presbyterian college in 1977 debated whether it should continue receiving government funds for student aid if doing so could restrict its religious freedom and a Methodist organization the same year challenged an ordinance that prohibited it from hiring only Methodists in staff positions. In subsequent decades, many similar cases of course would come before the courts concerning religious freedom and the rights of gays and lesbians.[48]

Progressive faith communities' role in advocating for affirmative action in the late 1970s and early 1980s, then, played a role in these groups' efforts to promote racial justice, principally by asserting their support for policies that would elevate the likelihood of disadvantages incurred by racial minorities being addressed. Faith communities' advocacy focused less on what exactly should be done and more on the fact that racial inequality was a systemic reality that could not be overcome simply by assuming everyone enjoyed equal opportunity. This advocacy, however, faced the significant obstacle of affirmative action having to be advanced by somehow acknowledging race without employing racial quotas, and thus arguing for *diversity* rather than for racial justice. There was also the obstacle of the increasingly powerful religious right, which mobilized against affirmative action as part of its larger concerns about abortion, sexuality, and gender.

Following as they did on the busing controversies of the early 1970s, these affirmative action cases cast into sharp relief how much—or how little—progressive religious groups could hope to accomplish under considerations of equal opportunity. The courts were willing to permit remedial policies for specific legacies of institutional discrimination, as in the case of segregated school districts. The courts were not willing to address the injuries inflicted on whole classes of people—namely, the descendants of enslaved persons—at the expense of other individuals. Religious groups could abide comfortably with these judicial interpretations by affirming that everyone was not only ideally equal in the sight of God but was in fact also sufficiently equal that no special provisions need be made to achieve equality. But religious groups' teachings about justice and mercy required doing more. Faith communities were supposed to give preference to the needy and to victims of injustice. That was a hard message to share compellingly if the prevailing cultural norms adhered to the idea that race did not matter, only the rights and freedoms of individuals.

The ambiguity about what affirmative action meant also left open the possibility for any group that felt its interests threatened to call for banning all programs concerned with racial inclusion. Banning such programs was easier to mobilize constituents for when affirmative action was popularly understood as racial quotas. In the decades after the *Bakke* decision, numerous attempts were made to outlaw affirmative action, including a lawsuit in Virginia and ballot initiatives in California and Michigan.

The Virginia case—*Richmond v. Croson* (1989)—was decided by the US Supreme Court in language determining that the city council of Richmond had acted illegally by requiring companies with city construction contracts to subcontract 30 percent of their business to minority business enterprises. The decision attracted attention from religious leaders as well as from civil rights organizations. Most notably, a Boston-based group called the Organization for a New Equality convened an interfaith consultation that issued a pastoral letter calling the nation to recognize its "pervasive racial and ethnic discrimination" and to work toward "race-conscious remedies which provide expanded economic opportunities for minority communities." The consultation included Episcopal, African Methodist Episcopal Zion, Southern Christian Leadership Conference, and Operation PUSH representatives as well as scholars from major seminaries and divinity schools.[49]

The ballot initiative in California—Proposition 209—prohibited state government institutions from considering race, sex, or ethnicity in areas of employment, public contracting, and public education. California voters in 1996 approved the initiative by a 54 percent to 46 percent margin. Exit polls recorded approval from 62 percent of Protestant voters, 54 percent of Catholic voters, and 42 percent of Jewish voters. The measure was opposed by the American Jewish Congress, the California Catholic Conference, and the National Black Presbyterian Caucus. Jesuit scholar William C. Spohn published an essay in *America* in response to the California ballot initiative in which he argued that the Christian gospel required challenging the culture of individualism, racism, and sexism and identifying with the poor, the weak, and the needy.[50]

The vote in California encouraged lawsuits to be filed in other states in the hope that affirmative action would be banned in those locations as well. As it happened, this hope was realized in Charlotte, where busing had begun. In 1997, seven White parents sued the Charlotte-Mecklenburg school system, alleging that a student who was Anglo Hispanic had been barred from a magnet program because of school policies allocating a percentage of the admissions slots to Black students. In ruling for the White parents, the judge ordered the school system not only to abandon quotas but also to terminate busing.[51] Public reaction to the ruling was generally favorable, although a thorough study evaluating the effects of busing demonstrated its positive effects on academic achievement—and, busing notwithstanding, White students' continuing privileges in access to greater educational opportunities.[52]

In national polls, opposition to affirmative action ranged from 60 percent to 75 percent depending on how the questions were asked. California's anti-affirmative action initiative earned the support of candidates in other states and in the national election in 1996. Washington state passed a ban on affirmative action in 1998, and Florida did a year later. The Church Council of Greater Seattle campaigned against the ban in Washington and church leaders organized a pro-affirmative action march in Tallahassee. There were also local rallies, including one at Ebenezer Baptist Church in Atlanta responding to an anti-affirmative action proposal in that city, and an interfaith "Celebration of Diversity" rally in New Jersey to counter an "Independence from Affirmative Action Day" rally organized by a White supremacist group.

Michigan became the focus of affirmative action attention through a 1998 lawsuit against the University of Michigan that the US Supreme Court decided in *Grutter v. Bollinger* (2003), followed by a proposed constitutional amendment in 2006 to ban the use of race- and gender-based preferences in government hiring and contracting and university admissions. A coalition of Jewish organizations filed an *amici* brief in the *Grutter* case, quoting from the Talmud, the writings of Frederick Douglass, and social science research, and supporting the university's contention that the use of race along with other considerations in evaluating the qualifications of individual candidates was within its constitutional rights.[53]

The ballot proposal in 2006 to ban affirmative action in Michigan was opposed by an interfaith coalition of Catholic leaders joined by hundreds of Jewish, Muslim, and Protestant leaders, who distributed more than a hundred thousand copies of a brochure arguing against the proposal, and who asked clergy to discuss the issue in sermons and leaflets and hold meetings to inform members about the issue's implications. The argument for opposing the ban emphasized religious teachings about justice and mercy. As one of the rabbis involved in the effort explained, "Scriptures implore us to oppose any attempt to keep some people on the margins of life."[54] Despite this opposition, Michigan voters opted to ban affirmative action. Nebraska followed suit in 2008, Arizona in 2010, and New Hampshire and Oklahoma in 2012.

The Supreme Court rulings in *Bakke, Grutter,* and similar cases allowed the race of applicants to be considered in university admissions policies on narrow grounds that avoided quotas but that included a consideration of race among other characteristics that might distinguish applicants, such as gender, where they had been raised and gone to school, and what they may have done through extracurricular activities. The stated argument for considering characteristics of these kinds was that diversity was beneficial to the educational process. Students learned better in the context of students and faculty with diverse ideas and backgrounds, it was argued, and as a result they would become better informed as citizens in an increasingly pluralistic society. Race was not considered in categorical terms or as a means of remediating inequality but strictly as one aspect of diversity that might contribute positively to students' individual growth and personal fulfillment.

The details of how universities were to implement these programs and the requirement that they be strictly monitored kept open the possibility for further lawsuits. In 2008, Abigail Fisher, a White applicant, filed a lawsuit against the University of Texas at Austin claiming that she had been denied admission because of her race. The US Supreme Court eventually ruled in the university's favor in a 2016 decision.[55] More than a hundred *amici* briefs were filed while the case was pending, mostly by universities, attorneys, and civil rights groups, but two were submitted by religious organizations—one by a coalition of Jewish groups and the other by a coalition of Christian groups. The Jewish coalition consisted of the American Jewish Committee, Central Conference of American Rabbis, and Union for Reform Judaism. The Christian coalition was composed of African Methodist Episcopal Zion, American Baptist, Catholic, Methodist, Presbyterian, Progressive National Baptist, United Church of Christ, and several interdenominational groups. Although both coalitions filed briefs supporting the university's affirmative action program, the briefs were quite different.

The Jewish coalition's brief built on the fact that Jewish organizations had supported Bakke in his opposition to affirmative action but had supported the University of Michigan in upholding its affirmative action program in the *Grutter* case. The Jewish coalition's brief emphasized the history of bigoted numerical quotas being used against Jews. These precedents gave the coalition an opportunity to focus in detail on how race-conscious and ethnic considerations could and could not be used appropriately in affirmative action programs. The Jewish coalition's brief also referred extensively to social science research demonstrating the limitations of certain inflexible quota-based programs and the measurable value of flexible, individualized programs for students' educational achievement. Drawing from this literature, the brief argued that "the race discrimination and race consciousness experienced by a minority student in our society can be a singularly formative experience . . . that will directly impact what insights he or she will bring to the classroom and the campus." In short, the brief was evidence-based, and it addressed race explicitly.[56]

The Christian coalition's brief argued that diversity was an inherent value consistent with religious teachings and that affirmative action was necessary to ensure that diversity was sufficiently present in higher education settings. The brief mentioned race only a handful of times, almost in passing, and did not mention racial inequality at all. Instead, the brief concentrated on the individual, individuality, and individual fulfillment, referring to something about individuals nearly four dozen times. It was individuals' leadership that universities sought to cultivate, individuals as whole persons to which campus ministries were oriented, and individuals' spirituality that God cared about. Picking up on the fact that the court in the *Bakke* case had argued for focusing admissions policies on individual characteristics, the brief argued that individuality was indeed consistent with religious teachings and that the coalition submitting the brief understood how diversely different individuals were from one another. "Every individual's unique gifts, talents, and spiritual formation" were what mattered. Colleges' role was to give "individuals the tools to mature in faith, compassion, and mutual understanding." The brief dealt less clearly with why certain kinds and quantities of diversity were essential to higher education, arguing mainly that a "critical mass of minorities" was necessary so that "members of each group can bring their individualized experiences to bear" on discussions.[57]

Whether the Christian groups' brief was guided by what its proponents thought would persuade the court, whether it mostly reflected the dominance of individualism in American culture and religion, or whether it strategically sought to bring the two together was unclear.[58] However, the contrast between the Jewish and the Christian briefs showed the extent to which progressive faith communities felt they could or could not argue specifically about race. The Jewish coalition's brief drew from precedents and research that distinguished among kinds of race-conscious affirmative action programs. The Christian coalition's brief shifted attention to the individual and to affirming that God was ultimately in favor of individuals' having the capacity to achieve personal fulfillment. Missing from both briefs was the call for redistributive justice that coalitions of Black clergy and civil rights groups were making at the time.[59]

Affirmative action, like school desegregation, was meant to remediate racial injustice—a goal that was consistent with religious teachings about caring for the disadvantaged and doing justice. But it was clear in the trajectory of both affirmative action and school desegregation that it was impossible to achieve that goal without also acknowledging that racial inequality existed in ways that affected an entire population. Affirmative action for the sake of exposing college students to diversity was a recipe for timid steps toward bringing individuals together in the hope of them learning from one another. That was worthwhile, but it fell short of the ideal that religious teachings held sacred and that true equality of opportunity required.

The progressive religious groups that supported affirmative action, then, played a role, but had relatively few options for influencing how affirmative action programs were conceived or implemented. Other than issuing public statements and filing friends-of-the-court briefs, religious leaders recognized that the determination of which programs were or were not valid was up to the courts. Public opinion was mostly against any form of race-conscious affirmative action, lawsuits repeatedly challenged it, hundreds of colleges and universities managed in small ways to implement race-conscious admissions programs, and yet federal and state policies narrowed the grounds on which these programs were approved, and the ambiguity of these policies kept the door open for legal cases claiming reverse discrimination. Public schools made headway toward reducing racial segregation, but busing continued to be controversial and entrenched residential patterns contributed to de facto segregation.

Religious groups' support could hardly be interpreted as having been as influential as civil rights advocacy and public policies were. For the faith leaders who played the most active roles, activism was exhausting, frustrating, and disappointing enough that it was unsurprising when some of them abandoned clergy roles and pursued other careers in which they could be more effective. However, faith communities were able to speak from time to time against segregation and to practice affirmative action within their own recruitment and employment practices. That meant redoubling their efforts to recruit minority applicants at seminaries, for clergy positions, and in staff and administrative positions at church offices. If there were obstacles in the way of faith communities' efforts to help achieve racial justice outside their own organizations, there were significant challenges to be overcome within these organizations as well. These internal challenges became the focus of many faith communities during the last decades of the twentieth century and first decades of the twenty-first century.

4

Racial Reckoning

FAIR HOUSING, BUSING, and affirmative action—all demonstrated that progressive faith communities were capable of advocating for racial justice in limited ways, and of making some headway when few sacrifices from White people were required. Equal opportunity meant leveling the playing field in the hope that whatever disadvantages Black people experienced from past discrimination would soon disappear. Religious leaders who argued that more should be done to combat racial injustice faced opposition on grounds that it was now unfair to White people if special opportunities were made available for Black people. Religious leaders interested in racial justice also faced the reality that their own power to influence the activities of other institutions was limited. The limitations included not only overt resistance but also the specialized knowledge needed to make a difference in housing authority meetings, educational policy negotiations, and the courts. Thus, it made sense that religious leaders' attention would shift back to tending their own flocks—working for racial reckoning in hearts and minds and among the composition of their own memberships.

The US Supreme Court's emphasis on diversity in the 1978 *Bakke* case reinforced the broader idea—long held as a basic principle of American democracy—that diversity was a desirable goal that could legitimately be achieved in ways that included Blacks, Hispanics, and Asians in the same way that Jews, Catholics, Muslims, and for that matter, rural and urban people, men and women, and various ethnic groups could benefit from coming together. The argument in the Bakke case pertained specifically to educational institutions, suggesting that diversity was valuable in those settings because differing perspectives enlivened the search for knowledge. As the court's ruling had suggested, a Black person was likely to bring a valuable perspective to a university setting in the same way that a farm-grown student or an immigrant might.

But was that argument valid in religion? There were plenty of reasons to believe that diversity in religion was beneficial on a societal scale, providing the checks and balances that lowered the chances of any one religion suppressing the others. However, there were counterarguments as well—for example, among those who believed that only Christianity was true and therefore saw no value in embracing other religions. There was also an argument against diversity within local congregations. One version of this argument held that congregations naturally attracted likeminded people. Another version suggested that church growth was best advanced by explicitly catering to ethnically, racially, and socioeconomically homogeneous groups. On that logic, a racially diverse congregation might be a worthy ideal but practically difficult to achieve.

The strategy that ecumenically minded congregations adopted was to form alliances among congregations—alliances that often included Black churches and White churches—and in this way to acknowledge the lack of racial diversity within congregations, while embracing diversity among the wider community of allied congregations. Many of these alliances took the form of interdenominational clergy councils, often dating to the early twentieth century, and then gradually expanding into interracial and interfaith coalitions. As we have seen, these alliances and coalitions were active in sponsoring fair housing initiatives, responding to busing controversies, and issuing statements in support of affirmative action.

In the 1980s, and continuing through the end of the twentieth century, interracial alliances among faith communities also formed to promote—or directed new attention to promoting—racial reckoning. Either in response to specific events, such as racist incidents, or simply to work toward greater understanding and cooperation across racial lines, these groups involved religious leaders meeting with one another and initiating programs geared toward creating better relationships and a more inclusive community-wide culture. The groups then were in position to respond to racial incidents when they occurred. The groups also challenged congregations in some instances to think about how to become more internally inclusive within their own memberships.

This chapter traces the trajectory of several community-wide racial reckoning efforts led by faith communities during the last quarter of the twentieth century. Well before multiracial congregations became the proposed method of solving racial problems, Black and White pastors were experimenting in small out-of-the-way places with attempts to bridge the racial divisions in their communities. These efforts, which included pulpit exchanges, interdenominational coalitions, and interracial ministries, reveal the crucial roles that individual clergy and lay leaders tried to play— and the precarious relationships of their participation to community events. Racial reckoning worked to keep alliances among congregations intact when community crises happened. However, racial reckoning was also limited in how it was understood and in what it was able to accomplish. Racism and racial misunderstanding were only part of the difficulties racial reckoning programs faced. There were also tensions that inhibited communities from working together owing to conflicting priorities.

Calls for Racial Reckoning

The 1983 March on Washington led by Reverend Jesse Jackson with some 250,000 people participating was the largest mass demonstration against racial injustice since the crowd that gathered for Dr. Martin Luther King Jr.'s "I Have a Dream" speech twenty years earlier. Jackson spoke of how much still needed to be done to achieve racial justice. School desegregation was slowly being implemented, but stark differences in the quality of instruction available to Black and White students remained. Joblessness and disparities in employment and housing remained. There was the added concern that the Reagan administration's appeal to White southern voters and Reagan's stated antipathy toward "big government" were threatening the public safety net that supported low-income minority families. The mood in 1983 among civil rights leaders like Jackson was gloomy—enough so to require an encouraging word. "Don't let them break your spirit," Jackson said. "From the outhouse to the statehouse to the courthouse to the White House, we will march on. March on!"[1]

Heads of national and regional religious bodies organized committees, hosted meetings, and issued statements signaling that they thought that racism and racial injustice were still issues worth addressing. In the late 1970s and early 1980s, nearly all major denominations offered ideas about why racism and racial injustice were important for faith communities to address. Among the largest groups, the National Catholic Conference for Interracial Justice criticized its member parishes for their "deafening disinterest" in desegregation and called for greater attention to racial reconciliation. In the same vein, the United Methodist Church's Commission on Religion and Race and its National Conference of Black Methodists for Church Renewal blasted the denomination's White leadership for failing to appoint Black pastors to White churches or as district superintendents.[2]

Other religious bodies expressed concerns about racial justice along similar lines. The southern and northern branches of the Presbyterian Church pledged their joint support of affirmative action, racial empowerment, and "recovenanting" in the "common struggle against all the walls which separate God's children based on race." The United Church of Christ at its annual synod meetings declared its abhorrence of racial violence, support of affirmative action, and concern about "urban problems." Among women's organizations, Methodist Church Women and Lutheran Church Women, among others, appointed committees to work for racially inclusive ministries. In calling for racial reconciliation, the initiatives religious groups announced typically mentioned racism as well. "Racism is an evil which endures in our society and in our church," the National Conference of Catholic Bishops declared in a pastoral letter. "Despite apparent advances and even significant changes in the last two decades, the reality of racism remains. In large part it is only the external appearances which have changed."[3]

Enough time had elapsed since Dr. Martin Luther King Jr.'s assassination in 1968 that progressive religious leaders realized that the national mood had moved on, leaving behind the difficult work of racial reckoning. The changing mood was signaled in the lessening popular acceptance of racial epithets and stereotypes and in the contention that White Americans were truly past the kind of racism about which they might need to feel guilty, even though the durable structures in which racial inequality was based remained in place. This was the message that leaders like Jesse Jackson and the Catholic bishops wanted to convey when they spoke about racism. It was also the reason an interfaith convocation in Boston—where the memory of busing-related violence was too recent to forget—addressed itself to "the systemic and institutional racism which infects the whole structure." It was the reason the National Council of Churches issued a "Call to the Nation" addressing the continuing struggle for desegregation and why Episcopal, Methodist, Presbyterian, United Church of Christ, and other groups convened meetings urging attention to racial reconciliation.[4]

Besides speaking to their own constituencies, the leaders of progressive faith communities also appealed to public officials about racial justice. A coalition of Jewish organizations composed of the Central Conference of American Rabbis, the Union of American Hebrew Congregations, and the Rabbinical Assembly urged the Reagan administration to take stronger action to curb violence against racial minorities. The National Council of Churches assembled a meeting of Catholic, Jewish, and Protestant advocacy groups that called on Reagan to address racism in domestic and international policies. Similarly, a coalition of Black clergy challenged Reagan to look beyond his pervasive optimism to see the fear and despair among Black Americans.[5]

Everywhere, it seemed, deploring racism was in vogue. The Reverend Jerry Falwell, whose leadership of the conservative Moral Majority movement had cast him as one of the nation's most quoted preachers, told a nationally syndicated talk show audience that he'd been wrong about opposing school desegregation in the 1970s and was now repudiating racism. Racism was a sin, he said, that could only be corrected by a personal encounter with Christ, like the one he'd experienced. He still considered himself a conservative who strongly supported Reagan, but Falwell hoped to form a coalition with Black clergy to struggle together against pornography and homosexuality. Reagan, speaking to the American Bar Association at a meeting in Atlanta, affirmed his own "unshakable commitment to eliminate discrimination."[6]

But were the calls for racial reckoning hollow? "At the present time there is very little real reconciliation between the races in this country; there is instead a fragile co-existence that can be tilted very easily. Even the rhetoric of the religious community about reconciliation is simply that—rhetoric," observed Black educator and columnist Catherine Meeks. Was the United States ready for racial reconciliation, she asked, or was everyone too much invested in not rocking the boat?[7]

The real work of racial reckoning had to happen within local communities—and, as far as religion was concerned, in local congregations. National religious organizations had many other priorities to address—apartheid in South Africa, conflicts in Central America, homelessness and poverty in the United States, and questions about women's ordination, not to mention the fact that immigration was bringing a new meaning to the concept of diversity. Membership in the mainline mostly White Protestant denominations and the Catholic Church was also declining, limiting church leaders' options in the social ministries that they felt they could afford to support. Thus, while national bodies pondered what little they could do, the front lines were in congregations where communities were facing racial issues. And when a community's image of itself was broken, it was sometimes the community's religious leaders who could piece it back together. Nowhere was this better illustrated than in Livingston County, Michigan.

A Dark Legacy

Livingston County in southeastern Michigan was dotted with farms and villages in 1960. The largest town was Howell, the county seat, with fewer than five thousand inhabitants. A decade later, in 1970, Howell's population was still only 5,224, and Brighton, the second largest town, had fewer than half that number. But in 1974, the US Supreme Court in *Milliken v. Bradley* determined that Detroit's desegregation plan had to be confined to Detroit and could not encompass the city's outlying school districts, thus preventing busing between mostly Black inner-city schools and predominantly White exurban schools from being used to achieve racial balance. As a result, large numbers of White families in Detroit—85 percent of whom in a survey said they would not cooperate with court-ordered busing—moved to those outlying school districts to escape busing. Howell and the rest of Livingston County were among those districts. And, with the completion of Interstate 96 in 1977, these families could easily commute to work in Detroit while residing in the security of an exurban enclave. Between 1970 and 1980, Livingston County's population grew from 58,967 to 100,287, a 70 percent increase. While Detroit's school-age population was 63 percent Black in 1970, it rose to 86 percent Black by 1980; meanwhile, Livingston County's population was 98 percent White.[8]

One of Livingston County's White residents was Robert Miles. Miles lived on a farm near Howell and until 1971 was the grand dragon of the Michigan Ku Klux Klan. In 1971, Miles was one of six men arrested for conspiring to bomb ten school buses in Pontiac, Michigan, in response to court-ordered busing, and then meeting immediately after the bombing at Miles's farm to relish in their success and to plan additional bombings. Miles spent most of the 1970s in prison, returning to his farm in 1979. In 1985, Miles held a cross-burning rally on his farm at which two hundred people participated, including members of the Ku Klux Klan, Aryan Nation, the American Nazi Party, and other White supremacist groups.[9]

Miles was not the only racist living in Livingston County. In 1981, two masked men attacked an Ethiopian immigrant, holding a knife to his throat and telling him to leave the area within three days. Then in 1988, a cross was burned on the lawn of Shirley Griffin and her husband, a Black couple. Shirley Griffin had been born and raised in Howell but had lived and worked in Detroit most of her life. So when she and her husband moved back to Howell to retire in the 1980s, their White neighbors regarded them suspiciously as undesirable newcomers. The cross burning made national news.

Having become known for its racism, Livingston County's leaders decided they needed to do something to change the county's image.

Following the cross burning, the community's leaders formed the Livingston 2001 Diversity Council. The reference to 2001 was to the year some of the children in the community would be finishing high school—by which time the council's founders hoped racism would be remembered only as the community's dark legacy.

Four of the community's leaders were instrumental in forming the diversity council. Two of the four were clergy. Reverend David Swink, pastor of the Chilson Hills Baptist Church, was a relatively recent arrival, having assumed the position in 1979 after growing up in South Carolina, where he had been active in civil rights demonstrations. Swink was White and his congregation was White, but he was working in a small way to bridge racial differences by bringing together White children from his church with Black children from Detroit for joint activities. The second founder was Reverend Ben Bohnsack, pastor of the First United Methodist Church in Brighton. Bohnsack also was new, having just arrived in 1988 after having served a pastorate in Detroit, where he had become interested in civil rights. The third leader was Thelma Lett, a Black woman, who with her husband moved from the South to Livingston County in 1976 and became active in Bohnsack's First United Methodist Church in Brighton. The fourth founder was Roy Westran, the president of Citizens Insurance Company of America and an active member of the community's lay leadership. Working together, the four represented racial diversity among themselves, had links with several of the county's longstanding civic groups, and saw the need to shape the county's image in a new direction.

The diversity council's work was cut out for them. In a county that was 98 percent White, it was difficult to persuade the population that racial reconciliation was important. One of the council's activities was simply to provide small seed grants to the local schools to start programs oriented toward racial diversity. A second was to build on Reverend Swink's cross-church exchange program. Reverend Bohnsack and Reverend Asriel McLain of Dexter Avenue Baptist Church in Detroit formalized an exchange program between their churches, at first consisting of the two pastors taking turns preaching occasionally at each other's churches, and then taking members from the Brighton church to participate in services at the Detroit church.

No sooner had the diversity council formed than Robert Miles issued a statement denouncing it. Pushback came again in 1993 when the council circulated a petition, signed by a thousand residents, calling on the county to further distance itself from its racist image by becoming a model of civil rights, interracial understanding, and harmony. The move prompted members of the Michigan chapter of the National Association for the Advancement of White People to picket the council's events. A White resident complained about the council: "Despite the high-sounding rhetoric, this is the opening salvo of a liberal, far-leftwing, politically correct multiculturalist organization whose only aim is to destroy our moral and family values and impose their own."

But the diversity council gradually made headway in altering the community's reputation. Having become known as a location where White supremacists could make headlines, Livingston County was selected by a Ku Klux Klan group from Indiana as the site for a rally in 1994. The announcement prompted Reverend Bohnsack, through the diversity council, of which he was now president, to urge the group to stay away. The rally went ahead as planned, although it was sparsely attended. In a symbolic act of cleansing, Bohnsack and seventy-five volunteers took brooms, brushes, and water and ritually scrubbed the area where the rally was held.

When the diversity council reached its initially planned goal-year in 2001, the council's membership of nearly two hundred residents were engaged in cultural-awareness training sessions in the schools and for the county's law enforcement officers, and had added gender, disability, and sexual orientation to its mission statements about racial equality. The county's population had grown by another fifty thousand residents, but less than half a percent of the population was Black. The council was still fielding calls from the few Black residents in the county and from visitors about being hassled. In April 2001, two White men attacked and severely injured an off-duty Black state trooper at a bar in the county.[10]

Livingston County was unique in having had to battle a reputation brought on it by a single White supremacist who happened to live in the county. But it was not unique in being composed of White residents who lived where they did because they had fled from desegregation or who wanted race relations to be a problem in other communities rather than theirs. The Livingston diversity council is of course not unique either. It illustrates several things about racial reconciliation: first, there is an opportunity to engage in racial reckoning when a community that doesn't want to be regarded as racist feels it has to do something to refute that legacy; second, it may take only a handful of dedicated leaders to initiate a program concerned with improving race relations; and third, religious leaders are sometimes well-suited to play a leadership role because of their training and experience and because of their networks in and beyond the community. However, the Livingston example also demonstrates the difficulties an effort to engage in racial understanding faces when the community is overwhelmingly White and includes activists intent on upholding White supremacy.

Pulpit Exchange

The pulpit exchange in which Reverend Bohnsack in Brighton and Reverend McLain in Detroit participated in the early 1990s was one of the most common ways for White and Black religious leaders to work on racial reconciliation. The precedent for these exchanges was set in the eighteenth and nineteenth centuries, when White preachers would share pulpits with other White preachers and Black preachers would trade pulpits with other Black preachers. On the frontier or in small towns, exchanging pulpits was sometimes necessitated by a church building being under repair or a preacher being ill. Exchanging pulpits was also a courtesy, signaling respect across denominational lines, especially to a new minister in town. As a minister in Boston explained, "The man on the ground ought to make the advance and extend the greeting to the newcomer, and he is lacking on courtesy, whoever he is, high or low, who fails in this direction. Then follows the courtesy of pulpit exchange."[11]

By the 1920s, pulpit exchanges were occasionally being initiated between White and Black churches, often through citywide church councils and clergy federations. The Baltimore Federation of Churches, for example, instituted an annual pulpit exchange day in which pastors paired themselves with pastors of different races and different faiths. The Chicago Church Federation took a similar step, calling the initiative "interracial Sunday." One of the White ministers explained the reasoning behind the initiative: "We are dealing with a new Negro, no longer content with hearing nice platitudes about gentle southern mammies. The Negro doesn't want to be patted condescendingly on the back. He knows he is not inferior. And he is not."[12] One of the Black ministers in Baltimore, though, saw the matter differently. "The Whites can't take it," he said, noting that a Black preacher would be praised at a White church if he made a few stereotyped utterances and said nothing about race relations, but would elicit no response if he spoke about racial advancement.[13]

In the 1990s, pulpit exchanges were still the most convenient ways for White and Black churches to engage in racial reconciliation. According to a Gallup Poll, 81 percent of Whites and 65 percent of Blacks belonged to churches of predominantly one race. And the 1990 US census reported that 86 percent of Whites and 61 percent of Blacks lived in racially segregated neighborhoods. If racial separation of this kind was the prevailing pattern, reconciliation implied a Black preacher from a Black church in a Black neighborhood occasionally speaking at a White church in a White neighborhood and the White preacher reciprocating at the Black church. Of course, there were instances in which Black and White churches existed in close geographic proximity with one another, but when that was not the case, an annual pulpit exchange could be arranged at a distance.[14]

An individual pastor might pair with a pastor who happened to have been a personal acquaintance, but pulpit exchanges more typically evolved from a clergy federation or from several religious leaders planning a program involving multiple faith communities. Reverend Bohnsack's pulpit exchange in Livingston County, for example, was subsumed into a "city of youth" program that included Black and White churches throughout the Detroit area. Pulpit exchanges usually did not consist only of preaching, either, but referred to events that often included visiting choir performances, guest lectures, and sometimes even an award given in honor of someone known for working on racial justice. An impressive endeavor occurred in Cincinnati, for example, where Dr. Orlando Yates of Union Baptist Church—the city's oldest Black congregation—launched a "race relations" day, invited pastors of Black and White congregations to participate, and within two years grew the initiative into the Race Relations Council of Greater Cincinnati involving pulpit exchanges among more than a hundred churches and a student exchange program for Black and White youth. Other examples included interfaith exchanges, such as the one in Connecticut organized by the Community Relations Council for the Jewish Federation of Greater Hartford to promote dialogue between synagogues and Black churches about poverty and unemployment and a similar initiative in Chicago.[15]

The incentives prompting pulpit exchanges varied. Some originated from racial incidents, as illustrated in Livingston County. The racial unrest that erupted in Los Angeles in conjunction with the police beating of Rodney King in 1992 provided an incentive in other communities. For example, a Black minister and a White minister in Winston-Salem, North Carolina, decided it was time for them to do what they could to prevent racial unrest from happening in their community. Another round of pulpit exchanges occurred in 1996 in response to a wave of arson against Black churches across the South. In other instances, pulpit exchanges grew out of small study and fellowship groups, led to committees that planned how to cultivate closer relationships among congregations, and stood ready to intervene when the next racial incident happened. Clergy earned credit for putting their ideals into practice. As the pastor of a mostly White congregation in Maryland that was holding a joint service periodically with a Black congregation put it, "Our goal is for this community to see that [our church] believes in being one in Christ." He continued, "Most churches are either European American, African American or Hispanic. What we want is a diverse community that God called us to have through Jesus two millenniums ago."[16]

Short of pulpit exchanges, clergy found other ways of showing their interest in racial reckoning. One was to sign a "pastoral covenant" declaring their commitment to eliminating racism among their follow-ers. Another was to hold a rally or participate in a march, not to protest anything but to publicize that a spirit of unity existed among Black and White religious leaders. The Austin, Texas, Pastors' Prayer Fellowship, for example, did both in 1996. Its three dozen members signed a covenant expressing their opposition to racism and some of their members par-ticipated in a march aimed at displaying their anti-racism.[17] Indianapolis's pastors went further. They brought in Reverend James A. Forbes Jr., the distinguished pastor at Riverside Church in New York City, organized a 500-voice choir, and held a massive worship service at the Market Square Arena.[18]

Burnishing the community's reputation was sometimes as impor-tant, if not more so, as demonstrating a particular congregation's or tradition's spiritual ideals. No matter what the community's history of racial inequality may have been, no community wanted to be known as a center of racism. That concern had been especially important in Liv-ingston County. It was a significant consideration for community lead-ers in larger communities as well. Demonstrating in some small way that race relations were harmonious was good for business. On the off chance that racial conflict could be avoided, that was even better.

Jacksonville, Florida, was one of the more interesting examples of a community-wide effort to enlist the churches in a program designed to benefit the community by promoting good relationships between its White and Black neighborhoods. The Jacksonville Community Council Inc. (JCCI) had been created in 1974 with the aim generally of bringing people together to learn about the community and engage in problem solving. In 1985, JCCI initiated an annual community indicator project that conducted surveys, held meetings, and issued reports on such top-ics as transportation, employment, business opportunities, and popula-tion growth. Race relations were rarely mentioned, although there had been racial conflict in the 1960s and again in the early 1990s. In 2002, JCCI turned its attention to race relations, spending nine months study-ing the topic and issuing an urgent call to action.

JCCI was not a religious organization, but the report on race rela-tions was released at a Black Baptist church and, among other things,

Jacksonville's mayor hosted a meeting at another church in which he challenged the city's clergy to take the lead in working on racial reconciliation. Two hundred of Jacksonville's churches and synagogues responded. The congregations included Baptist, Episcopal, Jewish, Lutheran, Presbyterian, and Unitarian organizations. Over the next two years, these organizations engaged in pulpit exchanges, periodic interfaith dialogue meetings, "study circles" that met weekly throughout the period, and "congregational twinning" in which congregations paired with each other to sponsor joint worship services and community outreach projects.

While pulpit exchanges of these kinds crossed denominational lines, they also took place within denominations—which was often more comfortable for churches that hewed closely to the distinctiveness of their own traditions. Southern Baptists had for decades held meetings at which Black Baptist preachers spoke to White Baptist audiences. The same was true within Assemblies of God circles. Among Pentecostal churches, many had embraced both Black and White participants from the inception of Pentecostalism at the start of the twentieth century. Pentecostal churches at a national meeting in Memphis in 1994 also pledged to renew their commitment to interracial cooperation, issuing what they called the "Racial Reconciliation Manifesto," and outlining specific steps to take, including pulpit exchange and joint worship services.[19]

The impetus behind the Memphis meeting also illustrated what many critics saw as the weakness of pulpit exchange programs. Hosting a Black pastor at a White congregation or a White pastor at a Black congregation once a year was a symbolic act of racial reconciliation that meant little if that was all that happened. Worse, brief exposure to a different style of preaching and an unfamiliar liturgy could underscore separation rather than harmony. Brief exposure was a recipe for moving too easily to the conclusion that nothing further needed to be done. As a Black minister in Minneapolis observed, "There can be no reconciliation until someone says, 'You hurt me,' and the other one listens and says, 'I accept responsibility. I ask your forgiveness,' and they agree to make a new start together."[20]

Interracial Congregations

Interracial congregations were the attempt to go further than settling for intermittent pulpit exchanges. Some mixed-race churches grew spontaneously because of residential integration. Others stemmed from religious leaders consciously seeking to create worship spaces in which White, Black, and possibly Hispanic and Asian participants interacted intentionally and with sufficient duration to break down racial barriers. Making multiracial congregations work was difficult because of having to overcome fears of the unknown, as well as preferences for interacting more comfortably with friends and neighbors who shared similar life-styles, tastes, and economic advantages. For these reasons, although the ideal of achieving racial reconciliation through congregations in which Black and White worshippers participated together had a long history, putting this ideal into practice evolved slowly.

The historic First Baptist Church, founded in 1698 and located at the corner of Seventeenth and Sansom Streets in Philadelphia, is credited with being the first to establish itself explicitly as a multiracial congregation. A mostly White congregation throughout its history, in October 1935 approximately 900 Black members and 300 White members participated in a service at which White and Black ministers officiated and Black and White singers filled out the choir. Dr. Mordecai Johnson, president of Howard University, delivered the sermon. "We cannot live in racial compounds," he declared. "Covered up under every skin and language, though beaten down by adversity, there are the same ambitions to live and to achieve."[21]

Over the next three decades, other congregations became the first intentionally interracial churches in their communities. These pioneering ventures included the Church for the Fellowship of All Peoples founded by Presbyterian and Black Baptist leaders in San Francisco in 1944, a joint Baptist and African Methodist Episcopal (AME) congregation calling itself the Church of All Peoples in Cleveland in 1946, an African Methodist Episcopal Zion (AMEZ) and Baptist venture in Louisville in 1956, a nondenominational church in Indianapolis in 1957, and a racially integrated Presbyterian church in Miami in 1965, among others.

These churches evolved in several directions. First Baptist in Philadelphia kept true to its mission of racial reconciliation even as its resources diminished. In 2006, an observer wrote, "The building was covered with soot, and membership decline had made it impossible to raise funds for cleanup and restoration." [22] In 2014, dwindling financial resources forced the building to be sold to another church, but the congregation continued to meet there under a lease agreement. The Church for the Fellowship of All Peoples in San Francisco, where Howard Thurman served as its first preacher, struggled in the 1960s but survived as a place of interracial fellowship and worship. The nondenominational church in Indianapolis veered into the cult, led by its pastor Jim Jones, that committed mass suicide in Guyana in 1978.

The reason that churches could become the first interracial congregations in their communities was of course that most congregations were segregated. The First Baptist Church in Norfolk, Virginia, for example, could have been the flagship in interracial worship because its White and Black members worshipped together when it opened in 1800. But it became segregated in 1848 and did not attempt to become integrated until 1962. Other congregations tried to be interracial and failed. One such example was the Church of the Assemblies of Jesus Christ, founded in Charlotte, North Carolina, in the late 1940s. Charlotte's resistance to desegregation two decades later made it an unlikely place for an interracial church to take root, which indeed it was. As the church began holding services, its White neighbors circulated a petition and obtained a lawyer to seek an injunction to prohibit it from meeting. When that failed, the minister began receiving death threats. The congregation prevailed briefly, growing to two hundred members, of whom 15 percent were Black, yet it failed. [23]

There were scattered examples in the 1950s and early 1960s of congregations successfully initiating sustained interracial services. Two Presbyterian congregations in Chicago, for instance, merged in 1954, the resulting church being interracial. A few years later, a similar merger between two Presbyterian congregations occurred in Philadelphia. In Washington, DC, Lutheran leaders founded an interracial congregation in the late 1950s by recruiting members from existing White and Black

churches to launch the venture. Other examples included a nondenominational church in Los Angeles that grew out of a rescue mission whose
clients were Black, White, and Hispanic; another church in Los Angeles
that became interracial by recruiting new White members to replace the
White members who left when the membership became mostly Black;
and a new interracial church that Methodist leaders in Maryland
planned in anticipation of conflicts over school desegregation. As these
examples suggest, there was sometimes encouragement from denominational leaders but local circumstances were often the determining
factor.

In the 1970s, denominational leaders began more earnestly to talk
about interracial congregations as a means of facilitating racial reconciliation. However, plans for interracial congregations evolved slowly
because mostly White denominations separated their mostly Black congregations into separate administrative conferences and included Black
representation among denominational leaders only in token numbers
or through Black caucuses. Speaking about plans to become more interracial in these circumstances more often meant welcoming Black
congregations or evangelizing Black individuals than it did initiating
intentionally interracial congregations. The more common method of
interracial representation was experimenting with White clergy serving
in Black congregations or Black clergy serving in White congregations.
A study in 1978 found a strikingly high proportion of White Protestant
churchgoers nationally—32 percent—claimed Black people also attended at their church. However, the study failed to ask how many Black
attendees that may have been. The study also found that residence in
racially mixed neighborhoods best predicted Whites attending with
Black attendees.[24]

Sensitivities in White neighborhoods about school desegregation
and subsidized housing projects deterred many church leaders from
working out plans for interracial congregations. Mainline Protestant
leaders faced criticisms that their denominations were losing members
because they were too liberal on social justice issues. The possibility of
working on racial reconciliation through interracial congregations was
even less likely in the more theologically conservative Protestant

denominations. When progressive leaders in the Southern Baptist Convention sought to encourage harmonious race relationships by including a photo in Sunday school materials showing two White girls talking with a Black boy, the denomination banned the photo, deeming it "potentially inflammatory."[25]

By the 1980s and early 1990s, several cultural trends were working in multiracial congregations' favor. One was that distinctive denominational traditions were breaking down, driven by the fact that more participants in religious services had been raised in multiple traditions than ever before. A second was that large independent and nondenominational congregations were taking advantage of the suburban population's geographic mobility to provide worship experiences featuring contemporary music and upbeat preaching rather than traditional styles of worship. A third was genuine concern on the part of Black, White, and other groups that diversity was an ideal that should be realized in places of worship.

Less evident—and not unique to multiracial congregations—was the turn inward that had been gaining ground in American religion during the 1970s. This was the focus on personal fulfillment that inspired historian Christopher Lasch to write about the "culture of narcissism" and sociologist Robert Bellah and his colleagues to describe as "expressive individualism" in the 1980s.[26] However, the narcissistic individualism of middle-class White Americans was not the reason that prompted progressive religious leaders to focus on racial reconciliation within congregations. The shift toward working on what could be done in congregations was a realistic appraisal of religion's limited capacity to achieve the kind of large-scale societal change that an earlier generation of progressive leaders had envisioned. Working on fair and affordable housing projects, helping with school desegregation programs, arguing in support of affirmative action—these were all activities that required significant investments of time and energy outside the day-to-day tasks of congregational ministries. Working on activities within congregations was closer to what many religious leaders saw as their primary vocation and as the arena in which they could anticipate tangible results.

Studies of multiracial congregations suggested that an inward focus increased as congregations planned and implemented ideas about racial reconciliation. For some congregations, this inward focus on the congregation was driven by excitement about what was happening. Members perceived themselves to be accomplishing something important, were proud of what they were doing, and saw their congregation as being a step ahead of what other congregations were doing. White and Black members alike invited friends to come and they themselves became more involved. But other congregations became paralyzed. They worried about conflict and devoted their energy to avoiding conflict and planning what to do if conflict broke out.[27]

Both tendencies were evident in a multiracial congregation in Dayton, Ohio, that Robert E. Jones studied in the early 1990s. As the congregation shifted from a mostly White membership to a nearly 50 percent Black membership, some of the members—especially Black members—increased their involvement, expressed enthusiasm about what was happening, and invited friends to become members. Some of the White members were excited about the changes, too. But the enthusiasm among both the Black and White members was in some ways what was left behind as less enthusiastic members dropped out. Among the White members who stayed, there was also a sense among the older members of waning involvement and increased time spent worrying about where the church was heading.[28]

Other studies suggested some of the same dynamics. It mattered that congregations were *voluntary* organizations. People were free to leave if they were uncomfortable with what was happening at their church. Thus, when studies focused on the positive things that may have been happening in a multiracial congregation, they missed the people who had exited and they witnessed only the dynamics among those who opted to stay. Additionally, interracial congregations were sometimes among the few churches that happened to be in a racially integrated neighborhood where members may already have known one another and perhaps had common interests such as sending their children to the same school. Close observation of social interaction in interracial churches also suggested continuing racial separation, as evidenced by who talked to whom and where people sat.[29]

Lakeview Presbyterian Church in St. Petersburg, Florida, offers an illuminating example of the ups and downs that even a successful interracial ministry may experience as it seeks to be a force for racial reckoning in its community. Enough was documented about its activities over the years that it provides an exceptional opportunity to grasp how an interracial ministry evolved. In 1967, Lakeview Presbyterian became the first congregation in the Southern Presbyterian Church with an interracial pastorate. Its senior pastor, Reverend Robert Miller, a White preacher from Tuskegee, Alabama, was new in 1965. Its associate pastor, Reverend Irvin "Mike" Elligan, who was Black, arrived in 1967, having previously served in campus and denominational ministries. Three developments coalesced to make this interracial pastorate possible. First, the neighborhood surrounding the church was undergoing change as Black families moved in and White families moved out, which resulted in several Black families starting to attend the previously all-White congregation. Second, Reverend Miller had gained attention in Alabama for serving communion to Black students against the wishes of the White leaders at his church and Miller was intent on making Lakeview a responsible ministry to its racially diverse community in St. Petersburg—among other things, by preaching about race and opening the church for the first Head Start program in the city. And third, Lakeview received an experimental ministry grant that enabled it to hire Reverend Elligan to expand its ministry to the community.

Between 1966 and 1968, Lakeview Presbyterian Church lost more than two hundred of its six hundred White members. Some of the White members and Black members who stayed were committed to advancing the congregation's ministry for social justice. The Head Start program, funded by the federal War on Poverty program, made it possible for the church to hire a social worker to work with families in the neighborhood. During a sanitation workers' strike, the church offered office and meeting space for the strike's leaders. When racial unrest broke out following the assassination of Dr. Martin Luther King Jr.,

Reverend Elligan worked to calm unrest in the streets. As busing started taking Black children from the neighborhood to schools in mostly White neighborhoods, the church started a program to support the families. By 1972, the church had started an interracial coffeehouse, an interracial youth council, and the county's first integrated boy scout troop. It had also experimented with a new style of worship, including rearranging the seating in a semicircle and replacing the traditional sermon with dialogues between its pastors.

Lakeview Presbyterian Church took the lead in these initiatives, but it did not act alone. It was supported in its efforts by the Council of Churches of Greater St. Petersburg. The council included only White churches until 1986, but under the direction of Reverend H. Robert Gemmer, a former chair of the Utica Inter-Religious Commission on Religion and Race in New York who arrived in 1967 and became a lay participant at the Lakeview church, its affiliates played a role in all the major events accompanying the changing racial composition of the metropolitan area. These included mobilizing what was called Operation Attack in support of the sanitation workers strike and a teachers strike, working with the St. Petersburg Council on Human Relations to implement the city's desegregation plan, and supporting the parents whose children were being bused.

Lakeview's interracial ministries continued, including its Head Start program, its involvement in Operation Attack, its community youth program, and its innovations in worship. However, the congregation's membership continued to decline, confronting it with serious financial difficulties, and forcing it to evaluate whether it would survive at all. By 1976, Reverend Miller and Reverend Elligan had left and another pastor had come and gone. With only a part-time interim minister, the congregation contemplated disbanding or merging with another church. However, the congregation opted instead to form a spiritual renewal task force, revitalize its Sunday school program, and cosponsor a childcare center with another church. For the next decade and a half, Lakeview focused internally on the spiritual nourishment and growth of its members, maintaining its vision for social justice by hosting an occasional lecture and affirming the individual efforts of several of its members who were interested in peace, community empowerment, and an AIDS ministry.[30]

On the verge of collapse, the Lakeview church nevertheless was able to participate in small ways with the racial reckoning activities taking place in its denomination and in St. Petersburg. Anticipating the 1983 merger between the northern and southern branches of the Presbyterian Church, the two branches formed a joint effort in 1980 that held regular meetings and provided information and financial support for racially inclusive ministries. In St. Petersburg, the Lakeview church began holding joint worship services with the First Baptist Institutional Church, a Black congregation; additionally, the council of churches formed a health center located in the Lakeview church basement, and in 1986 the council merged with St. Petersburg's two Black ministerial associations.

All of that was background for the racial conflict that erupted in St. Petersburg in 1992. The conflict stemmed from the firing of the police chief, who was White, by the interim city manager, who was Black. The firing followed accusations that the police chief had been favoring White officers for promotion, had canceled a cultural diversity training program, and had ordered an internal affairs investigation of high-ranking Black officers who were critical of his actions. White leaders said his firing resulted from pressure exerted by Black leaders and clergy. Black leaders said the firing was justified. St. Petersburg was already under stress from an economic recession, was experiencing an upsurge of racially motivated hate crimes, and was further divided when the terminated police chief added to the turmoil by deciding to run for mayor.

Shortly before the police chief was fired, the Lakeview church—now down to only 125 members—was selected by the General Assembly of the Presbyterian Church (USA) as a pilot project to further develop what the denomination's leaders recognized as a significant interracial ministry articulating the relationship of faith to community action in a changing neighborhood. The Jubilee program, as it was called, paired Lakeview in a mentoring relationship with congregations in St. Louis, Chicago, and Tampa that were undergoing similar changes in their communities. The program gave Lakeview access to new ideas, funding for summer interns, and a boost in morale. Among its activities, Lakeview's pastor, Reverend Earl J. Smith, worked with two dozen of St. Petersburg's ministers to organize Congregations United for Community Action. With training and consultation from the Miami-based Direct Action and Research Training Center (DART), Congregations United pledged its member congregations to work for issues of special concern to the community's low-income families. Its member congregations included African Methodist Episcopal, Baptist, Catholic, Episcopal, Lutheran, Presbyterian, and Unitarian churches.

When the St. Petersburg police chief was fired, Congregations United organized a community-wide prayer vigil in which hundreds of Black and White residents participated and worked through its network of affiliated churches to calm tensions, provide information about why the firing occurred, and monitor the street protests that took place. As the unrest quieted, Congregations United kept working on the community action that had inspired its formation. Its board brought together balanced representation of Black and White leaders, including clergy and laity from ten denominations. Its priorities focused on community safety from drugs and crime, racial tensions in the schools resulting from discriminatory suspension policies, and the needs of low-income families. As the coalition expanded, its affiliates included Catholic, Jewish, and Muslim groups and its activities included prayer services, anti-drug marches, and affordable housing meetings organized in conjunction with interracial civic groups, such as the Lake Maggiore Shores Neighborhood Association that routinely convened at Lakeview Presbyterian Church. In 1994, Congregations United formed an economic development task force that monitored predatory lending programs and provided support for low-income lendees. In 1996, the affiliated congregations again played a role calming unrest when protests erupted after police fatally shot Black motorist TyRon Lewis.[31]

Lakeview Presbyterian Church's history was of course unique, but its experience in interracial ministry illustrated the challenges that many such initiatives faced. It was one thing for a mostly White suburban congregation to decide that it would launch an interracial ministry by inviting a Black pastor to give a guest sermon on Martin Luther King Jr. Day or to exchange pulpits occasionally with a Black church. It was different when the congregation was in a racially transitioning neighborhood dealing with school desegregation and experiencing White flight among its own members. It was especially challenging when a congregation's small membership kept declining to the point of threatening the church's very survival. However, Lakeview's experience also demonstrates the value of a core of dedicated leadership, denominational support, and the strength of joining with other concerned congregations.

By the end of the 1990s, multiracial congregations were becoming of sufficient interest among religious leaders that social scientists began seeking to identify how many such congregations may have been initiated nationwide. In 1998, sociologist Mark Chaves devised an inventive means of studying congregations by first conducting a nationally representative survey of individuals and then asking the religiously involved among these individuals to provide the exact name and location of the house of worship they attended. Chaves then conducted a survey among a randomly selected sample of those congregations, asking one of the congregation's leaders an extensive list of questions about the congregation. Chaves's data confirmed the extent to which American congregations were racially segregated: in nearly 90 percent of American congregations, at least 90 percent of the participants belonged to only one racial group. Further analysis of the data by sociologist Michael Emerson identified congregations in which less than 80 percent of the members shared the same racial background. Using this metric, Emerson concluded that 7.4 percent of American congregations—about 5 percent of Protestant congregations and 15 percent of Catholic parishes—could be considered multiracial.[32]

That was an impressive number. While it meant that de facto segregation still characterized most American congregations, it pointed to far more than just a few congregations in which interracial relationships were being cultivated. Emerson and several colleagues proceeded to conduct an extensive series of quantitative and qualitative studies to learn as much as they could about these multiracial congregations.

The national survey that Emerson and his colleagues conducted pared down the number of congregations in which a significant percentage of Blacks and Whites were present to about a third of all multiracial congregations—or about 2 percent of all US congregations. An analysis of in-depth information from about twenty congregations demonstrated that each was unique, following a different path to becoming multiracial—reflecting different racial and ethnic groups, different denominations, and different locations. However, geographic factors were clearly an important consideration. Congregations were started or their leaders decided to turn existing congregations toward becoming multiracial because that was the key to their survival in a racially changing neighborhood or because they considered it a mission and an opportunity to serve in a racially diverse neighborhood. Another primary factor was a sense of purpose that grew out of leaders' training and background. Additionally, an external authority structure such as a denominational initiative played a role in some of the cases.[33]

Further examination of multiracial congregations employing quantitative measures documented several characteristics that enabled their successful adaptation to favorable diverse environmental conditions while other congregations failed to adapt. Unsurprisingly, having a racially diverse leadership team was an important enabling factor. Less surprisingly, the presence of small groups in congregations had an enabling effect. They did so, even though small groups in congregations often sort themselves into racially homogeneous gatherings, apparently because some of the groups facilitated closer cross-race interaction than during less personal worship services. The research also suggested a facilitating role for charismatic worship services, perhaps because the experiential style of these services transcended racial differences, or perhaps only because the Pentecostal tradition in which charismatic worship originated had been racially inclusive from the start.[34]

As scholars interacted with the participants who were actively involved in multiracial congregations, one of the conclusions that emerged was a clearer understanding of the power of discourse, stories, and metaphors. Talking about beliefs, ideas, and experiences could be dismissed as insignificant compared with doing something like building houses or passing laws. But talking was how preaching happened, how creeds were recited, how sacred rites were performed, and how congregants interacted when the services were finished. Unlike the brief statements that religious leaders issued in the hope of registering their support of some policy or court decision, the discourse that happened within congregations could be powerful because it was lengthier, improvisational, and cast in the familiar language of religious traditions.

Communication studies scholar Heather Entrekin's rich ethnographic study of a theologically conservative multicultural congregation in the Midwest in the 1990s probed deeply into the language, stories, and metaphors that emerged as the members of this congregation worshipped together and created friendships with one another. Whether knowingly or unknowingly, the leaders and members rarely used language that implied differences of status, and when they did, it was to deny these differences. As one participant said, "God doesn't put one person above the other. It doesn't matter what color we are. It doesn't matter what we look like." Words such as "with" and "together" that emphasized equality replaced up and down language that implied inequality. Similarities in dress and seating arrangements further symbolized equality both among the congregants and between them and the clergy. Togetherness was similarly expressed in metaphors of home, tables, families, heaven, and the community in which the church was located. These metaphors were embedded in stories that referred to events that individuals and the group had experienced—events that included food, activities, emotions, and shared memories—and the stories were often interlaced with references to biblical narratives about Jesus, God, and love of neighbor.[35]

Although storytelling and metaphors of these kinds are possible in multiracial congregations, many of the studies of these congregations have suggested a significant caveat. Eager to demonstrate that racial differences do not matter, participants in racially diverse congregations frequently avoid having explicit discussions of racism, racial inequality, discrimination, and racial justice. Rather, participants downplay these topics, speak euphemistically of diversity and inclusion, and rarely refer to their own or another person's race.[36] These modes of avoidance are common in other realms as well, where talking specifically about racial, sexual, socioeconomic, and religious differences is sufficiently uncomfortable that skirting around them is the easiest solution. When avoidance is the norm, participating in a multiracial congregation can be a way of feeling diverse without addressing the depths of diversity. Feeling diverse can even become the accepted norm when diversity is only modestly present, as for instance when clergy say their congregations are quite diverse, meaning only that a single person of color has been attending or that the congregation is composed happily of Swedes and Norwegians. Nonetheless, participating in religious services with worshippers of different races can be a reminder of those differences. And being reminded of racial differences is arguably an important step toward working more actively toward racial reconciliation.

The evidence from multiracial congregations also demonstrated the dual-faceted nature of racial reconciliation. On the one hand, reconciliation of any kind implies coming to an understanding about certain beliefs and values with which all can agree. On the other hand, reconciliation implies greater awareness of the differences and disagreements that underlie the desire for reconciliation in the first place. Both tendencies were present among the participants in studies of multiracial congregations. Black and White participants alike wanted to find common ground, but they also wanted their distinctive traditions and styles to be embraced. In these respects, multiracial congregations were less like melting pots and more like mosaics in which diversity was being maintained.[37]

As more studies of multiracial congregations were conducted, the evidence further suggested the continuing racial disparities that persist within many of these congregations. The senior pastor, for example, may be White while the associate pastor may be Black, as was true at the Lakeview church in the 1960s. Or the Black pastor may be the one assigned to work with low-income families, while the White pastor works with the upscale members. Insofar as how the congregation is financed, the White families may have more say in how the money is spent than the Black families, or the Black families may be the ones tasked with speaking about race while the White families get by assuming that race is unimportant. A congregation's image of itself may matter as well. It may pride itself on being multiracial, but it may prefer to be known as an "urban ministry" instead of as a congregation Black enough to be described as a Black church. Additionally, religious leaders and scholars who call for more participation in multiracial congregations may have in mind Black participants joining White churches more than White participants joining Black churches. All of these possibilities suggest that challenges persist even when racial reconciliation is facilitated in interracial ministries.[38]

Among the notable features of the racial reckoning efforts that faith communities initiated in the late twentieth- and early twenty-first centuries, then, the underlying assumption was that getting racially mixed groups together would contribute measurably to reducing racial injustice. This expectation was evident in study groups, pulpit exchanges, joint worship services, and multiracial congregations. Christian groups expressed the hope that racial reconciliation would be achieved as people from different racial backgrounds came to understand themselves as brothers and sisters in Christ. Interfaith groups pledged themselves to a clearer recognition of everyone being equal before God. Their hope was to battle racially biased behavior, beliefs, and attitudes. This hope was driven by the ideal expressed in sacred teachings of all people living in harmony. It was an ideal that by the end of the twentieth century also seemed to be the practical way for religious organizations to respond to a changing world. If communities were becoming increasingly diverse, then forward-thinking religious organizations also needed to be diverse.[39]

The strength of tackling racial reconciliation in these ways was that evidence could be found that interracial contact was indeed associated with less negative stereotyping, fewer conflicts, and lower likelihoods of engaging in discrimination. People who participated in interracial study groups and worship services learned that racism was wrong even when it may have occurred only from a thoughtless remark. Participants in interracial congregations benefited from opportunities to become personally acquainted with individuals whose backgrounds and experiences differed from theirs. Study groups and worship services were the occasions for moral convictions about fair treatment to be reinforced. The further strength of racial reconciliation efforts in congregations was that congregations could use their resources to sponsor racially inclusive programs without having to engage with the outside powers that managed housing programs, schools, businesses, and government agencies. Racial reconciliation was a way to focus internally on something a congregation could manage with an expectation of the participants benefiting.

These were among the reasons that interracial relationships among and within congregations were able to diffuse as widely as they did. Coalitions with nonreligious organizations specializing in housing, education, and government policies were not required. Congregations eager to avoid being perceived as being "political" could sponsor interracial pulpit exchanges and study groups without riling members' sensitivities about separation of church and state. Multiracial congregations were also a way that smaller congregations, new ministries, and churches in theologically conservative denominations could participate. Without seeming to side with religion's progressive wing, congregations could demonstrate their commitment to a biblical ideal of love for all.

Racial reconciliation's value also lay in the symbolism it provided. Congregations, neighborhoods, cities, and whole branches of the religious community could publicize their abhorrence about racist acts. When Black churches were burned in 1996, for example, interdenominational services told the public that these acts were unacceptable to the ways most faith communities thought about race. Religious leaders took the occasion variously to call for stiffer laws and a renewed commitment to religious principles. It mattered for religious organizations to publicly condemn racist acts, if only to demonstrate that there were people in the community who did not think racism could be justified simply as an excusable eccentricity or as freedom of expression.

All of that was commendable. However, racial reconciliation too easily focused on racism as if it were something that could be significantly reduced by individuals of different races interacting with one another or by individuals simply acknowledging to themselves that their attitudes were not always as pure as they should be. "We get comfortable in knowing one or two people of another culture" was how one pastor put it, "but there are masses of people we don't talk to and don't see and have no connection with. How can we be reconciled?"[40] Racial reconciliation was a fraught topic, too, when religious leaders claimed it was divisive to speak frankly about the continuing realities of discrimination and inequality—just "focus more on what we have in common than on our differences." Although institutional racism and systemic racism were concepts toward which racial reckoning was ultimately directed, the references to these forms of racism were too often left ambiguous, as if mentioning them would be enough to spark individuals' thoughts toward a deeper exploration of where racial inequality was present and what its sources were. In the breach, systemic racism meant simply that lots of individuals could eradicate it by thinking kindlier about their neighbors, rather than having to understand much of anything about housing policies, classrooms, financial institutions, or the courts. Church people who lived in White suburban communities could return from briefly interacting with someone of a different race feeling content that they had done their good deed for the day and that all was well.

Racial reckoning efforts were themselves limited by the societal structures that made it difficult for well-intentioned people to participate in the organizations most devoted to achieving reconciliation. Interracial congregations' success was limited by the fact that White neighborhoods and Black neighborhoods were so often geographically separate—that they were separated because of redlining and realtors' histories of discrimination and by developers' deals with planning commissions, as well as by White flight to escape school desegregation. Interracial ministries were further limited by the fact that for many congregations, racial reconciliation simply was not a priority—not one at least that competed effectively with clergy's overburdened schedules ministering to the sick, the needy, and the aspirations for spiritual solace of their most faithful members.

These limitations, therefore, were among the reasons that racial reckoning programs experienced difficulties in adequately responding to blatant instances of injustice, violence, and conflict. On the assumption that faith communities were populated with people who were not themselves racist, it was difficult to imagine that there might be unjust structures to which well-intentioned people contributed. Especially when law and order were at stake, it was hard to contemplate how these structures should be changed. Racial injustice perpetuated in the name of criminal justice was one of the most serious issues in which these questions needed to be addressed.

5

Criminal Justice

IN 1984, a gang of White men drove their car into a Black neighborhood in Franklin, Tennessee, just south of Nashville, and opened fire with shotguns, injuring six residents and beating three others. In Boston that year, four White men attacked a Black bus driver, kicking him, yelling racial slurs, and throwing him through the front door of the bus. In Philadelphia, at about the same time, three hundred White people in a predominantly White neighborhood gathered outside the home of a Black man and his White wife to register their disdain for the couple's presence in the neighborhood. In Portland, Oregon, after a White police officer choked a Black man to death, T-shirts went on sale bearing the slogan "Don't Choke 'Em, Smoke 'Em."

These were only the most recent acts of racially motivated violence. In 1980, three Ku Klux Klan members attacked five elderly Black women in Chattanooga in broad daylight, leaving them seriously injured with shotgun wounds. In the Bronx, the Klan burned a cross at the home of a Black family. At a bagel shop in Brooklyn, a White gang fatally assaulted a Black man. In Buffalo, six Black men were murdered, the hearts were ripped from two of the victims, and the killings were punctuated by a cross burning in the middle of a Black neighborhood. Over a two-year period in Atlanta, more than two dozen Black children were murdered. This was the setting for Jesse Jackson's appeal to the March on Washington participants in 1983, "Don't let them break your spirit."

Between 1978 and 1983, more than eleven hundred serious acts of racially motivated violence were committed—probably an undercount—and more than half were tied to members of organized hate groups. The magnitude and apparent increase in racially motivated violence prompted the US Commission on Civil Rights to issue a report on "Intimidation and Violence" in 1983 and the US Congress to initiate hearings on hate crimes in 1985. These reports and hearings opened a series of discussions, legislative proposals, and court rulings that would continue through the end of the century. These discussions, proposals, and rulings were meant to guide and redefine how the criminal justice system addressed racial violence and injustice.[1]

When religious leaders thought about criminal justice in the early 1980s, the issues uppermost in many of their minds were the rising crime rate, the seemingly unstoppable sources of crime, and the pervasive fear among their congregants of being the victims of crime. Religious leaders understood the need to address the apparent breakdown of law and order, the nation's penchant for violence, and the persistence of hate groups. Worries about drugs, family breakdown, and moral decline fueled these concerns. The venues in which faith communities addressed criminal justice concerns ranged from interdenominational conferences and clergy association meetings to special events in local congregations. Baptists, Catholics, Episcopalians, Jews, Lutherans, Methodists, Presbyterians, and the United Church of Christ all organized and participated in criminal justice events. Addressing criminal justice through church programs meant supporting victims' families, gaining greater appreciation of the complexities of the courts and law enforcement, and volunteering to visit inmates and speak with chaplains.

Few of the topics addressed at these events were new. Faith communities' legacies of support for law and order, care for the victims of violent crime, and ministries to prisoners served as the background for their contemporary discussions. The topics that they discussed focused on the personal and societal roots of crime, how better to steer young people away from drugs and alcohol, and how to continue their denominations' advocacy for penal reform, including in some cases advocacy against capital punishment. There were discussions of what the US Department of Justice was or was not doing and how congregations could work more effectively in supporting the police. There were small-scale events, too, such as ones that featured a role play about how to counsel the victim of a crime, a covered-dish dinner followed by a guest lecture from a reformed felon, and an optional tour of a correctional facility.

But the rash of cross burnings and killings, and news reports' tendency to treat racist violence only as hooliganism, prompted a response from some of the nation's top religious leaders. The National Council of Churches' Governing Board issued a lengthy policy statement in 1979 called "Challenges to the Injustices of the Criminal Justice System." In issuing the statement, the council sought to advance three objectives: first, to encourage Christian reflection on the biblical meaning of justice; second, to describe current racial disparities and other biases in the criminal justice system; and third, to guide Christian individuals and congregations in the ways in which they might contribute to a more equitable system of criminal justice.[2]

The biblical meaning of justice, the council's statement affirmed, was the divine principle set forth in the book of Micah, chapter 6, verse 8, "What does the Lord require of you but to do justice and to love kindness and to walk humbly with your God." This was a principle that directed concern toward the poor and the oppressed, including those in prison. The concern was meant to be expressed both in the behavior of individuals and in the society's laws. It implied both compassion and restitution.

The racial disparities and biases present in America's current system of criminal justice were the result, the council's statement said, of an evolution in how criminal acts were defined and how the penalties incurred were assigned and enforced. These definitions and penalties reflected the society's dominant norms and values, which in the best scenarios reflected a commitment to the fair and equitable treatment of all. However, the criminal justice system in practice was overburdened, subject to unrealistic expectations, and marked by conflicting goals, especially retaliation, prevention, deterrence, and rehabilitation. These conflicting goals enabled the criminal justice system to be applied—and indeed, misused—in ways that treated racial minorities and the poor unfairly.

The statement's agenda for individual citizens and congregations to be involved in facilitating a more equitable system of criminal justice emphasized the basic principles the system was meant to uphold. These included restraining acts disruptive of law and order, implementing penalties fairly but also flexibly, and avoiding discrimination based on race, ethnicity, social class, and other characteristics. The statement called for a greater understanding of the extent of bias and discrimination not only in the penal system but also in the society's basic institutions, including schools, economic structures, and religious groups. Individuals could play a more active role, the statement suggested, in supporting programs addressing drug abuse, marital problems, and other sources of antisocial behavior. Congregations were encouraged to promote greater awareness of difficulties within the criminal justice system and join with other groups in advocating for measures to strengthen the system's adherence to values of dignity, equality, and justice.[3]

In the various faith communities' gatherings that followed, addressing issues of criminal justice sometimes meant grappling with the fact that crime rates were high in Black neighborhoods, that Black men made up a disproportionate share of the incarcerated population, and that acts of racial violence were being committed not only by White gangs but also by the police. For example, at a meeting in San Francisco in 1984, delegates from American Baptist, United Methodist, Lutheran Church in America, Episcopal, United Church of Christ, and Presbyterian churches discussed strategies for addressing racial violence. In Georgia, the Christian Council of Metro Atlanta teamed with the NAACP to plan an interfaith meeting about racial violence after shotgun blasts were fired into the home of a Black resident. Each February since 1979, Presbyterian churches had observed Criminal Justice Sunday with sermons, guest lectures, study groups, prison visits, and discussions of racial violence.

But churches' responses to racial violence were fraught with uncertainty about how best to address the problem. The conference in San Francisco paid little attention to White violence against Blacks because its primary concern was about violence toward Asian Americans who were more often present among the members of predominantly White congregations. The meeting in Atlanta was postponed when some of the leaders objected to how it was planned. The Criminal Justice Sundays at Presbyterian churches often emphasized White fears of being victimized even as events sometimes also sought to focus on concerns about racial injustice.

"Considering the staggering crime rate in our country," explained a speaker at a 1982 Criminal Justice Sunday event, "it is most likely that every person has been a victim or is acquainted with a victim of crime. And so a call for prison reform is really a call to love our enemies. For those of us who have been victims of crime, prisoners symbolize in a very real way enemies. These are people who have abused us—who have literally hit us on the cheek, stolen our coats, and worse. So, it's not an easy challenge to love these people."[4]

The National Council of Churches by this time had also become the target of critics on the right to such an extent that what it said about criminal justice was easily dismissed or misinterpreted. The call for criminal justice reform seemed part of the council's left-leaning agenda to challenge the basic principles of free enterprise and to replace them with radical ideas about redistribution. Said one conservative critic of the council, "Its stands on criminal justice, abortion and school prayer are typical of the permissive, secular attitudes toward these subjects and are contrary to what most American church members believe to be a Christian approach."[5]

Such criticisms notwithstanding, between 1980 and the end of the century a wide variety of civic, social action, and watchdog groups introduced major initiatives to address criminal justice and the need for reform in new ways. These initiatives had four principal foci: hate crimes, police reform, racial profiling, and incarceration. Hate crimes included instances of racial violence and racial intimidation deemed to be in violation of equal protection laws and hence classifiable as crimes. Police reform was shorthand for concerns about the use of excessive force by law enforcement officers against individuals and groups among whom racial minorities were very often the ones targeted, injured, or killed. Racial profiling was the procedure that police officers used in the hope of identifying suspects by improperly stopping Black motorists.

Incarceration referred to the dramatic increase in the imprisoned population, which disproportionately affected Black families and communities.

Progressive faith communities—at least a few—were involved in all these initiatives. However, religious organizations were rarely as effective or even as significantly involved as their leaders often hoped them to be in the early 1980s. When faith communities did respond effectively, they usually did so by working under the auspices of other nonprofit organizations or governmental agencies and often by participating in this work as individual citizens or through small initiatives in congregations. Despite general agreement about the need to advocate against racial violence and intimidation, progressive faith communities were also influenced by the priority that White religious organizations devoted to protecting predominantly White communities from crime. The trajectory of initiatives introduced in these years and the limited results they achieved provide much of the context in which to understand how progressive faith communities—especially White churches—would still be struggling to respond to racialized violence during the early decades of the twenty-first century. How these late-twentieth-century initiatives came to be understood and how faith communities responded is the focus of this chapter.

Hate Crimes

Calling something a "hate crime" was a relatively new way of categorizing racist behavior in the early 1980s. Before that, acts of physical violence and verbal intimidation that involved racial slurs and attacks went under rubrics such as racial violence, racial intimidation, racial incidents, or simply racism. The concept of "hate crimes" stemmed from concerns about "hate groups," such as the Ku Klux Klan, neo-Nazi organizations, and White supremacists. Hate *crimes* pertained to acts committed by these groups or to similar acts done by individuals that violated the law and thus could be prosecuted as crimes. Hate crime legislation and advocacy against hate crimes was meant to identify and thus raise awareness of the extent of such activities and to stiffen earlier civil rights legislation by imposing harsher penalties on the perpetrators of these activities.

The Civil Rights Act of 1968 had made it a federal crime to willfully injure, intimidate, or interfere with or to attempt to injure, intimidate, or interfere with someone because of their race, religion, or national origin. The legislation pertained especially to examples of violence or intimidation associated with schools, public places, places of work, the courts, and opportunities for voting. These had long been the kinds of violence and intimidation to which Black students, shoppers, employees, and voters had been subjected. The legislation was meant to elevate the seriousness with which such acts were taken and the severity of the penalties incurred.

However, closer monitoring, new legislation, and stiffer penalties were needed to curb hate groups' activities. The hate groups' freedom of speech and assembly protected them from prosecution in instances not involving violence, as did interpretations of civil rights laws that narrowed the laws' relevance to protecting only specific violations of access to public facilities and voting rights without addressing the wider implications of speech and violence intended as intimidation. These acts of intimidation were directed not only at Blacks but also at gays, women, and Jews. Ku Klux Klan groups were most visibly involved, but there were also various neo-Nazi, Aryan, and White supremacist groups. While the sheer number of violent and intimidating acts these groups committed prompted public concern, it was the unanticipated effect of several specific events that generated a response from religious groups.

In 1968, when the Lakeview Presbyterian Church in St. Petersburg, Florida, organized a "pray-in" to support the striking sanitation workers, one of those present was Reverend William Land. Reverend Land— who had been trained by civil rights leader Fannie Lou Hamer and been a leader during the 1965 sanitation strike in Memphis—was the Community Organization Director for the United Church of Christ (UCC) Committee for Racial Justice Now.[6] The committee with which Reverend Land was working had been formalized in 1963 in support of units within the church and interdenominational agencies seeking to lead the church and the nation toward racial reconciliation. In 1969, the church expanded the committee's work, renamed it the Commission on Racial Justice, and allocated $500,000 for its support. The commission was to be led by Black clergy, was to work toward fuller participation among the denomination's 70,000 Black members, who represented approximately 3.5 percent of its total membership, and was to engage the denomination more actively in civil rights activities.[7]

While the denomination's leaders were putting the commission's financing together, Reverend Land was supporting strikes in Virginia and North Carolina and finding himself under investigation by the FBI and spending time in jail for his efforts. The commission's staff were also involved in monitoring the case of a teenage Black girl on death row in North Carolina, challenging "no knock" police entry rules in Washington, DC, and questioning the treatment and sentencing of inmates in Arkansas and Florida. In 1970, the commission's executive director Reverend Charles E. Cobb, issued an appeal for prison reform, declaring, "The American judicial system is being used by those in power to systematically dehumanize and brutalize Black men and women."[8]

In 1971, the UCC Commission on Racial Justice's engagement with the criminal justice system took an eventful turn when it sent Reverend Land and two other pastors to assist Reverend Eugene Templeton, the White pastor of the mostly Black Gregory United Church of Christ in Wilmington, North Carolina. Reverend Templeton and his family had been driven from their home by bomb threats and gunfire after Templeton had given refuge inside the church to Black students who were boycotting the high school in protest of its discriminatory policies. The emerging spokesperson and organizer for the protest was a 23-year-old Black leader named Ben Chavis.[9]

Chavis was the regional North Carolina and Virginia field organizer for the UCC Commission on Racial Justice. A graduate of the University of North Carolina in Charlotte, Chavis had been an activist as a student, was among five candidates who ran unsuccessfully for the city council during Charlotte's court-ordered desegregation crisis in 1969, spent the following year teaching high school chemistry in his hometown of Oxford, North Carolina, and, following the killing by the Ku Klux Klan of a childhood friend, joined the staff of the Commission on

Racial Justice. When court-ordered busing began in Wilmington, the busing consisted primarily of Black students being bused to previously all-White schools, where they were denied participation in athletics and student government, and several were expelled without reasons for their expulsion being given. The boycott began when the school administration refused Black students' request to hold an assembly in honor of Dr. Martin Luther King Jr.'s birthday.[10]

In response to the boycott, four days of sniper violence broke out as a paramilitary White supremacist hate group called Rights of White People and members of the Ku Klux Klan drove through Wilmington's Black neighborhoods shooting at residences, at the Gregory United Church of Christ, and at Reverend Templeton's parsonage. In the ensuing melee—about which reports by the police and Black residents differed—a Black teenager named Steve Mitchell was shot dead by police, a White motorist named Harvey Cumber was killed by a sniper, and a White-owned grocery store near the Gregory church burned to the ground. A month later, another Black teenager, Clifton Wright, was killed by a shotgun blast from an unknown assailant. Black residents reported that their appeals to the police department for protection had gone unanswered.[11]

While the investigation of the Wilmington events was under way, Chavis and activist journalist Earl Grant were arrested and charged with conspiring in Charlotte to help two persons indicted for illegal possession of firearms flee to Canada. Chavis and Grant were also charged with illegally manufacturing and possessing firearms, which they denied, resulting in Grant being convicted, and, although Chavis was acquitted for lack of evidence, the case put Chavis under suspicion in Wilmington. In 1972, Chavis along with eight Black men and a White woman—the Wilmington Ten—were arrested, convicted, and sentenced to lengthy prison terms. Chavis was convicted of having conspired to set the grocery store on fire and was sentenced to thirty-four years in prison.

In 1973, the United Church of Christ's general synod voted to borrow funds to provide bail for Chavis and the other nine who had been sentenced. The general synod further directed the Commission on Racial

Justice to "maintain an ongoing program of organization, training, and mobilization in the Wilmington communities." In so doing, the United Church of Christ was taking a risk that its action would be resisted by its politically conservative congregations—which soon happened. However, the UCC's action was consistent with the denomination's history of concern for racial justice, extending as far back as New England Congregational leaders' engagement in abolition, selected leaders' activism during the civil rights movement, and the procedures through which Black congregations were able to gain dual affiliation with the UCC. Two years later, having posted $400,000 bail, the general synod urged the denomination's congregations to request educational resources from its national agencies to better understand the continuing efforts to appeal the convictions. At that meeting, the general synod also adopted a statement on racial and economic justice affirming the denomination's commitment to the biblical heritage of "seeking justice, correcting oppression, healing the sick, feeding the hungry, [and] loving our neighbor."[12]

The Wilmington Ten became known nationally and internationally. While on bail, Chavis spoke at UCC rallies in Charlotte and New York and was named the new director of the UCC Commission on Racial Justice's Washington, DC, field office. The Black leader Angela Davis enlisted Chavis in the newly founded National Alliance Against Racist and Political Repression, describing Chavis as "one of those rare persons who believes in devoting every single moment of his life to working toward justice and equality for all people. His Christian beliefs are, for him, an imperative to social action—action against racist discrimination, needless poverty and all the prevailing inequities in our society." James Baldwin published an open letter to President Carter in 1977 calling for the Wilmington Ten's exoneration; that summer, UCC leaders organized a demonstration near the White House in an unsuccessful effort to persuade Carter to support the Wilmington Ten's parole; and in 1978, clergy alliances across North Carolina organized "Free-the-Wilmington-Ten" Sundays. In the interim, while Chavis had been on bail his car was firebombed, nearly killing him, and while he was in prison two of his fellow Black inmates were burned alive, and Chavis came close to dying twice, once from appendicitis and once from an extended hunger strike.

After repeated attempts to reopen the case, the circuit court of appeals finally overturned the Wilmington Ten's convictions in 1980. Among the reasons the court cited was the fact that the three witnesses for the prosecution had been pressured and basically bribed to give false testimony and to perjure themselves during the original trial. In addition, the Department of Justice filed an 80-page brief arguing that there had been due-process errors in cross-examination of witnesses and biases in jury selection. Extensive reporting about the case, including a thorough examination by an investigative journalist, as well as Chavis's own account, demonstrated the fabrications and biases that had been part of the case from the start.[13]

The Wilmington Ten case brought to national attention both the role of hate groups and the inaction of law enforcement in properly protecting the Black community and prosecuting the perpetrators of racially motivated violence. The case also solidified and publicized the United Church of Christ's dedication to criminal justice reform. Between 1971 and 1980, the church held numerous events at which the case was publicized and spent an estimated $2 million in defending the Wilmington Ten. During this period, the UCC Commission on Racial Justice also investigated cases of police brutality and participated in the Department of Justice's National Minority Advisory Council on Criminal Justice. Chavis, while in prison, completed a master of divinity degree from Duke University, was formally ordained as a UCC minister, and upon his release began lecturing widely about criminal justice reform. In subsequent years, Chavis chaired the United Church of Christ's Prophetic Justice unit, served as vice president of the National Council of Churches, held office as executive director of the NAACP, and wrote extensively about criminal and environmental justice.

As the Wilmington case was drawing attention to the need for criminal justice reform, the resurgence of the Ku Klux Klan and other White supremacist groups was raising additional concerns about the lack of effective law enforcement against hate groups. The 1978 neo-Nazi groups' march through the heavily Jewish community of Skokie,

Illinois, posed concerns about how far the constitutional protection of freedom of speech could extend when the intent was to promulgate anti-Semitism and to engage in racial and religious intimidation. A study by the National Jewish Community Relations Advisory Council reported high levels of concern among Jewish groups about anti-Semitism and anti-Jewish discrimination. Yet there was also concern among Jewish leaders about overreacting to neo-Nazi groups' activities. The Anti-Defamation League of B'nai B'rith, which kept the closest tabs on anti-Semitic hate groups, however, stressed the broader surge of Klan activity and Klan memberships—estimated in the thousands in South Carolina, Florida, Texas, and several other states—as well as a steady rise in anti-Semitic bombings, attempted bombings, arsons, and cemetery desecrations.[14]

In 1979, an interracial group in Greensboro, North Carolina, organized an anti-Klan demonstration during which the demonstrators were attacked by a nine-car caravan of Klan members and neo-Nazis. The attackers opened fire, killing five of the demonstrators and wounding ten others. Four of the five were members of the Communist Workers Party. One of the dead, William Sampson, who was White, was a recent graduate of Harvard Divinity School, and was currently working in Greensboro as a labor organizer among textile workers. One of the wounded, Reverend Nelson Johnson, who was Black, was the pastor of the nondenominational Faith Community Church in Greensboro. The attack, which was captured by a local television station's camera crew, resulted in three trials: a state and a federal trial in which the Klan and neo-Nazi members were acquitted, and the third, a civil trial brought by the widow of one of the victims in which the defendants were eventually found liable in 1985.[15]

Greensboro's Black churches protested the massacre and conducted the victims' funerals. Reverend Chavis—recently released from prison—led a march of some six thousand anti-Klan demonstrators urging justice against the perpetrators. Reverend Leon White of the United Church of Christ issued a statement calling for an investigation of the police department's conduct. And over the next year, White, Chavis, and clergy from Charlotte and Durham as well as from Greensboro held rallies and issued statements supporting the victims' families in their appeals for indictments and convictions.[16]

This show of support from religious leaders notwithstanding, the Greensboro shootings illustrated the fine line that faith communities feared crossing in advocating against racially motivated violence. Supporting the Wilmington Ten had been tenuous enough that only the National Presbyterian Church added significantly to the United Church of Christ's assistance, and even though Chavis was affiliated with the church and the Gregory church had been attacked, critics within the denomination, especially among its southern congregations, vehemently opposed the church's involvement in the struggle.[17] The Greensboro victims were more difficult for religious groups other than Black churches in the area to support because the media characterized the event, not as a racist hate group attack, but as a shootout between rightwing extremists and a "radical leftist" group.[18]

The Greensboro shootings were among a series of attacks—in Alabama, California, Maryland, New York, Tennessee, and elsewhere—that prompted civil rights groups, public officials, and religious leaders to step up efforts to counter the attacks. When plans were laid in 1979 for a National Anti-Klan Network to be led by Black Baptist minister Reverend Lucius Walker, supporters included the Southern Christian Leadership Conference, United Church of Christ, Presbyterian Church, and National Council of Churches, as well as scores of trade groups and ethnic associations. Local and regional groups mobilized anti-Klan activities as well, ranging from resolutions endorsed at clergy conferences to anti-Klan strategy meetings in church basements in preparation for public demonstrations. These efforts mobilized against attacks that were racially motivated and especially against attacks on churches, synagogues, mosques, and other places of worship and by "identity groups" that combined White supremacy with religious ideas. In the instances in which clergy-led groups were only minimally involved, religious messaging was often present in other ways, if only in the hymns demonstrators sang or the church fans they carried.[19]

The US Commission on Civil Rights' 1983 report, *Intimidation and Violence: Racial and Religious Bigotry in America*, was meant as a response to the widening variety of hate-motivated incidents as well as to the prevalence of racially motivated violence. Reports to the commission from around the country indicated violent acts that ranged from assaults on Black men and women and firebombing of Black homes to attacks on federal judges, anti-Semitic fliers distributed on college campuses, ethnic diatribes in political campaigns, and violence toward immigrants' businesses. While most racist incidents were fomented by Whites against Blacks, intimidation and violence was understood to be directed as well toward Jews, women, and immigrants and to consist of both verbal and physical abuse.

Notably, the report emphasized bigotry as the central concern in addressing intimidation and violence, defining bigotry as being obstinately or intolerantly devoted to one's own race, religion, or opinions. Bigotry was identified as the source of efforts to frighten, intimidate, injure, or kill another person. Bigotry was exacerbated by economic distress of the kind present at the time owing to inflation and unemployment. But bigotry was ultimately based on the teachings, ideas, and indoctrination to which people were exposed in their homes, communities, schools, and churches. The way to reduce bigotry, therefore, was by exposing people to different ideas. Different ideas likely to prove effective included better information about the extent of racist violence, a clearer understanding of the laws and likelihood of swift punishment against the instigators of violence and intimidation, a greater willingness in the media and among public officials to speak against acts of violence and intimidation, and better education in the schools, churches, and other community organizations.[20]

For faith communities, these ways of thinking about intimidation and violence had several implications: first, faith communities were themselves at fault if they instilled followers in narrowly doctrinaire ideas; second, faith communities could make a positive difference by promoting tolerance and lawfulness in the ideas and habits of their followers; and third, faith communities could also serve beneficially by speaking against intimidation and violence. Less obviously, emphasizing bigotry in these ways also implied that most acts of intimidation and violence were probably committed by extremists and not by upstanding members of religious congregations. A focus on beliefs and attitudes further implied that individuals could contribute beneficially rather than change needing to be made in basic systems and societal structures.

The 1983 report was less an innovation in how to think about bigotry than a reflection of understandings in the social sciences and among educators.[21] Addressing intimidation and violence in the ways suggested in the report was in fact how majority-White religious groups responded to many of the racist incidents of the 1980s. Their support of the National Anti-Klan Network was an example of furthering information about the extent of hate groups' activities and of speaking against these activities. Clergy in local communities frequently responded in similar fashion. When shotgun blasts were fired into the home of a Black woman who moved into a White neighborhood in Atlanta in 1984, for example, half a dozen local ministers issued a joint statement condemning the incident and declaring their support for residential integration. And when Hildegard Smith, a Black mother of five, was attacked by two White men in a mostly White New Jersey community in 1988, it was a local coalition of Black and White clergy who publicized the incident and assisted in securing financial support during her recovery.[22]

Interfaith conferences and denominational study guides were among the additional ways in which religious groups contributed to educating their members and the wider public about hate crimes. Examples of such efforts ranged from essays in church publications by Black leaders like Angela Davis calling for greater clarity about the extent of racial injustice, to news items informing readers about the resurgence of Klan activity, to essays taking the view that even Klan leaders could be deterred from racist activity through spiritual redemption. Conferences and study guides benefited increasingly from updated reports about hate crimes produced by the Anti-Defamation League of B'nai B'rith, Center for Democratic Renewal, US Commission on Civil Rights, Southern Poverty Law Center, the National Anti-Klan Network, and, after the 1990 Hate Crimes Statistics Act, the annual information compiled by the Department of Justice. Hosting conferences and distributing study guides were of course far less directly involved ways of advocating for racial justice than the kinds of intervention in which activist religious leaders like Reverend Chavis participated, but conferences and study guides were small ways of reaching distant majority-White congregations whose members may themselves rarely have been the victims of hate crimes.

If hate crimes were to be prosecuted, it was up to the criminal justice system to act. Legislation to stiffen penalties for hate crimes was enacted in nearly every state during the 1980s and early 1990s, although the bills failed in a few instances because opponents figured the measures would be used to combat discrimination against gay people. Legislation had to be tailored carefully to avoid being ruled an unconstitutional violation of freedom of speech. Thus, it depended not only on legislation but also on local human relations commissions, civic organizations, and religious groups to see that bias was monitored. The value of these programs was that they could sponsor informational meetings in the schools and at community gatherings in the hope of lowering the odds of violence occurring.

Police Reform

Although the US Commission on Civil Rights' 1983 report and the 1990 revision of the report stressed information and education, the report also called for reform within the criminal justice system. Law enforcement, the report said, "should intensify efforts to ensure that staff who confront incidents of racial and religious terrorism are broadly representative of the racial, ethnic, and religious makeup of the communities they serve."[23] Clearly, the law enforcement officers called to quell violence in Wilmington, Greensboro, and many other places were not representative of the Black communities in which these acts of violence occurred. The lack of representativeness was one of the factors in the lack of appropriate protection being provided. But inadequate representativeness was relevant not only in enforcement against "racial and religious terrorism"; it was also a concern in other realms of law enforcement. Inadequate representativeness was one of the factors in what had long been—and would increasingly be regarded as—the use of excessive force by law enforcement officers.

While instances of police officers cursing, beating, injuring, and killing Black men and women were as common, if not more common, than racially motivated violence committed by hate groups, these acts of police violence were less often the source of public outrage. The reasons for a lack of outrage included the fact that what had happened was often unknown or subject to differing interpretations from bystanders and the police; in addition, the police involved were rarely prosecuted and even more rarely convicted. Yet, when there was indisputable evidence that an innocent, unarmed person had been killed by the police, there was no question that an act of injustice had been committed. And the recurrence of such instances led to protests, hearings, and demands for police reform.

Faith communities' advocacy for police reform varied from playing hardly any role at all to being among the influential groups who successfully argued for police reform. These roles were strengthened by religious leaders' moral authority and in many instances by being acquainted with the victims and their families. Religious leaders were also connected with wider networks that provided resources and publicity. Of course, faith leaders did not have the legal authority that law enforcement officers did. Nor were religious leaders in a position to demand changes in police departments' affairs. What faith communities could provide was support for victims' and witnesses' credibility.

Solid Rock Church of God in Christ was a small frame building about the size of a small house in a Black neighborhood in Portland, Oregon. About 8 p.m. on July 14, 1980, Theodore Dixon was running an errand about a mile from the church when he passed a patrol car and saw an officer struggling with a Black teenager. By nine o'clock the next morning, Dixon—his face, neck, wrists, and knees bleeding—had been charged with inciting a riot, harassment, assault, and resisting arrest. Dixon gave an account of what happened to a reporter from Portland's Black newspaper, *The Skanner*, in which he claimed he was doing a Night Owl street ministry when he asked the police officer what was going on, received no explanation, and was soon surrounded by seven officers who verbally abused him and beat him. The police report said that Dixon had tried to free the teenager, struck one of the officers, and attempted to grab another officer's revolver.

Which story to believe depended on how the story was reported, who read it, and their previous experience with the Portland police. That much was obvious. But in addition, Dixon's credibility was enhanced by his relationship to the church. Solid Rock Church was well known in the neighborhood for helping families in need and ministering to people who were sick. Dixon was a deacon in the church and was known for his street ministries. He stated in his account, "I tried to tell [the police officer] I served the Lord and I was trying to help." The officer, Dixon said, replied, "God don't hear [n-word]. I am your god. Why don't God help you now."[24]

Dixon's encounter was an example of a pattern in which the victim or the victim's family and friends being publicly identified with a religious organization was a means of adding credibility to the victim's side of the story. Whether that added credibility made a difference depended of course on many other aspects of the case. Despite Dixon's association with the church, and despite the police department promising that a thorough investigation would be conducted, no further action was taken, and the Portland police department continued to be the focus of complaints about police brutality. The outcome in the Ernest Lacy case was different.

Ernest Lacy was a twenty-two-year-old Black resident of Milwaukee. He was walking on a downtown street on July 9, 1981, when three White Milwaukee police officers stopped him, saying they were searching for a rape suspect. The police officers said he resisted arrest. Witnesses said he was treated roughly. That evening, Lacy died in police custody. The police report said he "just died." The family said his body was badly bruised. Another person was eventually arrested for the rape. Instead of Lacy's death being dismissed, a coalition formed to pursue the case. After a coroner's inquest and two trials, one of the offending officers was found guilty of using excessive force and fired, four others were suspended, and Lacy's family won an out-of-court civil settlement in 1985.

The Lacy family prevailed because of the evidence, the circumstances of Lacy's death, character witnesses, and the publicity surrounding the event over the four years of court proceedings. The sociologist Laura Woliver, who examined all aspects of the case, including the conditions in the community and the social networks among those involved in the coalition calling for justice, argued that religion also played an important role. Lacy's immediate family members were deeply religious, and they told Woliver that their minister was one of the first persons they called. That minister, the pastor at a Black congregation called the Church of the Living God, where the funeral was held, and another Black pastor at a Lutheran church led the effort to press the case and to use their networks in the community to win support.[25]

It was by no means a foregone conclusion that clergy would become involved in cases of alleged police brutality, other than to conduct funerals and comfort grieving family members. The odds of their becoming involved were significantly higher when a member of the clergy was personally attacked, injured, or killed—which happened with some frequency. Clergy were also drawn into hearings about police brutality because clergy were assumed to be law abiding themselves and were respected by the people in their congregations. Whether the hearings resulted in police reform or not, the clergy could speak to the biases and injustices they believed needing reform.

In 1983, Michigan's US Democratic Representative John Conyers Jr., who would lead the effort to secure passage of federal legislation to monitor hate crimes, was in Harlem convening a hearing about New York City's police department—which during the previous year was the subject of more than five thousand complaints, of which more than half involved the use of excessive force. The hearing pitted the city's White leadership, including Mayor Ed Koch and US Attorney Rudy Giuliani, both of whom denied that there was any evidence of police brutality, against Black leaders who testified that there was. The Black leader who prompted Conyers to convene the hearing was Reverend Calvin Butts, pastor of the powerful Abyssinian Baptist Church. Among the instances of police brutality that Butts cited was the beating of Reverend Lee

Johnson, a Black pastor. Against the credibility of Butts, Johnson, the testimony of additional clergy, and the support of Union Seminary president Donald Shriver, Koch and Giuliani found themselves on the defensive. When the hearing was over, Koch continued to insist that not a scintilla of evidence could be found of systemic police brutality but acknowledged that "there are some police officers who abuse their trust."[26]

Besides participating in community-wide hearings, the same clergy coalitions that sponsored affordable housing projects or worked to cultivate reconciliation among Black and White churches sometimes organized meetings of their own to discuss police brutality. The Greater Minneapolis Council of Churches organized meetings in 1989, for example, to discuss the troubled relationships between Black residents and the police in Brooklyn Park—the neighborhood that would become the focus of national attention for police brutality again more than a quarter of a century later. Other examples included a "concerned clergy" coalition in Long Beach, California, that addressed the need for better human relations training among police, and church forums in Boston, Chicago, Philadelphia, and Tampa focusing similarly on improved interracial police training.[27] There were also scattered experiments with clergy and lay members serving on citizens' police review boards, taking part in complaint oversight panels, assisting as neighborhood volunteers, and working as police chaplains.[28]

Religious leaders became involved in advocating for police reform most aggressively when the brutality was particularly heinous and when the officers who committed the brutality went unpunished. The roles that religious leaders played in these situations ranged from participating in hearings and issuing statements to mobilizing demonstrations. Religious leaders' participation in community-wide demonstrations depended to a considerable degree on how infuriated the community may have become when the latest act of police violence occurred. Their participation varied greatly owing to their relationship to the local community and their networks beyond the local community. This variation was evident in the incident of police brutality that received more national attention than any other such case in the early 1990s.

On the night of March 3, 1991, a neighbor filmed four officers of the Los Angeles Police Department beating a Black man who they had stopped after a high-speed chase. The officers beat Rodney King with billy clubs more than fifty times while he was on the ground and shocked him with a 50,000-volt stun gun. "Oops," one of the officers radioed, "I haven't beaten anyone this bad in a long time." A year later when the officers were acquitted on charges of having used excessive force, South Central Los Angeles erupted in six days of civil disturbances during which widespread looting occurred, homes and buildings were burned, sixty-three people were killed, and more than two thousand were injured. Faith communities' responses fell into three categories.[29]

The first category was composed of the congregations in the immediate area. Six of the congregations were Black churches with a longstanding presence in the community. Two of the six church buildings were burned. During the year before the attack on Rodney King, these six churches held weekly worship services, conducted weddings and funerals, planned Sunday school lessons, and hosted the kinds of events that reflected the neighborhood, including choir performances, guest lectures, and meetings at which civil rights, Black history, and race relations were discussed. During the year between the attack and the officers' acquittal, many of the same activities continued, demonstrating that to a considerable extent business was being carried on as usual, although one or two of the pastors joined the growing consensus that the Los Angeles police chief should be fired. Everything changed when the acquittal was announced and the civil disturbances began. The congregations' role was to respond to the crisis itself. They provided a haven for families who were displaced, organized street patrols, provided legal services, and became locations where congregations outside the affected area brought food and clothing.[30]

The second category was made up of religious leaders outside the immediate area who perceived a need to offer statements about what was happening. In late March 1991, the leaders of nine denominations in southern California issued a statement calling for an independent citizens' commission to recommend changes in the training of law enforcement officers. The statement was issued on behalf of the Los Angeles Council of Religious Leaders, the membership of which included the Catholic archbishop and the heads of the region's American Baptist, Brethren, Episcopal, Lutheran, Presbyterian, United Church of Christ, and United Methodist denominations as well as the leaders of Conservative and Reform Judaism. The leaders commended the decency of the great majority of the police while condemning the recent occurrences of brutality. These leaders' statement was echoed in comments from national figures, including one by Reverend Billy Graham, who also deplored the violence and called for a restoration of harmony.

The third kind of response was from religious leaders who addressed the crisis by emphasizing that racial justice was the primary lesson to be learned by this latest act of police brutality. Other than Reverend Jesse Jackson, Reverend Chavis was the leading spokesperson for this response. Now serving as the UCC Commission on Racial Justice director, Chavis did more than any other person to speak and write about the connection between what was happening in Los Angeles and the pervasive persistence of racial injustice. As he told a *Washington Post* writer shortly after the officers' acquittal, "The denial of justice in the Rodney King case is fundamentally related to the historical denial by this society of the existence and prevalence of institutionalized racism. In the absence of racial justice, the call for law and order in Los Angeles is an exercise in futility."[31]

In January 1991, six weeks before Rodney King was beaten, the United Church of Christ issued a statement called "A Pastoral Letter on Contemporary Racism and the Role of the Church." Chavis and a team of UCC clergy had worked on the statement for two years, believing the church needed to speak forcefully, as it had attempted to do in the past, against the rising tide of racially motivated violence against racial minorities. The statement, issued from the denomination's top leaders, was sent for study and discussion to each of the UCC's six thousand congregations. Racism takes two forms, the letter said. "The first consists of overt acts by individuals, which cause death, injury or the violent destruction of property." Those acts were hate crimes of the kind that had been so much in the news for years. The second type "is enforced and

maintained by the legal, cultural, religious, educational, economic, political, and military institutions of societies." That was institutional
racism.[32]

On the fifth anniversary of Rodney King's beating, a scattering of
Black churches in Los Angeles and around the country held commemo-
rative services. A few took the occasion to organize marches demanding
police reform yet again. In the interim, a new police chief in Los Angeles
who was Black had been appointed and a few reforms had been made.
The Catholic bishops had issued a statement about racism. A Black
Baptist ministers' council had protested the police department's use of
excessive force in Cincinnati. A council of Methodist leaders had called
for a common commitment to basic human values, an Episcopal diocese had convened a summit on racism, and Criminal Justice Sunday
happened annually in Presbyterian churches, as it had for decades. An
editorial in *Christianity Today* criticized White churches' indifference to
racial diversity. There was plenty of evidence that mostly White faith
communities had not been completely oblivious to the persistence of
racial issues. But it would have been a mistake to assume that the brutality against Rodney King had been a wakeup call. With a few exceptions,
most of the response was among Black leaders in Black communities
rather than among White churches.

Racial Profiling

Between 1992 and 1998, racial profiling became another issue posing the
need for police reform. Racial profiling was law enforcement's practice
of stopping individuals for questioning on suspicion of having committed a crime simply because of their race or ethnicity. As a practice, stopping and questioning and then sometimes arresting and using excessive
force against persons because they were Black was hardly new in the
1990s. But it was in these years that racial profiling became the term
used to describe the practice.

In August 1991, four Black Delaware residents were stopped on Interstate 95 outside Philadelphia by the Tinicum Township police. When
the motorists asked why they were stopped and why the police were

searching their car, one of the officers said, "In order to make this a le-
gitimate stop I'm going to give you a warning for obstruction of your
car's rearview mirror," pointing to a thin piece of string from a disinte-
grated air freshener. The other officer allegedly said they had been
stopped "because you are young, Black, and in a high drug-trafficking
area driving a nice car." The American Civil Liberties Union (ACLU)
filed a lawsuit claiming the group had been stopped improperly simply
because they were Black. The group happened to be returning from a
church meeting in Philadelphia when they were stopped. Other than
that, faith communities would not become involved in advocating
against racial profiling until the practice became a nationally publicized
issue several years later.[33]

By 1994, the ACLU's lawsuit against Tinicum Township was casting
light on a practice that was being used widely in and beyond the Philadelphia area. Defense attorneys in another case seeking to prove that
their clients had been stopped and arrested improperly on drug charges
argued that Black and Latino drivers were being subjected to racial profiling. An investigation conducted by a team of researchers at Temple
University supported this claim. The study compared drivers' race—
based on visual observation—along a stretch of the New Jersey Turnpike with the race of drivers arrested along the same stretch of highway
and concluded that the odds of Black and Latino drivers being arrested
were five times the odds of White drivers being arrested. A former New
Jersey state trooper confirmed that racial profiling was indeed com-
monly practiced. It was the best way to make arrests, he said.[34]

The New Jersey case continued until 1996, with testimony from thirty
witnesses and additional statistics, when the court ruled that racial profiling had in fact been used. The court concluded that the New Jersey
police did not practice racial profiling as a formal policy but that officers
were encouraged informally to use the procedure. The case emphasized
the pressure that the police were under to make drug arrests as part of
the national crackdown on drugs that was being emphasized at the
federal and state levels of the criminal justice system. Responses to the
case fell along the same lines that the case had been argued: on the
one hand, critics of racial profiling argued that Blacks' constitutional

rights were being violated; on the other hand, supporters argued that law enforcement was simply using an efficient means to implement the war on drugs.[35]

The New Jersey case received less attention than it would have were it not for another incident that occurred two years later. On April 23, 1998, two New Jersey state police officers pulled over a late-model van on the New Jersey turnpike that appeared to be speeding. Three of the men in the van were Black and a fourth was Latino. The officers fired eleven shots into the van, wounding three of the passengers. Police and passersby accounts differed. The police said the van backed into the officers, injuring one and necessitating the use of deadly force. A witness said the van was moving forward when the officers fired shots into it. The publicity surrounding the incident posed the larger question: was this yet another case of racial profiling?[36]

In the weeks that followed, Black clergy played a leading role in focusing public attention on the case and arguing that measures needed to be taken to halt racial profiling. Members of the Black Ministers Council of New Jersey organized a prayer vigil near the site at the turnpike where the incident happened and continued the rally at a church in Trenton. The ministers' council met with the state attorney general and the state police superintendent to demand that patrol cars be equipped with video cameras. The council also pushed for the incident to be investigated as part of a larger pattern of racial profiling and lobbied for the state to hire more Black law enforcement officers.[37]

The Black ministers' group was still meeting with public officials about racial profiling in 1999 when a Black driver on Interstate 80 near Parsippany, New Jersey, was shot and killed. Although the details of the shooting (as in other incidents) were in dispute, faith communities in Morristown where the victim lived rallied to challenge the state's continuing use of racial profiling. The interfaith coalition that formed included the communities' mostly Black AME, Baptist, and Churches of God in Christ congregations and its mostly White Christian Science, Episcopal, Jewish, Methodist, Presbyterian, and Unitarian congregations. "At a time when racial profiling is an established fact in our state," the council said in an open letter to the community, "this tragic event, whether racially motivated or not, only serves to intensify the fear, anger, and mistrust felt within the community as a whole."[38]

The Black ministers' group and the support that they received from other clergy did not end racial profiling in New Jersey, but their efforts contributed significantly to the reforms that were made. In 1999, the New Jersey attorney general and the Civil Rights Division of the US Justice Department launched investigations of the state police illegally targeting minority motorists, concluding from these investigations that the practice of racial profiling could no longer be denied. The Justice Department appointed a federal monitor to watch over the New Jersey state police's efforts to root out racial profiling.[39]

To a considerable degree, racial profiling was interwoven with the wider protests against police brutality and the advocacy for police reform that were happening with increasing urgency during the 1990s. Insofar as faith communities were active in these protests and advocacy efforts, it was Black leaders who stood at the forefront of the work being done. White leaders came along in supportive roles when incidents of injustice happened in ways that could not be ignored. It was also the case that making a difference in how police departments conducted their affairs was grindingly slow. That was also true when faith communities attempted to tackle the racial injustices embedded in the structures of mass incarceration.

Mass Incarceration

The number of incarcerated Americans held steady between 1960 and 1975 at about 300,000, but after 1975 the number climbed. By 1990, it exceeded 1 million, grew to 1.5 million by 1995, totaled nearly 2 million in 2000, and was more than 2.2 million in 2010. Although Black Americans accounted for only 13 percent of the US population, they comprised 40 percent of the incarcerated. The imprisonment rate for Black females was 1.8 times the rate for White females; the rate for Black males was 5.8 times the rate for White males.[40] Counting those who were on probation or parole as well as those who were currently incarcerated, millions of Black families were affected by the criminal justice system, with measurable consequences for family relationships, finances, job prospects, the ability to vote, children's health, and children's performance in school.[41]

Following biblical teachings about care for prisoners, faith communities had long been engaged in prison ministries. These ministries included visits with inmates, holding services in prison chapels, and caring for prisoners' families. Prison ministries also included advocacy for penal reform. For example, in 1973, in response to reports of violence in prisons, recent prison riots, and high rates of recidivism, the United Church of Christ formed a Criminal Justice Priority Team to investigate prison conditions and make recommendations to state legislators about pretrial work release projects, standards for setting bail, and community-based rehabilitation programs. As another example, also in 1973, the Episcopal diocese of Georgia established a diocesan council to hear from former inmates and make recommendations about penal reform.[42]

Religious groups' interest in the racial injustices associated with mass incarceration increased as mass incarceration escalated. In the 1970s and 1980s, religious leaders' attention to incarceration emphasized ideas about punishment and sentencing. When the National Council of Churches issued a policy statement on criminal justice in 1979, for example, the council's chief recommendation was to reduce incarceration by shifting punishment toward fines and community service and to emphasize restitution to victims. By the 1990s, religious groups were taking greater account of the racial disparities in incarceration rates and the treatment of prisoners. For example, in 1992 newly appointed Attorney General William Barr—answering a question about the large number of Blacks in prison—stated unequivocally that "our system is fair and does not treat people differently," but Black clergy at a national conference in Washington, DC, criticized federal sentencing guidelines. The clergy also discussed what their congregations could do to reduce crime, provide counseling for recently released prisoners, and strengthen mentoring programs. A model to be emulated, they said, was Reverend Jeremiah Wright's at Trinity United Church of Christ in Chicago, where eighteen programs were being offered to provide job training and thereby elevate the trainees' self-esteem.[43]

Much of the attention that prison reform received from religious groups in the 1990s was of this kind—providing job training, counseling, and support of other kinds for recently released prisoners. The "One Church One Inmate" initiative founded in Chicago in 1995, for example, linked lay volunteers in congregations with soon-to-be released prisoners to facilitate their transition. Similar programs were initiated in Georgia through Catholic Social Services and the Prison Commission of the Christian Council of Metropolitan Atlanta. Additionally, interest grew in programs providing Bible studies and prayer ministries within prisons, such as the ones initiated through Prison Fellowship, founded by Watergate conspirator Charles Colson. With government funding, these programs raised concerns about separation of church and state, but they were popular among evangelical faith communities that believed spiritual conversion to be the only sure way of rehabilitating prisoners. The prisoners to which these programs ministered ranged from first-time juvenile offenders to long-term inmates.[44] Other faith-based initiatives tried to raise awareness of prisoners' needs by organizing visits at correctional facilities and by hosting conferences at which correctional officers spoke.[45]

Critics said that these initiatives dealt too little with the conditions underlying mass incarceration. Associate editor of the *Black Commentator*, Bruce Dixon, for example, said that "many serious people in our communities [are] involved in churches and voluntary organizations that try their best to offer services to the families of inmates, that lobby and agitate against drug and incarceration policies, [and] that attempt to offer counseling and re-entry services." But that was different, he said, from mobilizing "to change America's policy of selective policing and racist incarceration."[46]

There was, however, growing interest in the practices underlying inequitable incarceration. The Presbyterian Church (USA), for example, passed a resolution in 2003 calling its Washington-based advocacy committees to lobby for the abolition of for-profit private prisons. The resolution included a detailed analysis of why for-profit prisons had grown, what their relationship to mass incarceration had been, and how the church had addressed the issue in previous deliberations. In challenging these private prisons on ethical as well as economic grounds, the church argued that concerns about racial, ethnic, and gender discrimination clearly needed to be addressed. Other faith-based advocacy groups tackled different aspects of criminal justice reform that also had implications for racial concerns. These initiatives included the Interfaith Drug Policy Initiative and the Interfaith Criminal Justice Coalition, both of which advocated for sentencing reform for drug offenses; the Episcopal Church's resolution for the repeal of mandatory federal sentencing guidelines; the United Methodist Church's resolution to advance practices of restorative justice; and the Unitarian Universalist Association's 2005 statement of conscience encouraging congregations to advocate for such specific reforms as terminating the relocation of prisoners to out-of-state facilities and eliminating post-prison restrictions on voting rights.[47]

By the 2010s, religious leaders who had been advocating in other ways against hate crimes and police brutality were focusing more directly on the racial impact of mass incarceration policies. Nearly every progressive Protestant, Catholic, and Jewish organization offered statements about criminal justice, the incarcerated, and law enforcement. The statements varied—from affirming that the accused should be given timely trials and fair sentencing, to calling on congregations to care equally for victims and offenders, to reminding their constituencies of scriptural teachings about justice and mercy. Besides issuing statements, religious groups also engaged directly in criminal justice activities.

For example, in 2010 a group of Jewish, Black Protestant, and White Protestant leaders in Cleveland began meeting in small planning groups and after nine months launched Greater Cleveland Congregations—a coalition of forty AME, Baptist, Disciples, Episcopal, Jewish, Lutheran, Presbyterian, UCC, and Unitarian congregations—that dedicated themselves to criminal justice reform, education, jobs, and healthcare. Through meetings with the county prosecutor, mayor, and other public officials, the coalition advocated for correcting racial disparities in criminal charges, formed a civil rights unit that succeeded in reducing overcharges for nonviolent offenses by 25 percent, and played a role in Ohio passing a major sentencing reform bill that evened penalties for crack and powder cocaine and diverted first-time offenders into community-based rehabilitation programs.[48]

The increase in wider attention to mass incarceration was partly because the numbers imprisoned had grown to such magnitude. There was also a shift in understandings of how anti-drug policies were contributing to the problem and why these policies needed to be rethought. Some of the attention was attributable to the popularity of civil rights lawyer Michelle Alexander's book *The New Jim Crow: Mass Incarceration in the Age of Colorblindness*, which Alexander spoke about to faith communities and for which a network of progressive Black churches developed a study guide for use in congregations. There were new voices within the churches as well, such as Reverend Marilyn B. Kendrix, pastor of a United Church of Christ congregation in Connecticut and member of a National Council of Churches working group on advocacy and justice, whose focus was on raising awareness of mass incarceration to suburban congregations. There were also new local and regional coalitions like the one in Cleveland working for justice reform, "just reentry," "human integrity," action, and hope.[49]

Interest in criminal justice reform had met resistance in the past—and this new groundswell was no different. Controversies about slogans like "defund the police" were still in the future, but in smaller ways criminal justice reform that seemed like compassion to some sounded threatening to others. For example, in 2010 an interfaith coalition of Catholic, Lutheran, Methodist, Presbyterian, UCC, and Unitarian congregations formed in Appleton, Wisconsin, to promote rehabilitation and to provide healthcare and housing for nonviolent offenders, but the initiative seemed wrongheaded to some of their neighbors. Soon a group formed, calling "solid prolife, profamily, patriotic Christians" to oppose the initiative.[50]

Progressive faith communities' response to hate crimes, racially motivated violence, other acts of intimidation and injury, and mass incarceration during the half century after the Civil Rights Act of 1968, then, was mainly voicing support for the victims of injustice while to some extent also considering the racial inequities built into the criminal justice system. Black clergy and Black congregations were front and center in these efforts. White churches were a step removed. White churches' support was mostly through Black clergy who were affiliated with the mostly White denominations and in statements that the heads of mostly White denominations issued when extreme instances of racially motivated hate crimes and police brutality occurred.

Unlike the racial reconciliation programs that religious leaders promoted within multiracial congregations, the issues concerning the criminal justice system were sufficiently outside religious leaders' power that protests were rarely effective in bringing about institutional reform. Protests were effective in registering to the wider public that yet another injustice had been done. Protesting injustice was the means among those most affected of demonstrating resolve that violence, injury, and death would not be forgotten. It mattered that faith communities supported leaders who carried forth the witness against these kinds of injustice.

The relative effectiveness or ineffectiveness of advocacy concerning hate crimes, police reform, and mass incarceration was indicative of the differing social arrangements that had to be confronted. Advocacy against hate crimes was relatively effective because hate groups such as the Ku Klux Klan were organized, and thus identifiable, and they were prone to acts that were clearly in violation of the law. Religious leaders could work with civil rights groups to bring action while congregations played an educational role about bigotry. It mattered, too, that hate groups' attacks, such as the ones in Wilmington and Greensboro, were the kind that prompted national outrage. In contrast, police reform and advocacy against mass incarceration, while also occasioned by killings and other violent events that drew national attention, necessitated working on a case-by-case and state-by-state basis and involved making demands that frequently evoked resistance from law enforcement agencies. The complexity of criminal justice itself required advocating for racial justice through these varied means.

How advocacy for racial justice within the criminal justice system happened effectively was in most cases not a matter only of mass mobilization, although there were exceptions. Advocacy that mattered had to be strategic, whether that meant giving support to the victims of hate crimes, serving on citizens' police review boards, or providing training to recently released prisoners. Advocacy of this kind was most visible in the work of the dedicated few rather than in the contributions of the many. It happened when particular leaders responded to events within their own communities. And yet the activist few would not have been able to play their part without the mostly invisible support that they received from congregations.

It was understandable that faith communities would support one of their own who had been unjustly accused, beaten, or killed, and equally understandable that faith communities worked on programs where they could see results, such as helping to exonerate someone who was falsely convicted or easing the transition of someone imprisoned to nonprison life. These were activities at the edges of the criminal justice system that made a difference one life at a time. Congregations were good at mobilizing volunteers to lend their hand to these endeavors. Congregations were also capable of contributing when they reminded their participants about loving their neighbors.

Compared with these acts of mercy, religious bodies issuing resolutions in the often-vain hope of influencing criminal justice legislation was harder to imagine being worth the investment. Issuing public statements rarely had any tangible effect on the actual functioning of the criminal justice system. What mattered more often was legislative reform, in which religious leaders were reluctant to become involved. However, there were reasons that religious bodies spent their time issuing resolutions. One was to be a witness to the truth of their own traditions—that the ministry of the faithful was to proclaim the justice and mercy that was meant as God's design. The other reason was pragmatic. The study, reflection, and deliberation that went into the statements that religious bodies issued were the practice through which consciousness was raised about issues of common concern. The process of crafting statements of public witness—statements that were often lengthy, research-based theological and policy documents over which participants deliberated for months—drew at least a small number of leaders and activists to these issues.

Although there were Black religious leaders and a few White religious leaders who consistently raised their voices against hate crimes and injustices within law enforcement, the difficulties that they faced in bringing about major criminal justice reforms were part of the background for the outrage that would erupt against the continuing racial injustices and deaths of Black men and women during the early decades of the twenty-first century. But there was also the *political* context to be considered in which Black and White faith communities attempted to address racial injustice—and how the election of a Black president would matter.

6

Politics of Hope

BETWEEN REAGAN'S VICTORY in 1980 and George W. Bush's victories in 2000 and 2004, religion's role in presidential politics was dominated by the Religious Right. Leaders such as Reverend Jerry Falwell, Reverend Pat Robertson, and Reverend James Robison embraced Reagan's policies, and Reagan responded warmly to their support. Theologically conservative anti-abortion and anti-same-sex marriage groups continued to be active in Republican politics through the end of the century. Progressive religious groups were frequent critics of Reagan's economic policies, his policies in Central America and South Africa, and his apparent lack of support for civil rights. These groups lent their support more enthusiastically to Bill Clinton, who convened meetings at the White House with Black Baptist, National Council of Churches, and mainline Protestant clergy; included leaders like Reverend Benjamin Chavis in his transition team; and reached into progressive religious circles through Hillary Clinton's Methodist connections and advisors such as Anne Wexler and Reverend Joseph Duffey. However, progressive religious groups were also critical of Clinton's welfare policies and the administration's ineffectiveness in addressing police brutality. Having rallied with the rest of the nation after the 9/11 attacks, much of progressive religious groups' attention during the first years of George W. Bush's administration was directed against the US military intervention in Afghanistan and Iraq.

After a largely ineffective effort to mobilize liberal White Christians in 2004, Democratic strategists launched a more deliberate effort to draw religious progressives into the 2008 campaign. Their efforts were significantly assisted by the fact that Barack Obama was more willing to talk about religion and spirituality than John Kerry had been. The fact that Obama was Black, though, had mixed implications for the role that people of faith would imagine themselves being able to play in advocating for racial justice. On the one hand, Obama was relatively assured of winning the Black vote and the support of Black churches. On the other hand, the strategy that emerged to broaden Obama's appeal deemphasized racial justice for Blacks relative to issues that included Whites, such as poverty, unemployment, and healthcare. Progressive White leaders' emphasis on racial advocacy followed this pattern, focusing less on racial justice per se while supporting Obama's policies on economic issues and healthcare reform.

This chapter examines what progressive faith communities tried to accomplish through electoral politics and public policy during the 2008 campaign and the first term of the Obama administration—the principal foci of these efforts being the election, economic recovery, healthcare reform, and voting rights. With attention to what was different and what was the same from progressive religious leaders' activities during the previous eight years under the George W. Bush administration, I argue that there was reason for hope that public policy would bend toward the ideas that progressive White and Black leaders wanted to advance. However, the entanglements of partisan politics resulted in detours and roadblocks that got in the way of more activist engagement in racial justice advocacy. I suggest that these detours and roadblocks contributed to the more activist mobilization among a new generation of Black leaders that would emerge during the last years of the Obama administration.

The 2008 Campaign

Analysts credited George W. Bush's victory over John Kerry in the 2004 presidential race to several factors: the loyalty Bush had earned in the immediate aftermath of the 9/11 attacks, Republicans' "swift boat" campaign to discredit Kerry's military service, placing a constitutional amendment against gay marriage on state ballots to mobilize turnout among conservative voters, and the advantages characteristically associated with the incumbent candidate. Despite the increasing unpopularity of the Iraq war, Bush won 51 percent of the popular vote. Among the additional factors contributing to the president's win, Bush picked up 11 percent of Black voters, which was 2 percent more than in 2000, and 44 percent of the Hispanic vote, up from 35 percent in 2000. Although the Black vote for Bush was small, it played a role in several key battleground states, including Ohio, where Bush received 16 percent of the Black vote, up from 9 percent in 2000, and Florida, where 13 percent of the Black vote went to Bush compared with only 7 percent in the previous election. Moreover, polling of Black voters showed that regular churchgoers opted for Bush in significantly higher numbers than Black voters who did not attend church regularly.[1]

Bush's appeal to Black churchgoers was attributable partly to the faith-based community initiatives that had benefited Black churches' social service ministries. Appealing to Black churchgoers was also an integral piece of the emphasis that Bush strategist Karl Rove had placed on "values voters," which was directed primarily at White evangelical Protestants, but was labeled in a way that included conservative Catholic, Black Protestant, and Jewish voters as well. The appeal to values voters was framed in terms of Republican opposition to abortion, same-sex marriage, and stem cell research. Although pollsters challenged the idea that these issues had been decisive compared with more standard issues such as the economy and foreign affairs, the polling did show that frequency of church attendance was one of the most powerful predictors of how people voted in the election—with Bush receiving 64 percent among "more than weekly" attenders but only 36 percent among "never" attenders.[2]

The takeaway for Democrats was that more needed to be done—as Democratic National Committee chair Howard Dean noted in 2005— "to do religious outreach [to] Americans of all faiths." Many of Kerry's supporters had criticized the campaign for not finding ways to capitalize on progressive faith communities' capacity to mobilize Democratic voters in the same way that conservative faith communities were contributing to the Republicans' campaign. Said one, "If you listen to Bush and Kerry talk, you would be excused for thinking Bush is an incredibly religious man and Kerry is not [religious] at all." Local grassroots "People of Faith for Kerry" groups did sprout get-out-the-vote efforts, and there was at least one group—called Mobilization 2004— that traveled the country speaking about pro-Kerry issues, and yet the leaders of progressive groups like the Interfaith Alliance and Americans United for Separation of Church and State cautioned against bringing religion into the campaign and others worried that Kerry's support of abortion rights would evoke even stronger criticism from anti-abortion Catholic leaders if the campaign drew more attention to religion. Only late in the campaign did Kerry speak more openly about his faith, cautiously describing it as something that sustained his values and gave him hope but refraining from saying much more. When the votes were tallied, the exit polls showed clearly that next time around the Democratic campaign would need to enlist emissaries who could reach more effectively into the religiously involved population.[3]

The person that Howard Dean enlisted as chief emissary to faith communities was Reverend Leah Daughtry, pastor of the House of the Lord Church in Washington, DC, and daughter of the prominent Black Brooklyn minister Reverend Herbert Daughtry. Leah Daughtry had served as managing director of the 1992 Democratic National Convention, worked as a consultant for the Clinton-Gore campaign, held senior management and development positions in the US Labor Department, and since 2002 was the Democratic National Committee's chief of staff. Daughtry's task was to bring Howard Dean up to speed on the possibilities for putting outreach to religious groups into practice, meet with congressional leaders, and strategize with possible presidential candidates—one of whom was Senator Barack Obama. By fall 2006, there was a faith working group in Congress under the direction of Representative James Clyburn and a faith advisory team of religious leaders under Daughtry's supervision.[4]

During the 2008 presidential campaign, Reverend Daughtry developed a six-person Faith in Action team that worked in conjunction with a sixty-person advisory board composed of Protestant, Catholic, Jewish, and Muslim leaders. The team's objective was to develop networks within the various faith communities who would work to showcase Democrats' values in a way that would combat the Religious Right as well as to produce radio ads for Christian stations and publish voters' guides in newspapers. In several states, volunteers blanketed churches with a letter from Obama describing his Christian faith, and in others campaign staffers organized "faith forums." As a Pentecostal minister, Daughtry hoped to make inroads among evangelical voters who normally voted for Republicans while also demonstrating to secular leaders the virtue of cooperating with faith communities. In her speech as CEO and chief of staff to the Democratic National Convention, she introduced herself as a pastor and pastor's daughter, praised the interfaith gathering that had been held the day before, thanked all the people who "know the power of faith in their personal lives," and encouraged them to continue being active citizens as people of faith.[5]

Obama's candidacy moved effectively in the direction of speaking about his own faith, combating the far-right activists who accused him of being secretly Muslim rather than Christian, benefiting from Reverend Daughtry's Faith in Action team, and receiving warm endorsements from religious leaders who reminded voters of their duty to vote. Journalists embedded in the campaign noticed interfaith political action committees like the Matthew 25 Network knocking on doors to encourage voters to think about the "gospel mandate" to work for peace and justice and the campaign's strategically orchestrated visits in congregations where Obama answered questions about his faith and asked parishioners' about theirs.[6]

However, Obama's outreach to faith communities found itself confronted with two potentially serious challenges. The first was an investigation launched by the Internal Revenue Service in February 2008 stating that the United Church of Christ had engaged improperly in partisan electioneering by allowing Obama to speak at the denomination's general synod meetings the previous summer. Although the investigation might have deterred the campaign's outreach to faith communities, the IRS dropped the investigation when the church pointed out that Obama had spoken as a member and not as a candidate. The second challenge was the media frenzy over an inflammatory statement uttered by Reverend Jeremiah Wright, the pastor of Obama's home church in Chicago, which resulted in Obama resigning his membership from the church.[7]

The Reverend Wright controversy was consequential for Obama's relationship with progressive faith communities, but it was consequential in heightening rather than diminishing the support that many leaders expressed for Reverend Wright—and, by implication, for Obama. Within the United Church of Christ, Wright had always been controversial for his outspoken claims about race, but he was widely regarded as one of the denomination's most successful preachers. "When I look at the Trinity model in Chicago where the Reverend Jeremiah Wright is the pastor," a speaker at the 1999 UCC general synod had said, "it is a model that connects spirit work with biblical work, with justice work that empowers a people spiritually and prophetically."[8] A decade later, with eight thousand members, Wright's church was still a powerhouse within the denomination and Wright was a preacher its leaders were willing to defend. As UCC president Reverend John Thomas said in a 1,400-word statement to the press, "It's time for us to say 'No' to these attacks and declare that we will not allow anyone to undermine or destroy the ministries of any of our congregations in order to serve their own narrow political or ideological ends."[9]

Religious leaders outside the UCC also spoke to the controversy, both to defend Reverend Wright and to focus on the underlying persistence of racial inequality with which Wright was concerned. The Black church was "born of slavery and Jim Crow," influential Richmond pastor Dr. Lance Watson reminded his congregation at St. Paul's Baptist Church, for example. "This is an attack on the Black Church's historic prophetic concern for social justice." Others made the same point. "There is a deep well of both frustration and anger in the African-American community," Reverend Jim Wallis wrote in *Sojourners Magazine*. "Those feelings are born of the concrete experience of real oppression, discrimination, and blocked opportunities—opportunities that most of America's White citizens take for granted." It was the Black church, Wallis said, that most often spoke truthfully and prophetically about the Black experience.[10]

The other consequence of the Reverend Wright controversy was racial issues becoming more explicit in Obama's campaign. In a major speech at the National Constitution Center in Philadelphia on March 18, 2008, Obama acknowledged the controversy surrounding Reverend Wright's remarks, distanced himself from those remarks, addressed Black anger and White resentment, and pledged himself to work toward racial reconciliation. The controversy demonstrated that he could not, historian Barbara Savage wrote, "move beyond or transcend race, despite his eloquent employ of his biracialism and his transnational heritage."[11]

The response to the speech among pundits and in the polls was generally favorable, praising Obama for speaking frankly about his relationship with Reverend Wright and crediting Obama with effective damage control, but in some cases also asking if Obama would follow through in working for a "more perfect union" if he were elected.[12] Among supportive faith leaders, the speech furthered their conviction that religious organizations should be part of the conversation. Reverend Otis Moss III, who took the pastorate at Reverend Wright's church when Wright resigned, reaffirmed the congregation's commitment to working for racial justice. The United Church of Christ announced a denomination-wide "sacred conversation" on race and racism. The National Council of Churches' leadership promised to support the effort. In congregations and at seminaries, anecdotal reports surfaced of discussions about the differences between Black and White perceptions of race and racism, why these topics were so often neglected, and what it meant, after all, for a conversation to be "sacred."[13]

The faith leaders who had quietly rooted for Obama applauded his victory. The head of the National Council of Churches called for the nation to come together in unity to uphold Obama in its hearts and prayers. The national leader of the United Church of Christ congratulated Obama on his vocation of public service and praised his concern for justice and compassion. In Harlem's Abyssinian Baptist Church, Reverend Calvin Butts—who had endorsed Hillary Clinton in the primaries—invited the congregation to stand and praise God for the election. At a Black church in Raleigh, North Carolina, a journalist observed one of the congregants marching joyfully among the pews blowing a ram's horn in celebration and in Los Angeles ushers walked the aisles passing out tissues to worshippers who wept openly. National polling, showing that White evangelical Protestants and White Catholics voted in slightly higher percentages for Obama than they had for Kerry in 2004, gave some indication that the campaign's outreach to faith communities had paid off.[14]

It was less clear, though, whether progressive faith leaders' investment had made much of a difference. As predicted, Black Protestants voted overwhelmingly for Obama, just as they had for Kerry, but White non-evangelical Protestants tilted slightly toward John McCain, just as they had toward Bush in 2004. While pleased with the election's outcome, some of the campaign's observers wondered if the "faith-in-action" effort had been too much of an inside-the-beltway idea and not an authentic expression of grassroots interest. There were also lingering questions about the likelihood of faith groups and secular groups who differed about issues such as religious freedom and priorities such as abortion and same-sex marriage being able to work together in the future.

These questions continued during Obama's first months in office. In February 2009, the new president appointed a "faith advisory council" that was partly a continuation of the outreach work that Reverend Daughtry had headed during the campaign, partly the administration making good on its promise to work with faith communities, and mostly a committee tasked with revising the previous administration's faith-based and community initiatives. The council's twenty-five members included progressive activists like Sojourners' Jim Wallis and Reform Judaism's David Saperstein and Black clergy like AME bishop Reverend Vashti McKenzie and National Baptist Convention president Reverend William J. Shaw. The membership also included Latino, Muslim, White evangelical, Catholic, interfaith, and nondenominational leaders whose diverse interests were important for any program of partnerships between government and faith-based service organizations to consider. The council's remit was to make recommendations about the six issues to which the revamped program was to be devoted: reform of the faith-based and neighborhood partnerships office, economic recovery and domestic poverty, fatherhood and healthy families, interreligious cooperation, environment and climate change, and global poverty and development. Hot-button issues such as abortion and homosexuality were off limits. The council submitted a lengthy list of recommendations in 2010 and then disbanded. Racial justice was implied among the recommendations but not explicitly addressed.[15]

Race, though, was the issue that journalists, faith leaders, and scholars were keen to know about: was it being neglected, was racism still an important national problem, or was having a Black president an indication that America was becoming postracial? The scholarly consensus was that racism and racial inequality were very much a part of the nation's institutional fabric, so deeply interwoven with ideas and power that Obama's election was no reason to rest easy in addressing these problems—although there was one strand of thinking that suggested that Obama's policy agenda would be better served by downplaying race rather than emphasizing it. Journalists covering the major news events of the day were struck by the rise in racially motivated church burnings, killings, and other hate crimes following the election and by the disrespect with which Obama was being treated by opposition leaders compared with previous presidents. Faith leaders' opinions fell along a spectrum from voicing hope that a new era had dawned to offering a more sober assessment of current affairs. For example, an AME pastor saw Obama's election as an event that "reinforces the scriptures that say there is always hope" and a Church of God pastor mused, "It's almost taking away anybody's excuse for using racism and bigotry [as a] reason for not achieving." In contrast, a Presbyterian pastor counseled his congregation, "The sin of racism continues to distort our world. . . . Generations of institutional racism, including slavery, the intentional dismantling of the family unit, segregation, and the effective segregation today [in] the public school system are not fixed by the election of Barack Obama."[16]

Among those who saw institutional racism as a continuing reality, Obama's election did inspire new efforts to work for change. Abyssinian

Baptist Church, for example, launched a series of forums to bring Black and White leaders together to attack groups more aggressively on the right promoting unfairness and inequality. Another example was in North Carolina, where the recent exoneration of Edward Chapman, a Black man who had spent fourteen years on death row, prompted a movement to address the fact that a disproportionate number of capital offenders who were Black were sentenced to death. The Racial Justice Act, which was passed by the legislature and signed into law in 2009, made it possible for a judge to replace a death sentence with a sentence of life in prison if it could be demonstrated that race had played a role in the initial sentencing. A coalition called Christians for a United Community was one of the leaders promoting the measure. "As a nation, we decided last year that the White House is a racism-free zone," one of the coalition's pastors explained. "We need to decide the same should be true of the courthouse."[17]

On January 17, 2010, Obama offered his own assessment of how things had gone during his first year in office, speaking at the Vermont Avenue Baptist Church in Washington, DC. "You know, on the heels of that victory over a year ago," he said, "there were some who suggested that somehow we had entered into a postracial America." They had argued that way, he said, because he had spoken about the need for unity, but "That didn't work out so well." Indeed, "as we meet here today, one year later, we know the promise of that moment has not yet been fully fulfilled." However, as he had often done during the presidential campaign, Obama pivoted in the speech from race to problems of partisanship, greed, and irresponsibility. The pressing issues on his mind were unemployment, hardship, and the recent banking crisis from which the nation was still recovering. It was the need to keep traveling the hard road to achieve healthcare reform, put in place tougher rules on lobbying, work for clean energy, and build a coalition to protect voting rights. If the generation of leaders who had worked for civil rights in the 1960s had played the role of Moses in foreseeing the promised land, he said, then it was now the time for the "Joshua generation" to confront the challenges of a new era.[18]

Economic Recovery

When Obama took office, the most serious crisis facing the new administration was the Great Recession, which had resulted in the loss of nearly 3.6 million jobs as well as evoking serious concern about the collapse of the nation's largest financial institutions. For many homeowners, the recession meant not only unemployment but also the loss of household assets, most specifically through foreclosures on home mortgages. Although White non-Hispanic families accounted for most foreclosures, Black and Hispanic families experienced foreclosures at higher rates. One study, for example, estimated that 17 percent of Latino homeowners, 11 percent of Black homeowners, and 7 percent of non-Hispanic White families had lost or were at imminent risk of losing their home. Among the reasons for these differences were the greater proportion of high-cost loans among Blacks and Hispanics and fewer resources of other kinds for fending off foreclosures. Research also showed that Blacks and Hispanics were more vulnerable to the lack of transparency in the subprime lending market and that fair lending laws against discrimination had received scant attention.[19]

Faith communities responded to the Great Recession's impact on members' economic well-being by addressing their needs for short-term financial assistance, offering counseling on how to avert foreclosures, hosting workshops about predatory lending practices, and handing out food and clothing—all while grappling with shortfalls on churches' budgets. Although these were matters usually addressed within congregations, religious leaders also participated in public events concerned with government policies. A few days after the November 2008 election, for example, forty clergy accompanied by 135 church members facing foreclosures gathered at the US Treasury building to pray, deliver a letter to the treasury secretary, and launch a nationwide campaign to encourage modifications in mortgage loan protocols. Over the next six months, these and other faith leaders lobbied—including a cross-country "Recovery Express" bus caravan—with the new administration to take bolder action for economic recovery legislation and implementation.[20]

The Neighborhood Stabilization Program (NSP) administered by the US Department of Housing and Urban Development was one of the federal government's initiatives that held the most potential for helping families struggling to meet mortgage payments, facing foreclosure on their homes, or living in neighborhoods where home values were declining and infrastructure was deteriorating because of the economic crisis. Passed by Congress during the last months of the Bush administration, the NSP funds had to be administered by the Obama administration between 2009 and the cutoff date in 2013 when all the funds had to be spent. The major decisions about the allocation of funds were made by federal, state, and local officials with input from community groups. How the funds were allocated had important implications for low-income Black neighborhoods and, in turn, for how Black community leaders would view the administration. The program was also a means through which to show the administration's attentiveness to religious groups. As the president's Advisory Council on Faith-Based and Neighborhood Partnerships noted in its report, the NSP was "a prime example" of "investment in positive steps to stanch the enormity of the impacts and challenges of the foreclosure crisis in communities across the country."[21]

Faith-based groups played three roles in supporting the administration's rollout of NSP funds. The first was to spread word about the program. On some occasions in cooperation with the faith-based advisory council, but more often through local initiatives, churches were among the places in which interested homeowners, renters, developers, and heads of nonprofit organizations gathered to learn about and discuss the program. These meetings included homebuyer workshops, presentations by clergy and other local leaders serving on decision-making committees, discussions about staving off foreclosures, and information about new opportunities under the NSP.

Meetings of this kind served the politicians who were eager to take credit for the NSP as much as the recipients who might benefit from the program. While the bill was pending in Congress, Democratic leaders toured the country to promote its passage and then continued the publicity campaign in 2009 and 2010, both to showcase the NSP's benefits and to include similar provisions in new legislation. HUD secretary Shaun Donovan, Vice President Biden, first lady Michelle Obama, and Democratic leaders in Congress all issued statements about it, but few spoke about it more often than Ohio Senator Sherrod Brown, who visited each of the state's eighty-eight counties in 2008 and then in 2009 and 2010 held widely publicized meetings in Cincinnati, Cleveland, and Columbus. Each of these meetings was held at a Black church and each included representatives of the city's leading Black clergy.[22]

The second role that religious leaders played was to advise local officials on how the funds should be allocated. Because the important decisions depended on buy-in from banks and real estate developers, religious leaders' role was mostly symbolic, showing that community leaders had some say in the matter. But clergy did have information in local neighborhoods that municipal officials often lacked. Detroit was an interesting example. With as many as 67,000 derelict structures, the city had $4.5 million in NSP funds for use in demolishing buildings that posed the greatest danger to public safety either from their physical condition or having become locations for drug-dealing and violence. The funding was enough to demolish only about fourteen hundred structures, which meant that the selection process was going to be controversial no matter how the decisions were made. The mayor turned to the clergy—specifically to the mayor's hundred-member Office of Faith-Based Affairs. The Black clergy affiliated with the group took on the task of selecting approximately half of the nearly nine hundred houses that were demolished during the first year of the program.[23]

The third role that religious groups played involved participating in the rehabilitation and construction of housing newly made possible under the NSP. Faith-based nonprofits that had been engaged in affordable housing and community development projects were well-positioned to take advantage of the NSP's opportunities. The best example was in Chicago, where the city government contracted with a faith-based nonprofit organization called Mercy Housing to manage a large share of the NSP funds that the city received. Mercy Housing had been founded in 1981 by the Sisters of Mercy of Omaha and by 2008 had become one of the largest national nonprofit housing organizations, with low-income rental properties and rehabilitation-for-resale projects, management services, and low-interest loans serving more than 55,000 people in forty-one states. In 2003 and again in 2006, Mercy Housing had worked out mergers with two other large nonprofit service organizations in Chicago, making it the obvious choice to manage the revenue from the NSP. Mercy Housing's major activities in Chicago included rental management and renovation projects in the predominantly Black and Hispanic neighborhoods of Austin and Pullman.[24]

Although faith-based nonprofits and clergy coalitions contributed in smaller ways in many other locations to similar efforts, their financial participation in proportion to the federal government's expenditures on recovery and reinvestment was infinitesimal. Religious groups' participation was meaningful mostly in symbolic ways, showing that they were on board with Obama's policies, representing constituencies who stood to benefit from these policies, and in small ways helping to provide information, advice, and managerial skills. The administration's economic recovery policies were sufficiently controversial that small signals of support were always welcome. That was especially true in 2010 when Tea Party resistance to the administration sprouted across the country, often with support from conservative religious groups. Between April and September, as massive Tea Party rallies took place, progressive religious groups joined forces with union members, environmentalists, gay and lesbian activists, and peace organizations to stage counter-rallies.

Progressive religious groups also participated in criticizing the administration's policies. This criticism was directed mostly at the banks that were, on the one hand, benefiting from the government's bailout program and, on the other hand, initiating foreclosures against homeowners and failing to invest in neighborhood rehabilitation. One prong of faith leaders' efforts was to participate quietly in meetings with bank managers and public officials to negotiate ways to pressure the banks to assist underwater mortgage holders or, in some cases, to donate foreclosed housing units to nonprofit rehabilitation organizations. The other prong was to participate in person or by issuing supportive statements about the Occupy Wall Street movement that blossomed in late 2011 as a protest against economic injustice.

Healthcare Reform

The signature achievement of President Obama's first term in office was the Affordable Care Act (ACA), which he signed into law on March 23, 2010. Much of what is remembered about religious groups' relationship to the ACA's passage and implementation is the opposition it received from conservative Catholic and Protestant organizations that disagreed with its provisions for contraception and abortion. However, both that opposition and ACA's support from progressive religious groups must be understood in terms of the several decades of advocacy and debate in which religious organizations participated on behalf of healthcare reform. Considerations of race were never central to these debates but never far removed from them either.

The battle lines that formed in opposition to or support of the ACA among religious groups were already drawn in the early 1990s when healthcare reform was under consideration during the Clinton administration. The Catholic Health Association proposed a public-private partnership in which government-subsidized health insurance would contribute to the healthcare that providers like the large Catholic hospital system would offer. The Catholic proposal, though, stipulated that abortion coverage should not be included. The Southern Baptist Convention also endorsed Clinton's healthcare reform plan if abortion coverage was not explicitly included and SBC leaders sent fliers to churches in key congressional districts explaining the denomination's position. The Christian Coalition under Ralph Reed's direction came out strongly against the Clinton plan. In contrast, the Presbyterian Church, many Black churches, and the National Council of Churches supported the plan. The NCC's support was expressed as part of the Interreligious Health Care Access Campaign, whose secretary, Mary Anderson Cooper, was an Episcopal lay person who also served as the associate director of the NCC's Washington office. "We believe that the health of our nation's people has deteriorated to such a point that we cannot wait any longer for universal access to comprehensive health services," she said in her statement to the president's Health Care Task Force. "It is the NCC's belief that in matters of health the rights and well-being of one group in society cannot be secured without securing them for all."[25]

With the failure of the Clinton healthcare reform effort, much of the advocacy for healthcare reform in which religious groups participated shifted to the states. Between 2000 and 2002, the Greater Baltimore Clergy Alliance, for example, participated in the Maryland Citizen's Health Initiative—a coalition of religious, community, labor, and healthcare groups—to advocate for healthcare reform in Maryland. The West Virginia Council of Churches formed a similar coalition to advocate for universal healthcare in that state. And in Oregon, the Health Care for All Initiative—a single-payer plan that failed to win legislative approval—received support from Episcopal, Lutheran, Methodist, United Church of Christ, and Unitarian congregations and from Church Women United as well as from civil rights, labor, healthcare workers, and teachers organizations.[26]

Religious groups continued to participate in healthcare reform movements during George W. Bush's tenure in office. Religious leaders participated in universal healthcare debates among political candidates and in legislative sessions in California, Colorado, Missouri, South Carolina, West Virginia, and Wisconsin. Healthcare was something that congregations were intimately familiar with and concerned about, whether from the healthcare needs of their members or through ministries among the poor, chaplaincies, and social service programs. The variety of connections linking faith communities with the healthcare system was evident in the kinds of advocacy in which religious leaders participated. For example, clergy, business executives, and union leaders convened meetings to advocate for healthcare reform in Connecticut. Statewide forums and rallies were organized in Alabama, California, Illinois, and Indiana. Ministerial associations organized campaigns in strategic locations, such as in Janesville, Wisconsin—then house speaker Paul Ryan's hometown. And meetings were held at influential congregations, such as at the Dexter Avenue King Memorial Baptist Church in Montgomery, Alabama.

During the 2008 presidential election campaign, religious groups were active in promoting healthcare reform proposals both as specific state-level measures and as general platform issues. An example of a state-level measure was a bill in Pennsylvania to provide health insurance converge for the state's nearly 800,000 workers who were currently uninsured. In support of the measure, an interdenominational coalition of churches organized Cover All Pennsylvanians (CAP) Sunday, distributed postcards and bulletins, and secured about ten thousand letters supporting the plan. An example of religious groups supporting healthcare reform more generally was the Cleveland-based Faithful Reform in Health Care movement, a coalition that included national representatives of Buddhist, Christian, Jewish, and Muslim groups. The coalition was part of the broader Universal Health Care Action Network that sought to generate support of the kind that had taken place during the civil rights movement. The value that the network's leaders saw in religious groups' participation was to argue that healthcare was a moral issue related to religious teachings about justice, compassion, human dignity, and the common good.[27]

Between January 2009 and March 2010 when it was passed, the pending ACA legislation received support from religious groups in numerous venues both local and national. One of the most active locations was Hartford, Connecticut, the one-time insurance capital of the world, where health insurance was still a matter of frequent discussion. A movement founded in 2007 calling itself the Interfaith Fellowship for Universal Health Care under the leadership of Rabbi Stephen Fuchs organized informational sessions in churches and synagogues and at least one public rally with roughly a thousand supporters participating. The United Church of Christ at its denomination-wide general synod meeting in June voted unanimously to endorse a resolution submitted by its Council on Racial and Ethnic Ministries in support of the single-payer legislation under consideration in the US House of Representatives. "We lift up our [belief] that all persons deserve and must have quality, accessible, affordable health care and related social services," the UCC Minister for Health Care Justice declared as two hundred of the delegates participated in a public demonstration chanting "Health Care Now."[28]

By late summer 2009, a national organization called Faith for Health had formed claiming to represent approximately 140,000 people. Faith for Health was a coalition of more than thirty Protestant, Catholic, Jewish, Muslim, and Buddhist organizations aiming both to generate grassroots support for healthcare reform and to interact directly with Obama's Advisory Council on Faith-Based and Neighborhood Partnerships through two of its members, Jim Wallis of Sojourners and David Saperstein of the Religious Action Center of Reform Judaism. The coalition's grassroots reach depended on groups that had already been acting, such as the Cleveland-based Faithful Reform in Health Care movement, the PICO National Network of congregation-based community organizing activists, and the Catholic Social Justice Lobby. Through in-person prayer vigils, conference calls, and broadcasts, the coalition sent approximately 100,000 messages to members of Congress.[29]

Polling suggested that the public was evenly divided between supporters and opponents of Obama's healthcare reform proposal, with mainline Protestants and Catholics slightly more favorable than evangelical Protestants. The Faith for Health coalition included at least nominal support from the African Methodist Episcopal Church, Episcopal Church, Evangelical Lutheran Church of America, National Baptist Convention, and United Church of Christ, while some United Methodist and Catholic groups supported the proposal and others refrained from supporting it or openly opposed it.[30] The coalition that most vehemently opposed healthcare reform—the Freedom Federation—was largely devoid of denominational representation and was instead mostly composed of conservative activist groups such as Concerned Women for America, Eagle Forum, Family Research Council, and the Traditional Values Coalition.[31] Critics sharpened the debate by accusing the faith leaders supporting reform of violating separation of church and state, sneaking "death panels" into the legislation, relying on government rather than taking responsibility for themselves, and forging unholy alliances with radical left-wingers intent on undermining the faith. "Obamacare" was praised on one side as a move toward social justice and regarded by some on the other side who rejoiced that it was a death knell for Democrats in Congress and vilified by others as the work of socialists, baby killers, and race hustlers.[32]

When the Affordable Care Act passed, the administration had to redirect its efforts toward defending the legislation against challenges in the courts, working out revisions, and above all persuading the public to participate. Among other things, Obama turned to his faith-based advisory council and the clergy networks they represented for whatever help they could provide. "I think all of you can be really important validators and trusted resources for friends and neighbors to help explain what's now available to them," he said to the hundreds of religious leaders participating in one of the council's conference calls. Large organizations such as the National Council of Churches applauded the legislation, and there were some anecdotal reports of congregations holding sign-up rallies and information meetings. Although the rollout was slower and more contested than the administration hoped, the faith groups that had supported it in the name of social justice had reason to be pleased. A national study conducted after the main ACA provisions went into effect in 2014 found that the percentage of adults who were uninsured decreased by 7.1 points for Hispanics, 5.1 points for Blacks, and 3 points for Whites.[33]

Voting Rights

On June 22, 2009, the US Supreme Court ruled in a case brought by a small utility district in Texas in a way that upheld the Voting Rights Act passed in 1965, but which raised questions about the act's constitutionality. Those questions were decided in 2013 in *Shelby County v. Holder* when the court in a 5 to 4 decision determined that the major sections of the Voting Rights Act were unconstitutional. Thus, a major concern of the administration during Obama's time in office was how to protect the voting rights that had helped him win the presidency in the first place. Ironically, Black voters' impressive turnout in the 2008 election was part of the court's reasoning that "extraordinary measures" were no longer needed to prevent racial discrimination in voting.

Although the battle for voting rights during the Obama administration was waged primarily by the Justice Department and civil rights groups, just as the struggle for voting rights in the 1960s had been, religious groups that cared about voting rights did what they could to support these efforts. The possibility that voting rights would be subverted or that gerrymandering and voter suppression would be used in states and local jurisdictions was, in fact, of sufficient concern that progressive religious groups had continued to advocate from time to time and in small ways since the 1960s for voting rights. This was true especially among Black churches and for organizations like the National Council of Churches that had actively supported the civil rights movement.

Black churches' engagement with voter registration and voter turnout drives was documented clearly in a 1998 study of a nationally representative sample of US congregations. Black congregations were on average more likely to have involved their members in voter registration efforts than White congregations—a difference that the author attributed to Black church leaders' interest in social justice and the relatively low investment of time and energy required for voter registration drives, compared with, for example, organizing protest demonstrations or mobilizing lobbying campaigns. However, the study also stressed the importance of congregational size, finances, and staffing for all kinds of civic involvement, including voter registration, which meant that small, resource-strapped Black congregations were at a disadvantage relative to large, resource-rich Black or White congregations for mounting voter registration drives. Although the study did not address how Black congregations might work around this disadvantage, the presence of coalitions among Black churches in most cities was one solution to this difficulty.[34]

Why voting rights and voter registration efforts were needed was readily apparent at the time the study was conducted both in the differences between Black and White registration and turnout in southern states and in the attitudes that sometimes surfaced among White voters. A White polling official in Georgia, for example, complained in a letter to the newspaper, "Why do the people conducting voter registration drives think they are being good citizens?" He added, "The people who usually get registered in these drives are the people we should not want on the voter registration list in the first place. Many of them cannot read or write, know nothing about what is taking place in the city, state, or country, and could not care less. Many of them would sell their vote for a couple of bucks if a candidate would take them to register and then to the polls on Election Day."[35]

Besides voter suppression rooted in attitudes like this, conservative religious groups' get-out-the-vote campaigns provided a further incentive for progressive religious groups to do the same. After George W. Bush's hair-thin victory over Al Gore in 2000, this incentive was even stronger. When the Christian Coalition, the Southern Baptist Convention, and other conservative groups aggressively promoted voter registration in churches in conjunction with the Bush-Cheney campaign in 2004, a progressive interfaith coalition of some twelve hundred religious leaders calling itself the Clergy Network for National Leadership Change launched an effort openly devoted to unseating Bush.

During Bush's tenure in office, the US Department of Justice's focus on rights had shifted toward defending the rights of religious groups that claimed that they were discriminated against because they were being forced to hire gay employees or unbelievers or were being sued because of operating government-funded service programs, which prompted concerns among civil rights groups that the justice department was allowing the voting rights of Black voters to be diluted and failing to file cases defending voting rights. The National Council of Churches was one of the groups expressing these concerns. In anticipation of the Voting Rights Act coming up for renewal in Congress in 2007, the National Council of Churches also publicized a resolution reaffirming its longstanding commitment to voting rights.[36]

The on-the-street campaign that would play a lasting role in voting rights advocacy began in North Carolina in February 2007 under the leadership of Reverend William Barber. Barber was the pastor of a small Disciples of Christ church in Goldsboro, North Carolina, from which he also served as the state's NAACP president. The demonstration in February brought participants from across the state to present the state's General Assembly with the "People's Agenda," which included raising the minimum wage, abolishing the death penalty and mandatory sentencing laws, supplying affordable housing, providing affordable

healthcare, redressing discrimination in hiring and government contracting, and easing voter registration.[37]

Reverend Barber's movement campaigned for voting rights on several fronts in 2008. One front was challenging a Republican-led redis-
tricting plan that would jeopardize the seats of as many as sixteen Black
legislators in districts across the state. A second involved repeating the
previous years' march in Raleigh, pressing the same agenda, but this
time with a larger crowd and more affiliated organizations. A third was
to file a complaint with the state justice department about an automated
phone campaign offering misleading information meant to confuse voters and suppress the Black vote. And a fourth was to defend a group of
Black students whose votes had been challenged. But as the general
election approached, Barber's movement focused its main efforts on
mobilizing voter turnout, taking full advantage of North Carolina having same-day registration and no-excuse early voting.[38]

Get-out-the-vote efforts in other locations included a coalition of
fifty churches in Los Angeles with some 75,000 members that conducted a voter registration drive by placing literature in churches with
encouragement like "God's Plan for Registration" and "When God's
people are counted, it means something"; a "From the Pews to the
Polls" campaign in Texas encouraging people to vote after going to
church; a 32-page study guide on voting rights produced by the Presbyterian Church (USA) for use in its congregations; and pastors in Florida
pressing local election officials to more effectively implement early voting and ease access to voting sites. A post-election study showed that
early voting was significantly higher in 2008 than in 2004 or 2006 and
that 29 percent of Black voters had received information about the election at their churches compared with only 7 percent of White mainline
Protestant voters.[39]

Obama's victory in the 2008 election and the US Supreme Court's
signal in 2009 that it might be open to reconsidering the constitutionality of the Voting Rights Act prompted Republicans to engage in new
efforts to restrict voting access. The Brennan Center for Justice, which
monitored voting rights issues, documented at least 180 restrictive voting bills in forty-one states after the 2008 election and prior to the 2012

election. The center's report listed race as a significant factor: "Of the 11 states with the highest African-American turnout in 2008, 7 have new restrictions in place. Of the 12 states with the largest Hispanic population growth between 2000 and 2010, 9 passed laws making it harder to vote." The report also noted that nine of the fifteen states that had previously been covered by the Voting Rights Act passed new voting restrictions. The most common restrictions were requirements for photo identification, which many low-income and minority voters lacked, an increase in forms and documentary evidence required for voter registration, and cutbacks on early voting days and hours.[40]

Against these voter restriction measures, religious groups' options were limited beyond what they had done in 2008 to mobilize voter registration and voter turnout. Indicative of the difficulties was an effort to ease the process by which persons formerly convicted of crimes could regain their right to vote—a right that was denied to approximately triple the percentage of Black voters than White voters. Some headway had been made in Virginia, for example, when Democratic Governor Tim Kaine was in office, but under Republican Governor Bob McDonnell, appeals by the Virginia Interfaith Center for Public Policy in conjunction with the NAACP and ACLU fell on deaf ears.[41]

The most concerted anti-voter-suppression campaign in which religious leaders played a role was the Congressional Black Caucus's Faith Leaders' Summit on Voting Rights held in conjunction with the National Black Churches' 2012 National Consultation, which represented approximately two-thirds of all Black congregations. The gathering pledged support of Attorney General Eric Holder's attempts to combat gerrymandering and voting rights violations, developed toolkits for civic engagement in congregations, and organized voter registration drives. Loosely organized as the Empower Movement, these drives took place in African Methodist Episcopal, African Methodist Episcopal Zion, Churches of God in Christ, and nondenominational Black churches. These efforts were joined by Jim Wallis's Sojourners movement, the United Church of Christ, and the North Carolina Council of Churches. In preparation for the *Shelby County v. Holder* case, an *amici* brief was filed by a coalition of faith communities that included Church Women United, the National Council of Jewish Women, Central Conference of American Rabbis, and the Leadership Conference on Civil and Human Rights—an organization in which all the progressive denominations participated.[42]

Obama's 50 percent to 48 percent victory over Mitt Romney in 2012 was much narrower than his win against John McCain in 2008 (a 53 percent to 46 percent margin). Obama won 95 percent of the Black Protestant vote, according to a post-election study, but White non-evangelical Protestants and White Catholics voted for Obama in smaller percentages than they had in 2008. A statistical analysis of the results by Brookings Institution demographer William Frey predicted that Democrats could win in 2016 only if Black turnout and Black preferences for the Democratic candidate remained as high as they were in 2012. Wide publicity to the effect that Obama had been reelected only because of the Black vote gave Republicans reason to hope that Black voter registration and turnout could effectively be dampened.[43]

As the 2014 midterm elections approached, North Carolina Reverend William Barber followed the Moral Mondays campaign that had grown out of his People's Agenda movement with Voting Rights Sundays to support the Voting Rights Act. Under Reverend Raphael Warnock's leadership, Ebenezer Baptist Church in Atlanta initiated a fifty-state Voting Rights Project to fight voter suppression. The North Carolina Council of Churches supplied voters with up-to-the-moment information about how and where to register to vote and what kinds of identification might be required. Representative John Lewis called on Black clergy to assist in his efforts to restore the Voting Rights Act. The United Church of Christ enlisted its member congregations in the drive to restore voting rights and the Presbyterian Church (USA) created a study guide for its congregations to discuss how voter suppression was being conducted and what could be done about it. Among the recommendations in these and other studies were the value of Sunday voting to accommodate "souls to the polls" mobilization, the importance of religious groups providing transportation and help with obtaining photo identification well before the elections, and even such steps as encouraging parents to take children with them when voting to instill an early understanding of its importance.[44]

As hopeful as many Black and White progressive religious leaders had been about Obama's presidency and as supportive as they had been of his administration's policies, it was notable that prominent voices within the progressive community were critical by the end of his first term and even more critical by the latter part of his second term about his handling of issues concerned with racial justice. Sociologist and MSNBC political analyst Michael Eric Dyson was one of Obama's fiercest critics. "Every President before Obama has been forced to respond to the issue of race. President Obama says he wants to be treated like all other Presidents," Dyson wrote. "Well, then, you can't be exempt from the call of responsibility to race. You can't have it both ways. What we get is, 'I'm the first black President, and my personal discomfort with discussing race in public has made me mute.' And I think that's problematic." The central claim among the criticisms was that Obama's approach to racial justice was to downplay its importance by seeking to govern on the assumption that a colorblind approach was best. "We should all be proud that we now have President Barack H. Obama as the President of the United States," Reverend Benjamin Chavis wrote. "Black Americans however should avoid falling into the anti-reality pitfall that we are now living in a 'postracial' society and world."[45]

Clearly, the evidence demonstrated that Obama's candidacy for president and the major policy initiatives of his administration had succeeded by appealing to constituencies that were majority White as well as to Black voters. Playing to White voters whose inclinations were often quietly dismissive of Black voters' interests was a factor in winning the presidency. That was also true of the economic recovery and healthcare reform packages. While these packages benefited Black communities disproportionately insofar as Black families were more likely than White families to face foreclosures, need affordable housing, and lack health insurance, it was the case that the majority of those who benefited were White. The more trenchant concern that critics voiced was that less was done to assist low-income families of all races than to earn buy-in from the powerbrokers who ran the banks, real estate organizations, and health services. A study of the demolition projects in Detroit cast this concern in an illuminating perspective. Five years after the Neighborhood Stabilization Program ended, little had been done to rebuild or stabilize neighborhoods other than clearing space for community gardens. A major share of the money had been spent hauling in millions of tons of dirt to fill the basements left open from the demolitions.[46]

The ways in which progressive religious groups interacted with the Obama presidency does, however, illustrate an important point about religion and politics. Because so much media attention focuses on closely contested elections, it has become easy to conceive of religion's role in politics as primarily an influence on who wins or loses in these elections. Polling supplies us with constant information, for example, about White evangelicals' support for Republican candidates, reinforcing the idea that a large bloc of religiously motivated constituents can make or break an aspiring candidate's chances. But even though this conclusion may contain a grain of truth, it misses an essential aspect of the link between religion and politics. Religion's influence is rarely channeled directly from the pulpit to the pew to the voting booth. Religion's influence in the lives of its adherents is *organized* and it is meant to be communal, rather than only personal, which means that its influence is channeled through denominational agencies, interdenominational coalitions, nonprofit governing committees, community boards, and grassroots leadership groups whose job it is to represent collectively the faith community to the wider world. That influence is rarely decisive, because it takes place in the context of other groups that represent other constituencies. Its role consists chiefly of expressing—and enacting in concrete ways—the values and convictions of the faith community. And, although its role may not be decisive, this is the level at which faith leaders do have input in policy decisions.

The power structures through which democratic governance in the United States is enacted operate much of the time on an implicitly colorblind basis—the exceptions being the many cases in which segregation, discrimination, racially motivated hate crimes, and voting rights are at issue. In these cases, race is an explicit consideration. But in many other instances, race is excluded from consideration, meaning that a policy aimed at subsidizing small businesses, for example, is unlikely to withstand legal challenge if it includes a provision that specifically benefits small business owners who are Black, no matter what the history of discrimination against Black businesses has been. Obama-era policies followed this pattern. The Neighborhood Stabilization Program, as a case in point, benefited Black communities like the Austin and Pullman neighborhoods in Chicago, but did so under a policy that was officially race neutral.

Whether it was fair or unfair to say that Obama should have done more, racial justice was the issue that returned to public consciousness with great significance during the last half of his presidency. The tragic events responsible were in many ways continuous with previous events but became the focus of greater outrage as the Black Lives Matter movement organized in protest against the racial injustice they represented. The response to these events must also be interpreted considering what the critics got right in criticizing the hopes left unfulfilled by Obama's policies. There had been hope that America truly could be a postracial society and that it could address racial justice at the same time. That hope had not been fulfilled.

7

Black Lives Matter

ON JUNE 1, 2020, when Donald Trump walked from the White House across Lafayette Square, positioned himself in front of St. John's Episcopal Church, and held up a Bible while federal officers used force to clear the area of peaceful demonstrators protesting the death of George Floyd in Minneapolis, some of the president's White conservative Christian supporters rejoiced. Here was a president who stood for what they did, a leader asserting that God was on their side. A Dallas megachurch preacher called the president's photo-op "faith-inspired." An anchor for the Christian Broadcasting Network praised the president's symbolic denunciation of "far left radicals." A visitor on the scene from Florida fell on her knees and began speaking in tongues.[1]

Reporters covering the event interpreted Trump's camera shoot as a signal of solidarity to his conservative Bible-believing base and saw it as a repudiation of the Black Lives Matter movement, which he had condemned since its inception a few years earlier and about which conservative religious leaders had mostly been silent or critical. Black religious leaders spoke quite differently about the event, focusing on how the Black Lives Matter protests were calling White and Black Americans to combat racial injustice. Faith in Action executive director Reverend Alvin Herring, whose interracial advocacy network included more than a thousand congregations in some two hundred cities, declared, "The nation and the world's attention is galvanized on the way anti-Blackness and White supremacy brings violence, brings trauma, to its Black citizens and to those who are also people of color. This is about fighting a battle to free your brothers and sisters and that you as a White person are instrumental in that fight."

White religious leaders who offered their views took the occasion to condemn the racism that they saw highlighted in the day's events. For example, the Evangelical Lutheran Church in America's Presiding Bishop, Reverend Elizabeth Eaton, declared, "As White people, we are spiritually stunted by our White privilege, our racism, and our White supremacy, which prevents us from living fully and deeply in our community. For every time we forget that each person is made in the image of God, we've moved further away from our own humanity." Similarly, a White Methodist pastor at a small church in Maryland confessed, "Even people who were silent are starting to become vocal. The more it's in your face, you can't ignore it." Other White pastors said it was time for White churches to start listening to Black people and begin speaking more openly against police brutality. "I'm tired of seeing my Black brothers and sisters brutalized for the crime of being Black," a White Presbyterian pastor in Chicago said. "It is against everything Jesus Christ has taught us."[2]

The loosely organized Black Lives Matter movement that mobilized protests across the nation in 2020 succeeded in focusing public attention on racial injustice in ways unseen since the civil rights movement. Black Lives Matter became a movement that responded to police violence, demanded reform, and enlisted a broad spectrum of activist groups in pressing these demands. The movement also challenged progressive White Christians' ideas about racial advocacy and led to some of them mobilizing anti-racism initiatives in their churches. But understanding that influence and the shape it took requires starting nearly a decade earlier. It was the killing of Trayvon Martin, an unarmed seventeen-year-old Black man, in 2012 that launched the movement in ways that could not have been fully anticipated at the time, and it was the movement's growth that challenged progressive White Christian groups to think about racial justice in new ways. The crucial phases of these developments included, first, the relatively patterned roles that Black churches and White churches played as the response to Martin's death grew from a local event into a national movement; second, churches' shifting pattern of responses to Black Lives Matter once it had become a national movement; third, the emerging focus among progressive White Christians on the fraught concept of White privilege; and fourth, the tenuous development in progressive White churches of deliberate anti-racist initiatives.

Much of the extensive writing prompted by Black Lives Matter has examined it as a social movement that made creative use of social media, benefited from on-site monitoring of law enforcement, and forged alliances among activist groups with overlapping agendas. Treatments of the movement have discussed the roles that Black churches played or failed to play in supporting it and how White Christian nationalists organized against it. Less attention has been given to the movement's relationship with progressive White faith communities and thus the complexities of this relationship—and the lessons to be learned—have not been satisfactorily examined. Especially in responding to a national movement organized by leaders who had serious doubts about churches' contributions, progressive White Christians faced an unprecedented challenge in determining how to respond. And yet the response did attempt to deal thoughtfully with racial justice even as it continued to be hampered by decades-old constraints.

This chapter traces the relationships that developed between the leaders of progressive White faith communities and Black Lives Matter—as a movement and as an idea—from the death of Trayvon Martin in 2012 through the protests following the killing of George Floyd in 2020. I show that the trajectory of this relationship evolved from the relatively weak supporting roles that some White churches in the vicinity of tragic events were accustomed to playing in conjunction with Black churches, through an interim phase during which activists among Black clergy developed a complementary division of labor with Black Lives Matter activists, and then a phase in which White faith leaders who wanted to do something struggled to find a place by showing up at rallies, issuing statements, participating in interfaith coalitions, talking about White privilege, and providing anti-racism study guides for congregations. Black Lives Matter, in these respects, propelled a new and often intense response from progressive White faith communities interested in racial justice, but this response also revealed how faith communities of necessity worked within their own limitations.

Trayvon Martin

When police arrived at the scene on the evening of February 26, 2012, seventeen-year-old Trayvon Martin was on the ground dead, and George Zimmerman, a twenty-six-year-old White man, was standing nearby, a gun in his waistband and blood seeping from injuries to his nose and the back of his head. Zimmerman told the police he was a neighborhood crime-watch leader, had called 911 to report a suspicious person, admitted to having shot Martin, and claimed self-defense. Zimmerman was taken into custody but released. The shooting drew little attention for more than a week, but on March 11, a small group of Black residents in Sanford, the central Florida city where Martin had been killed, and a few members of the New Black Panther Party gathered at the Sanford police headquarters to pressure the authorities to arrest Zimmerman. Two days later, the case was forwarded to the Florida state attorney's office.[3]

On Wednesday, March 14, nearly four hundred people—including local civil rights leaders and pastors—packed the small Allen Chapel African Methodist Episcopal Church located about three blocks from the police department in Sanford to call for Zimmerman's immediate arrest. The church's pastor addressed the congregation, and the mayor promised to conduct a full review of the case. The main speaker was Reverend Jamal Bryant, a prominent Baltimore evangelist. Almost immediately, the case drew national attention. After meeting with the Sanford police chief and the mayor, Florida Congresswoman Corrine Brown issued a statement calling on the US Department of Justice to open an investigation. *Orlando Sentinel* journalists published articles detailing the circumstances of Martin's death and linking it to the history of racial violence in the region. *New York Times* columnist Charles M. Blow posted a lengthy article about the case, including a photo of Trayvon Martin and describing how the teenager, who was visiting from Miami, had gone out to buy Skittles at a nearby 7–11 when he was killed.

Newspapers in Boston, Chicago, Cleveland, Philadelphia, Pittsburgh, San Francisco, and Washington, DC, as well as across Florida picked up the story.[4]

Faith communities' response to Trayvon Martin's death illustrated the gap in experiences with racial violence separating Black churches from White churches. For Black faith leaders, the tragedy was the latest in Black communities' history of subjection to violence. "Violence and its potentially deadly consequences," religion scholar Eddie S. Glaude Jr. wrote, "were constitutive of the horizons within which all African Americans produced and reproduced political and social identities."[5] The Sunday following the Wednesday gathering at Allen Chapel, the North Brevard Ministerial Alliance representing about two dozen Black congregations in the Sanford vicinity organized a march and hosted a series of speeches at St. James African Methodist Episcopal Church. The following Sunday, the Sanford clergy and civil rights leaders held a prayer vigil with hundreds of residents participating. The Associated Press reported that Sunday services at Black churches in Atlanta, Chicago, New York, and many other cities included preaching about the case, calls for Zimmerman's arrest, and churchgoers wearing hooded sweatshirts in Martin's memory. By mid-April, the National Black Church Initiative, representing approximately 34,000 congregations, joined in calling for Zimmerman's arrest and the US Justice Department to become involved."[6]

White churches' responses registered an awareness that this was a tragedy all too familiar in Black communities but one from which their own experience was a step or two removed. The presiding bishop of the Evangelical Lutheran Church in America's statement was typical: "Are we, who are White, ready to confront our power and privilege for the sake of a more just and inclusive society?" he asked. The pastor of a declining mostly White Methodist church in a racially mixed Florida suburb discussed sorting out his feelings and asking himself why he wasn't sensing outrage. "The system," he said, "has basically worked for me over the years and I trust it."[7]

White faith leaders' reckoning with racial differences was complicated by the conservative media casting doubt on whether the event suggested anything about race. Zimmerman himself appeared on Fox News's Sean Hannity program claiming that it had been God's will for him to kill Trayvon Martin. Evangelist Franklin Graham said it would take more time to know if a racial injustice had been committed. The Southern Baptist Convention's Ethics and Religious Liberty Commission president Reverend Richard Land accused leaders who were taking Martin's side of being "race hustlers."[8]

The differences in perspective between Black and White churches was evident, too, in Sanford, where the community was divided about how to think about Martin, Zimmerman, and the police. The Sanford Ministers Fellowship had been meeting off and on for twenty years in the hope of forging ties between Black and White churches. The fellowship discussed plans for a community-wide service that would bring Black and White congregations together only to discover that the congregations' leaders could not agree on how to structure a public event. However, the discussion did draw attention to the racial divide separating the community's churches. As one of the Black pastors observed, "We accepted the separateness, but the White community did as well. The prevailing race problem hinges on comfort."[9]

Although the Sanford Ministers Fellowship's hope to bring Black and White churches together failed, the group did not give up. Members continued meeting during the summer and through late September, this time with a different outcome. The eighty clergy who participated were Black, White, and Hispanic and from White Protestant, Black Protestant, Catholic, and Muslim organizations. Some of them met one on one, some had attended the group meetings enthusiastically, others less eagerly. They disbanded the earlier ministerial fellowship and formed a new group with a more intentional focus on building long-term relationships across racial lines.

Whether the new organization's plans would succeed was unknown, but what had brought the group this far was leadership from the outside. That leadership came in the person of Thomas Battles, a seasoned Black leader who headed the US Justice Department's Southeast Regional Community Relations Service—a unit established by the Civil Rights Act of 1964. Battles's job was to work behind the scenes to defuse tensions and build trust in communities during times of crisis. His task with the pastors was to listen, offer advice from the training and experience he had earned in other locations, and help restore confidence that racial reconciliation could be achieved.[10]

When Zimmerman was acquitted of the killing in July 2013, large protest demonstrations took place in response. The number of demonstrators in New York's Times Square was estimated in the thousands. Largely peaceful demonstrations also occurred in more than a hundred cities including Boston, Chicago, Los Angeles, and San Francisco. Marchers sang hymns, prayed, carried "Black Lives Matter" signs, and chanted "justice now." In her Sunday sermon at Allen Chapel AME Church in Sanford, Reverend Valerie Houston recalled Dr. Martin Luther King Jr.'s statement that "the daily life of the Negro is still in the basement of the Great Society." And today, she said, "The daily life of my people is still enslaved to a White supremacist society."[11]

Despite the attention that Trayvon Martin's death received, it was not obvious that a sustained national movement for racial justice would be the result. The immediate attention that the killing received from the media, clergy, and elected officials was driven by the tragedy itself but also by the fraught circumstances in Florida politics at the time. In 2005, Florida had passed a controversial "stand your ground" law that permitted the use of deadly force by someone who reasonably felt themselves to be at risk of bodily harm. Within five months of the law going into effect, thirteen shootings occurred in Central Florida in which self-defense was claimed. Of the six persons killed and four wounded, only one was armed. The law's proponents claimed it would deter gun violence; opponents said gun violence would increase. Shortly after the Martin killing, Florida Governor Rick Scott called for a review of the law, which prompted hearings and thousands of public comments but ended without the law being repealed or modified.[12]

Gun violence in 2012 resulted in more than 22,000 firearm homicides nationally, including 171 in the Orlando area where Trayvon Martin was killed. The rate of deaths per hundred thousand population was nearly twice as high among Black people than among White people, which had resulted in the NAACP becoming increasingly involved in investigating killings and pursuing complaints against police departments about the handling of cases. The Obama administration's Justice Department under Attorney General Eric Holder and Assistant Attorney General Thomas Perez was involved in several major investigations between 2009 and 2011 that drew public attention to shootings of Black victims and raised hope that public pressure would produce results. These included an investigation into the police shootings of eight Black men in Miami, the killing of an unarmed Black man by a White former transit police officer in Oakland, and the completion of an inquiry into an earlier murder of a Black man by police in New York City. These investigations were conducted against a crescendo of criticisms from right-wing pundits claiming that the Obama administration was implementing a kind of reverse racism against the White community.

Ferguson

The national attention that Trayvon Martin's death generated solidified into a national movement following the killing of Michael Brown by police officer Darren Wilson in the St. Louis suburb of Ferguson, Missouri, on August 9, 2014. Demonstrators, believing that Brown was surrendering when killed, filled the streets near where the shooting took place, organized a candlelight vigil the next evening, and continued holding protests through the end of the month. Demonstrations resumed in late November and early December as grand jury testimony leaked suggesting that an indictment of Wilson would not be forthcoming, and protests took place again the following March when the US Department of Justice decided against charging Wilson with a civil rights violation in the shooting. Faith leaders were an active presence in the community throughout these months.

Like their involvement in the Wilmington Ten case in the 1970s and the Rodney King case in the 1990s, clergy's roles in response to Michael Brown's killing differed between those who were local and those who responded from a distance. Eleven churches in the immediate vicinity offered their buildings as safe spaces where protesters could meet or come for prayer. One of the closest was the Greater St. Mark Family

Church, a Black Baptist congregation of about a hundred people, where the pastor, Reverend Tommie L. Pierson Sr., organized a rally the day after the shooting. Another was Christ the King United Church of Christ, pastored by Reverend Traci Blackmon, who worked among the protesters to keep the demonstrations peaceful and would later become a prominent figure in other protest demonstrations.[13]

At a slightly greater distance were clergy who pastored interracial or White churches but were close enough to have hosted prayer vigils or taken part in demonstrations. Episcopal bishop of Missouri Reverend George Wayne Smith was one of these clergy. He wrote a few months later: "We who are the church do well to learn from the rage present in Ferguson and surrounding communities, a rage which has spread throughout the nation and around the world. That rage did not come from nowhere, and it has something important to tell us all, but especially to those of us living with privilege. We can commit ourselves to honest and difficult conversation, in the presence of the racial wound in our community, made evident in the body of Michael Brown."[14]

Faith communities farther away sometimes sent leaders to support the churches in Ferguson and organized vigils in their own locations. In addition to her role at Christ the King United Church of Christ, Reverend Blackmon headed her denomination's Justice and Witness Ministries, which connected her to the UCC's activists in other congregations and affiliated denominations. Reverend Osagyefo Sekou, an ordained Church of God in Christ minister, came out from New York City to work with Blackmon and other local clergy in training local participants how to engage in peaceful confrontations with the police. In their own locations, congregations expressed care for Ferguson in acts of symbolic support, such as a church in Baltimore that collected signatures in a book of prayers for racial healing and a congregation in Boston that created and blessed a thousand paper origami cranes (symbolizing peace) and sent them to Reverend Blackmon.[15]

Much of faith leaders' activism in Ferguson was devoted to expressing while also containing anger about Michael Brown's death, guiding reflection about racial justice, and seeking to restore peace among Black and White neighbors and with the police. A reporter for the *Chicago*

Tribune described Reverend Blackmon's congregation as an "oasis of warmth and calm." That was a role Reverend Blackmon modeled in meeting with Brown's family, praying for Darren Wilson and the police, and serving on the commission that the mayor appointed to review the case and make recommendations for police reform. With deep roots in the community, Black churches like Reverend Blackmon's had legitimacy, making it possible to play these roles. Other churches had the capacity to bridge divisions in the city, as was the case with the interfaith coalition, Metropolitan Congregations United, whose member churches convened small gatherings encouraging cross-racial interaction. Churches also challenged the community to engage in spiritual reflection, as Reverend Tommie Pierson did in asserting, "If my community is going to get better, I must get better." However, the roles that faith communities were accustomed to playing were not the ones that formed the focus for the organizers of Black Lives Matter.[16]

The protests that broke out in cities across the country in the immediate aftermath of Michael Brown's killing expressed anger about the continuing, never-ending racial injustice of police abuse. Approximately 8 percent of all homicides nationwide were committed by police. Blacks were three to four times more likely than Whites to be the victims. Protesters chanting "Hands up, don't shoot"—in imitation of Michael Brown's surrender as he was shot—expressed the anger. "Black Lives Matter" was a prevailing refrain as well. Initially, it was a phrase posted on Facebook and Twitter, carried on signs, and used to frame events— including ones in which faith leaders participated, such as a nationwide effort for churches to affirm their support for racial justice. Reverend Jamal Bryant, the Baltimore pastor who met with the demonstrators protesting Trayvon Martin's death, for example, responded to Michael Brown's death by declaring his support for a "Black Lives Matter Sunday" and calling on Black churches and youth organizations everywhere to wear black in solidarity with the families of African Americans brutally murdered by the police.[17]

By the time the US Justice Department decided not to press civil rights charges against officer Wilson, Black Lives Matter (BLM) had evolved from a hashtag into a national movement. It was intersectional, appealing to queer and transgendered persons, women, and the poor, as well as to activists calling for racial justice. Its leaders distanced themselves from the civil rights movement, mobilized participation through social media, and attracted younger activists, many of whom were religiously unaffiliated. Some of the leaders were critical of the hierarchal and patriarchal connotations they associated with established religion. The movement was decentralized, confrontational, and adept at mobilizing in opposition to police violence.[18]

The question that BLM posed for progressive faith communities interested in racial justice was whether to join its ranks, keep distant from it, support it sporadically, or borrow from it selectively. During most of the past half century, progressive faith communities—White and Black—had worked cooperatively with racial justice groups that were not explicitly faith-based, such as the NAACP, ACLU, fair housing groups, and desegregation initiatives. There had been holdouts against supporting militant activists on the left such as Angela Davis and James Forman, but not since the Black Power movement had there been a movement as influential as BLM about which some progressive religious groups had doubts.

The doubts in some instances stemmed from BLM's aggressive tactics in staging confrontations with the police, interrupting public officials' speeches, and organizing street protests that led to violence and looting. The doubts in other instances had to do with BLM's embrace of intersectionality, which aimed to broaden the movement by enlisting the support of gay, transgender, and feminist activists, but which weakened its support among racial justice advocates who either did not agree with some of those activists or worried about trying to pursue too many agendas at the same time. The doubts about sexuality surfaced especially among campus groups and congregations that were divided about ordaining gay clergy.[19]

For their part, many BLM activists believed faith communities were too wedded to the status quo, too invested in nostalgia about the civil rights movement, and too intent on believing postracial ideology. As racial equity scholar Lawrence Brown observed, "Many in the movement perceive the Black Church as either sitting on the sidelines or, even worse, a buffer for or an accomplice in the systems of oppression leading to homicides at the hands of police." There were exceptions like Reverend Blackmon, whose work on behalf of racial justice was widely respected, but the BLM leaders Brown talked with saw Black pastors and churches calling for decency, dignity, and decorum while offering only scripted support of the movement.[20]

Advocacy for racial justice was always contentious, but BLM's far-right opponents succeeded in sowing doubts about the movement by arguing that it was totally against the police, an anarchist threat to law and order, a form of "race hustling," and extreme enough that supporting it meant siding with the "radical left wing" of the Democratic party rather than hewing to the moderate middle of postracial politics. In one of his first comments about BLM, Donald Trump remarked, "I saw them with hate coming down the street last week talking about cops and police. . . . I think it's disgraceful the way they're being catered to by the Democrats. I don't think it's going to end up good. The fact is all lives matter."[21]

In 2015, many of the churches that displayed Black Lives Matter signs did so less in solidarity with the BLM movement than as ways of expressing their support for racial justice. As the pastor of a Unitarian church in Florida explained, the Black Lives Matter sign in front of his church was "about naming racism in our community and recognizing that it exists." In other places, the message that Black Lives Matter signs conveyed was itself sufficiently controversial that other statements and clarifications had to be posted. To better communicate her congregation's support for racial justice, a pastor in Maryland, for example, swapped the Black Lives Matter sign for a new one with a line from John Legend: "Selma is now because the struggle for justice is now." Similarly, a church in Chicago swapped its Black Lives Matter sign for one reading "Life Matters, Risk Loving Everyone" after receiving a barrage of comments like "Nice that a church plays into the race card crap" and "Thank you for doing your part to support what is quickly becoming a terrorist movement."[22]

The problem with signage bearing a three-word slogan was that miscommunication was inevitable. An additional problem was the BLM movement's aggressive confrontational style. This problem became a major issue in Los Angeles when BLM chapter leaders disrupted a town hall meeting with Mayor Eric Garcetti at the Holman United Methodist Church, where venerated civil rights leader Reverend James M. Lawson Jr. had preached for years. Outraged by the disruption, Black clergy—including the president of the Baptist Ministers Conference of Los Angeles and Southern California and the president of the LA chapter of the National Action Network—held a press conference denouncing BLM for its disregard for the community and its disrespect for one of the most prominent historical churches in the community. A year later, *Los Angeles Times* journalist Angel Jennings found the city's Black clergy still skeptical about BLM. They disliked its brash, in-your-face tactics and considered it irresponsible and lacking in direction.[23]

The advantage of BLM being a decentralized movement was that a problematic situation in one community did not hinder faith leaders in other communities from adopting some of what BLM represented. For example, when 24-year-old Jamar Clark was killed by police in Minneapolis, faith leaders considered the occasion an opportunity to engage their congregations in conversations about racial justice. Black Clergy United for Change became the convening vehicle and was soon joined by the Interfaith Roundtable for Racial Justice, which had evolved from demonstrations for same-sex marriage. Several of the clergy also had loose ties with BLM leaders. The faith leaders in Minneapolis found the ideas of BLM compatible with what they wanted to accomplish but considered their efforts separate from any national movement.[24]

Church leaders' response to Freddie Gray's death—the 25-year-old Baltimore resident who died from injuries at the hands of police a week after his arrest in 2015—revealed an emerging division of labor between the churches and the Black Lives Matter movement in which the two played distinct and yet complementary roles. As BLM protests filled the streets, a coalition of Black clergy formulated a seven-point plan advocating for change in the police department, including the resignation of the police commissioner. In the following months, the clergy coalition met with city and state officials and worked with Maryland's US representatives in Congress to advance community-oriented criminal justice initiatives. The clergy's and the BLM protesters' demands were the same but the tactics were different, each group doing what it was most effective at doing.[25]

A closer relationship between BLM activists and faith leaders developed in Charlottesville, Virginia, in August 2017 when White nationalists and neo-Nazis rallied in the community to protest the removal of Confederate statues. Reverend Blackmon and an official from the National Council of Churches flew in to support local clergy and teamed up with BLM activists in a counter-rally. "The message of faith leaders in Charlottesville was not about statues," Blackmon told a reporter for the *Christian Century*. "It was about love. We understand that the removal of statues is merely a symbolic gesture unless we commit ourselves to the transformative work of eradicating racist statutes, revisionist history, and white supremacy in this land."[26]

Cooperation of a sort between BLM activists and clergy happened again on the one-year anniversary of the Charlottesville confrontation, as White supremacists planned a "Unite the Right" demonstration in Washington, DC. The event failed to draw many supporters, but faith-based activists mobilized a large "Unite to Love" rally on the National Mall instead. Organized by the Baltimore-Washington Conference of the United Methodist Church, the rally included clergy, lay activists, and seminary students who sang hymns, prayed, held banners reading "Standing on the side of love," and offered to supply pastoral support to the BLM movement. "You're seeing more and more people getting involved—there are churches all over the region today who maybe aren't here, but they're having vigils, they're preaching sermons. . . . Everybody is coming alive," one of the participants said.[27]

BLM did win support from faith leaders when demonstrations mobilized, but many congregations' reticence about the movement's tactics shaped how White faith communities tried to address racial justice. Explanations of this reticence varied. One version emphasized congregations' attachment to respectability, which appeared to characterize a great number of Black as well as White congregations and meant keeping on good terms with the police and elected officials. A second version, which did not pertain specifically to churches, suggested that

White people tended to regard anyone who was Black—no matter how well-educated and successful—as an inferior person. This mindset, sociologist Elijah Anderson wrote, assumes "that all black people start from the inner-city ghetto and are therefore stigmatized by their association with its putative amorality, danger, crime, and poverty. Hence, in public a black person is burdened with a negative presumption that he must disprove before he can establish mutually trusting relationships with others."[28]

Yet another interpretation emphasized congregations' queasiness about disturbing members' levels of comfort, which afforded opportunities to discuss how they felt about race, how they might behave differently around a person of a different race, and what that might say about their relationship to God but stop short of thinking about racial justice as a societal issue. Social scientist John Delehanty's research on faith-based social justice activists, for example, provided an illustration of this tendency in the congregations he studied. In response to police violence, the activist group that formed in one progressive congregation proposed displaying a Black Lives Matter sign outside the church. But the congregation's leadership rejected the proposal in deference to "a lot of [parishioners] who didn't know about the issue or maybe had their own feelings about safety and inclusion." As an alternative, the leadership suggested bringing the name of someone who had been killed by police and placing the name in a book for prayer. They considered this alternative much more appropriate than doing anything that might offend some of the congregants' feelings.[29]

White Privilege

The takeaway from Black Lives Matter demonstrations for majority-White faith communities concerned about racial injustice was a heightened interest in discussing White privilege. Although White privilege had been featured in deliberations about South Africa, Rhodesia, and a few other countries in the 1970s, not until the 1990s did it surface with much frequency in discussions about the United States. By the end of the decade, White privilege was an emerging theme in Whiteness studies programs, essays on White culture, and in the reports on the subtle advantages that some people enjoyed when purchasing automobiles or dealing with law enforcement simply because they were White. White Protestant groups started mentioning White privilege in the 1990s as well. For example, in 1994 the Episcopal Church's House of Bishops issued a pastoral letter to be read in all the denomination's pulpits reminding parishioners that "our primary experience is one of White privilege" and challenging them to move beyond making resolutions toward actively addressing social and economic inequality.[30]

The bishops' letter originated from the denomination's interaction with Anglican leaders in South Africa during the struggle against Apartheid. Other discussions of White privilege grew from interaction across racial lines in congregations and among clergy, such as at a Korean American church in Seattle, an interdenominational Community Congress on Racial Relations in Spokane, and an interracial campus ministry in Kansas City. Ideas about what might be done to remediate White privilege focused on reforms within religious organizations, such as giving greater liturgical expression to racial and ethnic diversity.

The protests that followed the deaths of Trayvon Martin, Michael Brown, and Freddie Gray foregrounded White privilege in ways that the churches had not grappled with before. The central claim was that racial injustice could not be effectively resisted by White people focusing only on the disadvantages affecting Black people. Instead, racism had to be understood as the structuring and maintaining of White privilege, which meant that White people needed to be more aware of their White identity and how the everyday behavior they took for granted contributed to the problem. This was a challenge that churches could address in their roles as moral guides concerned with the shaping of everyday behavior. But it was an idea that ran afoul of several deeply ingrained ways of thinking.

Whether they were liberal, conservative, or in between, many Christians liked to imagine that God was colorblind and wanted them also to be colorblind. That conviction got in the way of paying attention to the fact that race had to be recognized if racial injustice was to be reduced. A second difficulty was that White privilege implied taking a critical stance toward the church's emphasis on *helping* others, *serving* others, and *ministering* to others. Those ways of thinking took for granted that the people doing the helping, serving, and ministering were indeed privileged—and that was a good thing. But White privilege suggested a need to reflect about what White people did to keep their privilege intact and indeed to make it seem right. A third problem was dealing with the reality that many of the people the churches ministered to were *not* privileged by most standards of comparison—they were poor, jobless, homeless, and struggling to meet their families' needs but were also White. It was a hard sell to convince church groups that these White people enjoyed advantages compared with someone in similar circumstances who was Black, even though that was in fact true.

The deaths of Trayvon Martin, Michael Brown, and others created what researcher Garrett Naiman insightfully termed a "crack in the windshield" of colorblind ideology. As one of Naiman's interviewees explained, "I think the age of colorblindness might be shifting or going dormant or something. The visibility of White police officers murdering Black people has kind of really punctured a big hole into that whole thing." And as another interviewee told Naiman: "White people were like, 'Why do I have to care about racism? Why do I have to do anything?' And then after Ferguson and Mike Brown got killed, all of a sudden White people are like, 'What the hell can I do? Tell me what to do!'"[31]

Attention to White privilege among White faith communities grew from the demonstrations protesting the deaths of Black victims, the increased salience of race propelled by the Black Lives Matter movement, the publication of books and articles about White privilege, and meetings among racial justice advocates. The impetus was perhaps driven as well by the White supremacy that rose tragically to the surface in 2015, when White supremacist Dylann Roof killed nine church members at the Emanuel African Methodist Episcopal Church in Charleston, South Carolina, and again with the White supremacist march in Charlottesville in 2017. White supremacy was a warning sign to White progressives that they needed to look within their own ranks for resources to protect against it.

The United Church of Christ, the Sojourners community, and scattered Presbyterian, Methodist, and Episcopal leaders were among the first to call on White congregations to address White privilege explicitly. United Church of Christ president Reverend John Dorhauer, for example, issued statements and spoke at local UCC congregations about White privilege and the need for "White allies" with Black churches in combating racial injustice. The UCC commissioned Reverend Blackmon to create a study guide for congregations to use in their discussions about White privilege. Sojourners' Jim Wallis published a book titled *America's Original Sin: Racism, White Privilege, and the Bridge to a New America.* The United Methodist Board of Church and Society produced a resolution asking the denomination to acknowledge White privilege as an underlying cause of racial injustice and challenging "individual White persons to confess their participation in the sin of racism and repent for past and current racist practices." Congregations in Arizona, Georgia, Maryland, Minnesota, Missouri, North Carolina, South Carolina, and other locations where protests took place after the killing of Black men announced that they were convening study groups to talk about White privilege. "If there is a positive thing going on around the nation," the pastor of a White church in Florida said, "it's that the White community is finally waking up and realizing there is a little bit to this whole White privilege thing. When you are the majority group, you think everything is fine. We are unaware, we are tone-deaf and blind to things."[32]

Reflecting on White privilege was continuous with what many progressive faith communities had long been doing in advocating against excessive uses of police force, discriminatory sentencing, and racially biased incarceration and in welcoming persons of color into their churches. But it was challenging to turn the focus inward and to decide what that focus should be; thus, differing ideas emerged. At a Congregational church in Minnesota, for example, the discussion focused on the realization that White church members were far less likely than Black church members to be the victims of shooters like Dylann Roof and, for that matter, White churches probably were not saying enough to deter such shooters. At a Congregational church in Maine, the group discussing White privilege realized it could talk about Whiteness in a safe space without immediately thinking about racial justice at all. The discussion at a church in Atlanta, in contrast, led to reexamining its role in the South's long history of slavery.

Conversations that were mostly hidden from public view did—on occasion—result in published reflections that their authors hoped would prompt further thinking about White privilege. For example, Reverend Christopher Keating, a Presbyterian pastor in St. Louis, wrote, "It didn't take long for me to see that the shadow my privilege casts is invisible to everyone except persons of color. It's important to point out that identifying White privilege is not the same as inducing White guilt. Instead, it is a chance to discover how unconscious actions negatively affect everyone." This realization came to him from attending a pastors' conference about White privilege. He thought about growing up without having to be watched by store clerks and questioned by the police like his Black age-mates. "I'm now seeing racism in everyday encounters," he said.[33]

Anti-Racism

The hope among faith leaders discussing White privilege was that the discussions would impel action. "I'm talking about [a movement]," said Reverend Blackmon, "that has as its end goal the changing of systems and the dismantling of structures."[34] But there were impediments to be overcome for that to happen. Congregations intent on engaging more energetically in advancing racial justice would have to move past vague ideas about moral uplift and spend time studying what it meant to change systems and dismantle structures. They would need to decide if seeing racism in everyday encounters was adequate to the task, or only an initial step, and they would have to learn from seasoned activists like Reverend Blackmon.

There were questions, too, about how White privilege was implicated in White churches' attempts to enact anti-racist ideas. One of those questions concerned White churches' willingness to give up any of their cherished traditions in seeking to welcome greater diversity. As a Latino writer observed, "For me to worship at an Anglo church, I must accept White theology, pray in a White manner, sing White German songs, and eat meatloaf at the potluck." Those were barriers in the way of any churches hoping to be genuinely multicultural.[35] A related question was whether White churches were or were not appropriately trying to be anti-racist by incorporating Black styles of preaching and singing. "The power that White people exercise," wrote sociologist Cheryl Townsend Gilkes in commenting on popular White church singers capitalizing on Black music, "provides opportunities to exploit style and cultural artifacts for their own benefit."[36]

The anti-racism initiatives that grew out of the Black Lives Matter protests mostly resembled the racial reconciliation attempts that had been tried with limited success in the 1990s. White congregations and Black congregations forged sibling relationships, White and Black clergy exchanged pulpits, and coalitions of congregations participated in vigils and sponsored food pantries. These initiatives were subject to the same limitations and criticisms as the earlier ones had been. Such measures were short-term, token displays of racial harmony that usually faltered when congregants felt their attention needed to shift toward other priorities. Reconciliation too often was the watchword rather than reckoning and repentance. This time around, though, there were new participants and new hopes. And there were leaders who argued that new ideas should also be tried or that old ideas should be reinvented.[37]

Among the newer participants were coalitions seeking to bring White and Black Baptists from various traditions together for projects oriented toward racial reconciliation and social justice. To that end, a "New Baptist Covenant" association was announced with former presidents Jimmy Carter and Bill Clinton on its board and with participants from the Cooperative Baptist Fellowship—the breakaway group of some forty thousand Southern Baptists who considered themselves more moderate than the denomination's leadership. The Southern Baptist leadership also declared itself in favor of racial reconciliation and pledged to secure greater participation among Black and Latino clergy. Among the old ideas that were tried again were reparations programs, which several institutions created to compensate for past involvement in enslavement and discrimination. For example, Princeton Theological Seminary set aside approximately $28 million of endowment funds for reparations-oriented scholarships, curricular reforms, and community outreach, and Georgetown University announced an annual $400,000 plan to fund reparations for the descendants of enslaved laborers.[38]

Anti-racism posed new challenges for Black churches as well as for White organizations. The challenge lay in rethinking the hope of a post-racial America in the light of having had a Black president but no apparent lessening of racially motivated violence. Anti-racism required attending appreciatively and critically to the distinctive strengths of Black churches and Black theology. There needed to be "an *integrative moment* in the development of Black people's apprehension of an anti-racist and holistically salvific faith," Reverend Raphael Warnock wrote, "*the flowering of a self-critical liberationist community*." This was a bold call for Black clergy to set aside the comforts of prestige and respectability and direct their attention to rediscovering the liberationist history of the Black church and renewing the church's institutional engagement with the injustices of homelessness, incarceration, and racial disparities in education.[39]

Nearly all the majority-White mainline Protestant denominations, for their part, launched anti-racism initiatives that invited churchgoers to sign up for in-person or online study groups to talk about racial concerns. The materials that the groups studied included policing, mass incarceration, housing, education, and economic inequality, as well as scriptural teachings about love of neighbor, justice, and kindness. Some of the materials, such as the one written by Reverend Blackmon, were produced and distributed by denominational staff. The United Methodist Church, Lutheran Church Missouri Synod, and Presbyterian Church (USA) also produced study guides for their congregations to use in a series of small group discussions over a period of several months. In each of these cases, the denomination staff's and volunteers' role was to deliberate about the goals to be accomplished, solicit input from racial justice leaders within the denomination, bring together educators and clergy to work over an extended period on the materials, assemble

appropriate readings, write sample introductions and discussion questions, and then publicize the materials through denominational web-
sites and newsletters. With only the power of persuasion, there were no
guarantees that the study guides would be widely used—indeed, there
was reason to believe they would *not* be widely used—but they were a
resource for congregations where even a handful of members were interested in doing more to understand racial injustice.[40]

Sometimes, the congregations' anti-racism study groups also took
the initiative to create their own materials. For example, two Presbyterian congregations in New York state—one predominantly Black and
the other predominantly White—organized a year-long collaboration
involving twelve members from each church. From week to week, the
group focused on community building, educating themselves about
racism, watching a documentary film about mass incarceration, and
reading selections from James Baldwin and theologian James Cone.
While the group was local, it was conceived as a model that other congregations could use. A distinguishing feature of these anti-racism initiatives
was that the study guides were tailored to make them appropriate for
use in congregations where members might feel it was inappropriate to
spend time under the auspices of the congregation discussing secular
materials, especially if those materials were deemed divisive or anti-
religious. Although the materials typically included references to secular readings—and sometimes consisted of video clips from popular
writers—the focus was decidedly oriented toward a churchgoing audience. The genre resembled traditional Sunday school lessons in providing selected scriptural texts about God, humanity, and neighborly love
that could be applied to present-day discussions of racism. Some of the
study guides also provided brief histories of what the denomination—
or churches in general—had or had not done in the past to address racial injustice. In each of these ways, the study guides showed that talking
about race was an appropriate thing for church groups to do.[41]

Besides the materials produced for their own members, faith communities mobilized publicity campaigns to support activists' calls for
racial justice. Following the Charlottesville White supremacist demonstration, for example, the United Methodist Church launched a video

campaign and took out full-page ads in national newspapers citing the Bible and encouraging viewers and readers to "overcome evil with good." The US Catholic Bishops issued a widely publicized Pastoral Letter against Racism, declaring that "racist acts are sinful because they violate justice." Another widely publicized statement came from Bishop Michael Curry, the first Black presiding bishop of the Episcopal Church, who used his office to speak frequently about racial justice, most memorably in delivering the sermon at the royal wedding of Prince Harry and Meghan Markle. "When love is the way—unselfish, sacrificial, redemptive—when love is the way," he said, "then no child will go to bed hungry in this world ever again. When love is the way, we will let justice roll down like a mighty stream, and righteousness like an ever-flowing brook."[42]

Anti-racism initiatives, then, were an outgrowth of the tragic deaths of young Black men that brought Black Lives Matter into being as a nationwide movement and prompted faith communities to question whether they were at fault for not having done enough to combat racial injustice. Although these initiatives were not profoundly different from earlier racial reconciliation efforts, it was perhaps significant that "anti-racism" was a rubric with a more explicit acknowledgement of the continuing problem of racism and, in any case, that the study guides had the context of Black Lives Matter activism as a factor to be considered. Additionally, there were rallies, protests, and demands for police reform, all within the context of counter demonstrations staged by White supremacists and divisive rhetoric from the White House. However, there were deep doubts that any of the talk in White churches about White privilege and anti-racism was likely to endure or to have much of an impact. In addition to everything else it implied, White privilege for White churchgoers meant going to mostly White churches in mostly White neighborhoods where they could easily forget that racial justice was an important issue.

In May 2020, when George Floyd died under the knee of Minneapolis police officer Derek Chauvin, the anti-racism initiatives that faith communities had formed over the preceding five years were in full enough operation that leaders could update their materials to take account of the latest tragedy. The protests that mobilized across the nation in response to the death and that continued during the trial of officer Chauvin included hundreds of White as well as Black religious leaders who carried Black Lives Matter signs. More congregations were said to have been involved than ever before. Updating the language used to describe them, news reports referred to the protests as anti-racism rallies.

Four years of the Trump administration had done what it could to embrace White nationalism and to disparage and discourage the Black Lives Matter movement—going so far as to pressure the US Justice Department to file federal charges that carried harsher sentences against protesters than state or municipal ordinances did. Trump's Bible-holding photo appearance with St. John's church in the background took place as White supremacists tore down and burned Black Lives Matter banners from nearby churches. The day was to be a preview of Trump supporters' violent attack at the US Capitol on January 6, 2021.[43]

Anti-racism initiatives that began as discussion groups in congregations became sufficiently controversial that some clergy declared them off limits or treated them as the moral equivalent among progressives of Make America Great Again support among conservatives. Filtered through best-selling books like *White Fragility* and *Nice Racism*, White privilege came to be interpreted less in terms of systemic structures and more in terms of personal attitudes and person-to-person relationships between White people and their Black neighbors.[44] Opponents attached the label "critical race theory" to any anti-racism initiative that emphasized racial inequality or that suggested White people might be at fault. Banning critical race theory from public school curricula, calling for teachers to be fired and school board members to be replaced if any mention of racial equity was made, and erasing slavery from history textbooks became the new rallying cry among White conservatives. As part of the backlash, the Southern Baptist Convention's leading seminary presidents banned critical race theory from their institutions' curriculum.[45]

Important as they were, street demonstrations and anti-racism study groups had never been the whole of progressive faith communities' advocacy for racial justice. As demonstrations mobilized and study groups met, racial justice advocacy continued in other ways. In Louisville, for example, the Presbyterian Church (USA) Office of Public Witness sent a detailed position statement to the US Department of Housing and Urban Development opposing a revision in HUD policy stripping the agency of its capacity to enforce civil rights protections. In New York City, for another example, Odyssey Impact, one of the largest interfaith producers of films and videos, teamed with REFORM Alliance, one of the most influential nonprofit criminal justice reform organizations, to engage Gen-Z'ers whose participation in religious organizations was on a downhill slide in pressing lawmakers for prison and parole reform. These were among the many ways in which faith communities kept their sights on racial justice.

Faith-inspired advocacy continued in politics as well. In North Carolina, Reverend William Barber, heading the Repairers of the Breach coalition, continued the Moral Mondays fight against poverty, discrimination, and voter suppression. In Florida and Georgia, "Souls to the Polls" groups mobilized protests against voter restriction legislation. In Georgia, Reverend Raphael Warnock, senior pastor at Ebenezer Baptist Church, where Dr. Martin Luther King Jr. preached, twice ran and won hotly contested campaigns for a seat in the US Senate. In Washington, DC, the coalition of Christian, Jewish, and Muslim groups supporting the Leadership Conference on Civil and Human Rights advocated successfully for the George Floyd Justice in Policing Act.

With the past serving as prologue to the present, the leaders of these efforts knew that none of these initiatives would go more than a short distance toward ending poverty, erasing prejudice, and eradicating racial injustice. Police violence continued, incarceration and foreclosures took a disproportionate toll on Black families, and states effectively passed voter restriction laws. Institutions meant to protect against discrimination moved slowly. It was in the nature of systemic racism that the structures of power were fixed in place by their complexity as much as by discriminatory intent. It was the nature of faith, however, to believe that justice should be pursued even if it could never be finally achieved.

Conclusion

THE PERSPECTIVE that we gain from viewing progressive faith communities' advocacy for racial justice over the past half century reinforces several sobering conclusions. The most sobering conclusion is of no surprise to anyone familiar with the recent history of race relations in the United States. This is the fact that racial inequality has remained entrenched, not only because of the built-in systems that maintain it, but also because of the grinding pace at which the most concerted efforts to bring about greater racial equality move ahead. An equally sobering conclusion—as far as progressive faith communities' role is concerned—is the great extent to which advocacy well into the 1990s was still the work of leaders whose interest in racial justice had been inspired in the 1960s by the civil rights movement. As those leaders passed from the scene, the level of uncertainty about who would be inspired to carry on the work has increased.

Although the leadership that emerged toward the end of the twentieth century was less likely than its predecessors to have been inspired by the civil rights movement, these groups demonstrated the valuable contributions that dedicated leaders could make even when their numbers were few. With hardly any of the massive press coverage that focused on the Religious Right, progressive faith leaders worked in small ways to address racial inequality.[1] Late twentieth and early twenty-first century faith communities' advocacy for racial justice has focused strategically on building and managing fair and affordable housing projects, supporting school desegregation and affirmative action, sponsoring small racial reckoning ministries within congregations, marching in the streets against hate groups, protesting excessive use of force by the police, campaigning against voter suppression, and organizing voter registration drives. Year by year after the civil rights movement no longer captured national attention, faith communities with leadership from denominational agencies and local activists mobilized to address the structures in which racial inequality is embedded. Several features of these efforts stand out and are worth reviewing here for the lessons they offer to future leaders.

First, Black churches typically led the way, but they did not work alone. Black clergy and Black lay leaders were front and center in building and rehabilitating affordable housing in low-income, predominantly Black neighborhoods. Black clergy and lay leaders rode school buses to protect Black children from White supremacists angry about desegregation. Black churches hosted classes for neighborhood children when public schools were closed. Black churches were locations for food and shelter ministries and served as launching pads for get-out-the-vote drives. The continuing reality of residential segregation meant that Black churches' knowledge of the issues confronting Black neighborhoods was deeply informed compared to the typical predominantly White suburban church. However, progressive White churches also played an important role. White denominations and congregations provided funding, staff, and training for racial justice ministries, worked with housing authorities and builders to organize community development projects, participated in local clergy councils' support of desegregation, and worked on interracial police review boards. Interracial coalitions among churches and with nonprofit service organizations—layered together in local, regional, and national advocacy organizations that far outstripped the average congregation's efforts—were crucial.

Second, there were strategic local and temporal differences in how racial justice advocacy was organized and in how effective it was. What worked to create a fair and affordable housing project in Prince George's County, Maryland, for example, had to be different from what worked only a few miles away in Fairfax County, Virginia, and that was even more so between Detroit and Hartford and between Chicago and

San Diego. Supporting families during desegregation in Boston presented faith communities with challenges very different from the challenges in Charlotte, North Carolina. Communities' racial composition, histories, school policies, and governing structure—all influenced how faith leaders secured financial support, forged alliances, and developed the expertise to combat White resistance. Things changed from year to year too. School desegregation was different in the late 1970s than it had been earlier in the decade. Department of Housing and Urban Development policies were different in the 1980s than in the 1970s. Affirmative action rulings changed what could and could not be accomplished in colleges and universities. Having to tackle issues within specific local jurisdictions and in changing temporal settings required religious groups to adapt by working strategically. They could learn from what had worked in other locations but what they learned was mostly that local conditions mattered. The coalitions and partnerships that religious organizations formed were ad hoc, bringing together available resources and ideas. And then, as they worked with multiple funding sources and under multiple jurisdictions, these organizations dealt with constant shortages of resources, confronted mismatched priorities, and worked within uncertain and changing timetables. Everything had to come together just at the right time and in the right way for projects to succeed.

Third, despite the uncertainties that necessitated innovative ideas, faith leaders' racial justice advocacy benefited greatly from the enduring administrative structures and the financial support provided by stable well-established religious institutions. Although groups sprang into action when an instance of racial violence occurred or when a court decision was pending, they could do so because they were institutionally supported. Congregations paid the salaries that allowed clergy to spend time working on racial reckoning projects. Denominations staffed positions for leaders to engage full time in public witness, justice, and advocacy. Agencies like the National Council of Churches and the United Church of Christ's racial justice ministry preserved the institutional memory of what had worked last time around and convened deliberations about what to do next. Municipal ministerial councils typically predated the latest civil rights initiatives by decades. Recently formed advocacy coalitions borrowed models from their predecessors. In these important respects, faith communities were formal organizations with full-time staff who could, among other things, inform the communities they represented about important issues and work with other faith communities, nonprofit organizations, and elected officials. It was with good reason that they called themselves faith *communities*. Being a community meant working together.

Fourth, much of what faith communities did in the interest of racial justice was under the national media's radar. Compared with Religious Right leaders like Jerry Falwell and Pat Robertson whose names appeared in the media thousands of times, a faith-based nonprofit organization managing a low-income housing project in Nashville or a pulpit exchange project in Detroit was rarely of interest to the national press. Faith leaders like Jack Quigley, Darius Swann, Charles Glenn, Ben Bohnsack, and Leah Daughtry—whose work for racial justice was so important at the time—were hardly known in wider circles and remain unknown in most accounts today. Exceptions like the Wilmington Ten drew national attention only because of violence and well-organized protest. The typical news coverage was local, sporadic, and heavily dependent on local journalists who filed stories in Black newspapers. Therefore, the public—religious leaders, too—believed that the Religious Right was a cultural juggernaut but failed to notice what progressive groups were doing.

Fifth, there were remarkable achievements, but the payoff was often small. Of the hundreds of thousands of low-income housing projects constructed and rehabilitated and of all the families owning homes through low-interest loans, the ones sponsored by faith-based organizations accounted for only a small percentage. The percentage of congregations that launched multiracial ministries was small and churchgoers' role in protest marches and voter registration drives was usually small as well. Faith leaders' activism was always small enough that it had to be leveraged by other organizations to be effective. Faith communities did what they could, and they often did more than other congregations did, but leaders understood that making a huge difference was not the point. It was rather to show that something needed to be done, and that something could be done, whether that was hosting an interracial meeting, signing on to an affirmative action brief, putting together a study guide about mass incarceration, or showing up at a rally. The idea was to be a witness to justice and mercy.

Why progressive faith communities have failed to accomplish more is a large question that can only be answered in the context of the challenges they faced—as they dealt with pushback from angry citizens in a St. Louis suburb or disgruntled church members in Florida or racial profiling in New Jersey or demolition projects in Detroit or police violence in Minneapolis. Part of the answer is that faith leaders' time and energy were spread thin. Part of the answer is prejudice and indifference. But if racial injustice was systemic, then it bears summarizing what that meant for faith communities working for racial justice. Systemic injustice presented itself in three kinds of impediments: cultural barriers, social barriers, and political barriers.

The *cultural barriers* that get in the way of faith communities doing more to advocate for racial justice are concerned only in part with race. The point about racial injustice being rooted in systemic aspects of society is to emphasize the importance of wider, indirect, and often subtler influences. Among these influences, the one that affects faith communities the most appears to be individualism—an orientation that emphasizes personal narratives, personal spirituality, a personal relationship with God, and the personal rewards that come to the individual in the form of meaning, purpose, emotional gratification, insight, self-esteem, and self-fulfillment. Individualism of this sort has been identified in numerous studies that attribute it to tendencies in American culture, in studies that associate it with long-term trends in Western societies, and in accounts that locate it squarely within the history and teachings of Protestant Christianity.[2] The irony of religious practices bending in this direction has not been missed by writers observing that individualism and "community" run in opposite directions. Yet the issue is not that individualists are social isolates devoid of concern for others. They do care, but they care for others as they care for themselves: as individuals. Caring in this way is personally rewarding because it evokes an emotional response and makes a difference.

Caring of this kind is also consistent with biblical narratives in which the poor, the stranger, and the hungry are cared for one person at a time. The problem is that caring for one person at a time misses the categories and structures that operate behind the scenes to put some individuals more in need of care than others.[3]

Individualism can be regarded merely as a self-obsession that can be cured by teachings about neighborly love. But individualism is built into the structures with which we evaluate ourselves and to which we unthinkingly conform. We learn in childhood to promote ourselves, and in school we are evaluated on the basis of our individual achievements. Most significantly, public policies are driven by the kind of individualism that economists call "neoliberalism," meaning that economic incentives are in place to reward entrepreneurial effort, keep governmental intervention at bay unless it benefits economic growth, and prevent the remediation of social injustice from being seriously considered. It has been precisely this kind of individualism that faith-based social justice activist groups have had to challenge.[4]

The cultural barrier that amplifies the problem of individualism is colorblindness. Colorblindness characterizes individuals who believe themselves to be caring, unprejudiced, reasonable, moral, accepting of everyone, and having long since moved past the kind of blatant stereotyping and racial epithets that may have been common in the past. Colorblindness is also a rosy narrative about an ideal America that, to be sure, once enslaved millions of people but got over that long ago and ever since has treated everyone the same. In religious discourse, colorblindness is a prominent motif in narrow interpretations of the Bible in which teachings about treating everyone the same means denying the realities of oppression and the scriptural requirement to work for justice. Colorblindness is also present in progressive versions of interfaith diversity that neglect the differences in power and privilege among faith communities. Versions of colorblindness variously hold that racial inequality no longer exists, does exist but is the fault of someone else, or does exist and yet is more a matter of style than of substance. From the perspective of the colorblind person, racial inequality is not a problem, or, if it is, tackling it without saying anything about race is the best way to proceed. To speak about racial inequality is from the perspective of colorblindness to be divisive.[5]

Colorblindness has been challenged in studies showing how it impedes people from acting against racism—because colorblind people see no need to advocate against racism or because they think that being friendly is all that matters.[6] Combating colorblindness has thus become one of the tasks for faith leaders interested in racial justice.[7] To that end, faith leaders have emphasized churches' need to talk about White racism and White privilege. As Evangelical Church in America Advocacy Director Amy Reumann observes, "I think we have a collective responsibility to confess our involvement and our complicity. It's still going on in the church. We see it in our denomination. We see clergy of color waiting longer for positions. They are still battling for acceptance."[8] Another strategy has been post-colorblind study groups in congregations. An interdenominational church in Boston, for example, initiated a ten-year plan to shift the congregation's implicit culture from being colorblind to being explicitly multicultural, aware of racial and ethnic differences in the church and its community, and engaged in working for social justice across these racial and ethnic groups. As a first step, the congregation examined biblical texts about "neither Jew nor Greek" and other distinctions from which colorblindness derived and looked more critically at what these texts may have been meant to imply.[9] These initiatives have of course drawn criticism, especially from political operatives who argue that any attention to racial inequality is itself a form of racism.[10]

Although congregations' colorblindness can be challenged internally, faith communities' engagement with racial justice emphasizes the value of coalitions that link congregations externally with specialized organizations. Advocacy organizations have become increasingly professionalized and formalized in the kinds of services they provide.[11] Advocacy is organized into specialized sectors, such as health and housing, and is dependent on the kinds of specialized knowledge required to address complex housing policies, curricular issues, sentencing procedures, and even the intricacies of voter registration. This is knowledge that the typical pastor or priest cannot be expected to have mastered but is exactly the kind of expertise that faith communities can benefit from and support if they conceive their roles to include strategic referral networks and interorganizational cooperation.[12]

The *social barriers* that impede faith communities from achieving as much as they want to achieve are grounded in de facto residential segregation. Although it has diminished, residential segregation profoundly affects the life chances of persons concentrated in low-income minority neighborhoods as well as the social interaction that happens—or fails to happen—between these neighborhoods and residents of advantaged majority White communities. Residential segregation reduces the chances that Black churchgoers and White churchgoers will be members of the same congregation, be acquainted with one another, attend the same school and after-school functions with their children, and shop at the same grocery stores. Residential segregation's economic costs for Black families include lower increases in home values when home values are rising, greater chances of families or their neighbors experiencing foreclosures on their homes, lower access to convenient healthcare services, and higher crime rates. Residential segregation reduces advantaged White families' exposure to all these disadvantages. Yet residential segregation has hidden costs for advantaged families. As Douglas Massey explains, "Despite the efforts of White Americans to escape through segregation, inevitably they will end up paying the costs—directly in the form of higher expenses for insurance, healthcare, criminal justice, security, and education and indirectly in the form of reduced competitiveness on world markets, a diminished quality of life, and a retreat from American ideals."[13]

Incremental decline in residential segregation has made it easier for congregations to initiate interracial ministries. However, research comparing levels of segregation in congregations with levels of segregation in those congregations' neighborhoods indicates that segregation is still significantly higher among congregations than in neighborhoods. Research also shows that neighborhood segregation remains high even when people surveyed say they would be happy living in a less segregated community. This result is consistent with other research showing that attitudes may change without affecting behavior—a challenge especially to religious organizations seeking to promote behavioral transformation through changes in attitudes.[14] When a congregation discusses "loving your neighbor," for example, the "neighbor" who implicitly comes to mind is going to be the people known and seen in one's neighborhood, which for many White suburban churchgoers will be White and middle class. Moreover, congregations seeking to change attitudes embark on sensitive territory when the attitudes being addressed are characterized in moral terms or, as is often the case, as sin. While there is clearly room for moral and theological criticism, those attitudes are also shaped by where a person lives and thus are best addressed by taking account of those influences in addition to the moral and theological arguments made about them.

Residential segregation is the reality that faith communities interested in racial justice have had to confront with little anticipation of effecting major change. Research shows that the structures keeping residential segregation in place include the overall proportion of various racial and ethnic groups in an entire metropolitan area, the region's history of race relations, residents' levels of income and education, the area's major sectors of industry and employment, population growth or decline, and residents' preferences for in-group versus out-group social interaction. Faith communities' capacity to work for racial justice within these constraints is facilitated by the fact that interreligious coalitions do provide opportunities for resources and interaction to cross racially divided geographic boundaries, whether in small ways such as intercongregational alliances or through larger endeavors such as community development projects. Research demonstrates that White flight and White community resistance is lower when integration occurs incrementally, as it does with dispersed affordable housing projects, and that affordable housing projects generally do not dampen property values.[15]

Faith communities have worked within the constraints of racial segregation by doing what they can in small ways. Although meager in number, faith-based affordable housing projects were ways to ensure that fairness was part of these projects, that some could be in low-income inner-city neighborhoods where loans might otherwise not have been possible, that prospective homeowners could receive training in home maintenance skills, and that advocacy for tenants' rights was available. Community development has included faith-sponsored initiatives in targeted economic zones but has also taken shape in environmental justice programs such as the United Church of Christ's work on race and toxic waste exposure. Support for school desegregation acknowledged the fact that busing was necessary because of residential segregation and that children and parents could be supported in small ways. Tackling the challenges of criminal justice required working at multiple levels of governance, including protesting police violence, advocating for sentencing reform, and organizing local support for post-prison rehabilitation. The idea of serving on zoning boards that a few faith leaders experimented with in the early 1970s is still one of the ways that faith communities are making a difference. Particularly in expanding suburban communities where decisions are being made about land use, public transportation, and kinds of housing units, serving on zoning, housing, and economic development committees can be a way to advocate for racial justice.[16]

The *political barriers* to racial justice are most obviously the ones that disenfranchise Black and Hispanic citizens through gerrymandering, voter suppression, and intimidation. The vast number of legislative acts in Republican states after Donald Trump's defeat in the 2020 presidential election increased the difficulties that low income, minority, elderly, and disabled citizens faced in seeking to obtain necessary identification for voter registration, to ensure that their names had not been purged from voter rolls, and to gain access to voting sites in their neighborhoods. Worsening these problems, concentrations of low-income Black and Hispanic residents in segregated communities in the South and Midwest made it easier for Republicans to focus voter suppression efforts on these communities. Privately funded election audits, unsubstantiated claims of voter fraud, taking election management out of the hands of local officials, and reducing the number of voting sites could all be accomplished more effectively when minority voters were concentrated in segregated gerrymandered districts than if they were scattered more evenly across all election districts. Because voter turnout tends to be higher among homeowners than among renters, the decline in Black homeownership also played a role in reducing Black voter turnout.[17]

The colorblindness that appears as a cultural barrier is also a political barrier. Colorblindness is easily weaponized by opponents of racial justice who argue that voter suppression laws certainly are not meant to be racially discriminatory even though they are discriminatory in practice. In this understanding, colorblindness implies that only racist intent is subject to prosecution and that the doctrine of disparate racial impact should not apply. But colorblindness has also been a longstanding policy instituted in anti-poverty laws that demand resources to be allocated without respect to race and in affirmative action rulings that drastically limit how institutions can take account of race. In these respects, democratic standards of treating all individuals equally—worthy as these standards are—create difficulties for addressing racial injustice unless race is explicitly acknowledged.

The federated nature of US government has both positive and negative implications for faith-based groups working to promote racial justice. The positive contribution has been that federal laws and the federal judiciary have repeatedly intervened to monitor and protect civil rights. The negative impact has been the disproportionate power held by southern, rural, less densely populated, majority White states in the US Senate, which has impeded passage of civil rights legislation. The federated structure of government has also necessitated activism at multiple levels, sometimes providing opportunities and sometimes posing barriers. Among other things, neighborhood segregation has meant that decisions affecting Black neighborhoods frequently rest in the hands of county, municipal, and state-wide officials who consider it their job to balance multiple interests that reflect the power structure of their majority constituents.

Faith communities bring their own limitations to the barriers built into the political system. Separation of church and state limits how religious leaders can make political endorsements without risking their organizations' tax-exempt status. Church–state separation, though, is often breached, such as by forming semi-independent faith-based nonprofit service organizations or by openly defying IRS investigations. Clergy more often monitor themselves, speaking on "safe topics" but avoiding contentious political issues. But when nearly everything has been politicized (even vaccines), it is difficult for clergy to address important issues if they fear saying anything political. Racial justice is certainly one of those issues and, as faith leaders address racial justice in the future, they will surely find it necessary to discuss its relationships with political barriers and remedies.

Survey results and recent studies of online sermon transcripts show that many clergy do in fact address issues of interest to voters, even when these issues are couched in partisan politics. Many faith leaders encourage congregants to vote, and congregations sometimes make study guides available without specifically mentioning issues from the pulpit. However, it is less clear that pastors make as much use of information from denominational agencies as they might.[18] These agencies— and advocacy organizations—have specialized knowledge of the kind that pastors lack. Increasingly, it takes specialized knowledge to navigate opaque voter registration laws, not to mention fair housing policies and school curricula. It takes more than superficial information, too, to understand why issues are often viewed differently in Black communities than in White communities.

These caveats notwithstanding, there is an ample research literature demonstrating that faith communities can and do change attitudes in ways that motivate participants to become involved in charitable, advocacy, and even political activities. Faith communities are venues in which teachings about justice and mercy are proclaimed, locations in which special information about needs and opportunities are shared, and spaces in which social networks can facilitate activist recruitment. Progressive faith communities, studies suggest, do a better job of connecting volunteers with outside organizations than conservative faith communities do, which more often focus internally on congregational activities. Moreover, it matters that congregations select particular causes in which to invest scarce time and resources—a food pantry, clothing drive, affordable housing project, prison visitation ministry, refugee resettlement plan, foreign humanitarian aid program, and so on—in addition to teaching broadly about love of neighbor. Thus, it follows that faith communities' grassroots mobilization for racial justice must similarly be oriented toward specific needs and opportunities.[19]

Progressive faith communities' advocacy for racial justice has become all the more important as politically conservative partisan activists, legislators, and governors have enacted rules preventing frank, honest, historically and sociologically accurate information about racial issues from being discussed in public schools and, in some instances, even in colleges and universities. Faith communities are free spaces in which racial inequality and injustice can be openly discussed. Moreover, faith communities' biblical traditions provide the authority to do so and the narratives in which to discuss, teach about, and enact ideals of equity and justice. The challenge is doing so courageously when the political culture seeks to turn every topic into a divisive issue. Fortunately, that challenge is being met by leaders within faith communities and by scholars intent on offering insights and guidance for faith communities. One thinks, for example, of such recent books as Jason Roach and Jessamin Birdsall's *Healing the Divides: How Every Christian Can Advance God's Vision for Racial Unity and Justice* and Donald Heinz's *Matthew 25 Christianity: Redeeming Church and Society*. Both are theologically informed, sociologically perceptive inquiries into the opportunities to which faith communities' can address themselves.[20]

The faith communities that have advocated most effectively for racial justice have made use of the ways through which religious institutions distinctively exercise power—prayer, worship, sacred rites, discourse, networking, the claiming of sacred space and time, and the shaping of individual and group identities. Local congregations' lay and clergy leaders have amplified the resources within their own memberships by drawing on denominational leadership, linking with other congregations, and working with leaders in nonreligious organizations, including school boards, teachers' organizations, parent groups, housing authorities, local chapters of the NAACP, county prosecutors, public defenders, and voter registration groups. With sparse resources, congregations' racial justice activity has always required strategic discernment, selecting a particular project, group, or issue on which to focus.

The difficulty that academic writers (like me, for instance) encounter when we shift from description to prescription is the temptation to suggest a one-size-fits-all list of recommendations—ideas drawn from our small corner of the world with perhaps only a smattering of practical experience. We want to say something hopeful and helpful about America when there are so many different aspects of America that we do not understand. With that qualifying note, I want to modestly suggest something to the part of America's faith communities I know best from firsthand experience and on which much of this book has focused. That is, the portion of American mainline Protestantism that is mostly White and mostly interested in trying to be progressive when it comes to racial justice.

My suggestion is to embrace more fully and more actively the collective vision of social responsibility that is woven so deeply into the narratives of Hebrew and Christian scriptures and has been such an important part of the progressive Protestant tradition in the past. This is the vision that Reinhold Niebuhr embraced when he called for realism in American politics in the 1950s and the one that Dr. Martin Luther King Jr. articulated when he spoke of realizing the dream of a beloved community. It differs dramatically from the view that God cares for individuals' souls but cares little about the condition of the world in which we live. It understands that the communities in which we live—beloved or not—are composed not only of individuals but also of institutions, and these institutions must be supported, challenged, and sometimes resisted if anything is to change.

In my view, it is unfortunate that the ideal of a beloved community has often been misinterpreted as a kind of warm blanket under which people of faith can huddle in search of comforting bonds of solidarity. That view may work in small fellowship groups where friendships and snippets of reconciliation are formed. It is the kind of place that religious leaders often have in mind when they speak of working to build right relationships. Those are valuable and yet turn too often toward the expressive individualism of a culture dominated by quests for personally fulfilling spiritual experiences and beliefs. Beloved community is better understood as the hard work of dealing with the entrenched macro-structures that distribute power and privilege unevenly. Beloved community includes the conviction that divine love is intended for humankind, but it is a vision that acknowledges the organized social bonds, norms, structures, and institutions of which the nation and the community of nations are composed.

The retreat from this collective vision of what scripture teaches may be understandable. The idea that people of faith should concern themselves with America as a nation veers too often toward an American exceptionalism or a version of Christian nationalism that ignores the religious, ethnic, and racial diversity of the United States and the world. Exceptionalism and nationalism of this kind exalt America's place in the world. And yet, it is difficult to imagine how peace and justice can be furthered without thinking of our nation as a whole entity whose constituent communities bear responsibilities toward one another. In this understanding, a beloved community is an interrelated society with all the complexities that questions about housing, schools, jobs, and families imply. Therefore, a theology that advocates for justice must reckon with the diverse gifts, interests, and skills that contribute to these interrelated connections.

The value of understanding diverse gifts, interests, and skills is abundantly evident when considering the many ways in which advocates for racial justice have contributed over the years. Some were gifted preachers who could mobilize crowds, others were pastors who worked quietly behind the scenes to comfort grieving families, and still others were skilled administrators who understood the challenges of financial and interpersonal organization. These were leaders whose gifts are recognized and encouraged within religious organizations. However, a theology of civic responsibility also requires religious leaders to acknowledge and encourage the work of people who have other callings—callings that go beyond volunteering in local congregations. An understanding of callings must be rediscovered that includes people doing God's work when the work is done outside the church—callings that may include planning an affordable housing project, registering voters, teaching second-graders, or serving on a police review board.

Understanding diverse callings is something that pastors in local congregations must think about when a share of their congregation's budget is allocated to support denominations' specialized racial justice ministries. Instead of keeping these allocations quiet for fear of offending some of their congregants, pastors might want to advertise the fact that the "body of Christ" includes the denominational efforts that their congregations have agreed to support through their denominational affiliations rather than implying that individuals' service in the congregation is all that matters. To be sure, pastors want to believe that their own preaching and committees matter most, but a vision of the beloved community must be larger if it is to be as effective as it can be.

A public theology of this sort need not be conceived in the same ways by different religious, ethnic, racial, and regional groups. It most assuredly will not be. Nor does this kind of theology imply a vision oriented toward uniting our country. As much as we may deplore the partisan disunity that divides the political community, vigorous disagreement about goals and policies strengthens American democracy. The value of a vibrant public theology is rather that there are contending ideas concerned with the collective good of the society. To that end, we can be grateful that there are conceptions of what it means to be a good society in all the major religious traditions. These are the teachings that incentivize the many faith constituencies to work for what they believe to be in the best interest of others as well as themselves. They are the teachings that cause conflict and at the same time propel constructive deliberation and engagement.[21]

A renewed emphasis on what a good society should be is relevant to the cause of racial justice only if the deep reality of racial injustice is part of that emphasis. The trouble with many thoughtful visions of America is that race has not been given due emphasis and its central role in American history and in the forming of American institutions has too often been ignored or suppressed. To give racial justice greater priority, there is much to be learned from the faith communities that have struggled to address it. In their failures as well as in their successes, it is possible to see the systems that work against racial justice and to gain a clearer vision of the avenues through which greater justice can be achieved.

NOTES

Introduction

1. Ruth Braunstein, Todd Nicholas Fuist, and Rhys H. Williams, "Religion and Progressive Politics in the United States," *Sociology Compass* 13 (2019), 1–16, is a valuable overview of the various meanings and forms of progressive religious action, values, identities, and theology; for a helpful discussion of the relationships among designations such as "mainline" and "progressive," see Todd Nicholas Fuist, Ruth Braunstein, and Rhys H. Williams, "Introduction: Religion and Progressive Activism—Introducing and Mapping the Field," in *Religion and Progressive Activism: New Stories about Faith and Politics*, edited by Ruth Braunstein, Todd Nicholas Fuist, and Rhys H. Williams (New York: NYU Press, 2017), 117–37; and for coverage of recent examples of political activism on the religious left, see Jack Jenkins, *American Prophets: The Religious Roots of Progressive Politics and the Ongoing Fight for the Soul of the Country* (New York: Harper Collins, 2020).

2. Our knowledge of the nuanced and diverse roles Black churches and White churches played in relationship to the civil rights movement has grown significantly thanks to such important works, among others, as Aldon D. Morris, *The Origins of the Civil Rights Movement: Black Communities Organizing for Change* (New York: Free Press, 1984); Charles Marsh, *God's Long Summer: Stories of Faith and Civil Rights* (Princeton, NJ: Princeton University Press, 1997); Albert J. Raboteau, *American Prophets: Seven Religious Radicals and Their Struggle for Social and Political Justice* (Princeton, NJ: Princeton University Press, 2016); and Barbara Dianne Savage, *Your Spirits Walk Beside Us: The Politics of Black Religion* (Cambridge, MA: Harvard University Press, 2008).

3. C. Eric Lincoln and Lawrence Mamiya, *The Black Church in the African American Experience* (Durham, NC: Duke University Press, 1999); Richard L. Wood and Brad R. Fulton, *A Shared Future: Faith-Based Organizing for Racial Equity and Ethical Democracy* (Chicago: University of Chicago Press, 2015); Richard L. Wood, *Faith in Action: Religion, Race, and Democratic Organizing in America* (Chicago: University of Chicago Press, 2002); Mark R. Warren, *Dry Bones Rattling: Community Building to Revitalize American Democracy* (Princeton, NJ: Princeton University Press, 2001); Jeffrey Stout, *Blessed Are the Organized: Grassroots Democracy in America* (Princeton, NJ: Princeton University Press, 2010); and Ruth Braunstein, *Prophets and Patriots: Faith in Democracy across the Political Divide* (Berkeley and Los Angeles: University of California Press, 2017). As far as grassroots' identities are concerned, polling estimates vary but the best guess from polling is that about 20 percent of White mainline Protestants claim to be "progressives" and, compared with those who do not identify this way, are more likely to be Democrats than

Republicans and want government policies to be concerned with economic inequality and social provision for the poor; see for example polling results discussed in Robert P. Jones, "1-in-5 Americans Are 'Religious Progressives,'" PRRI, July 18, 2013, prri.org; Robert P. Jones, *Progressive and Religious: How Christian, Jewish, Muslim, and Buddhist Leaders Are Moving beyond Partisan Politics and Transforming American Public Life* (New York: Rowman and Littlefield, 2008); and John C. Green, Robert P. Jones, and Daniel Cox, *Faithful, Engaged, and Divergent: A Comparative Portrait of Conservative and Progressive Religious Activists in the 2008 Election and Beyond* (Washington, DC: Public Religion Research, 2009). The role of White conservative faith communities in either promoting White privilege or failing to address racial justice is the focus of a large literature; for example, see Robert P. Jones, *White Too Long: The Legacy of White Supremacy in American Christianity* (New York: Simon and Schuster, 2020); Khyati Y. Joshi, *White Christian Privilege: The Illusion of Religious Equality in America* (New York: NYU Press, 2020); Andrew L. Whitehead and Samuel L. Perry, *Taking America Back for God: Christian Nationalism in the United States* (New York: Oxford University Press, 2020); and Anthea Butler, *White Evangelical Racism: The Politics of Morality in America* (Chapel Hill, NC: University of North Carolina Press, 2021).

4. Nancy Tatom Ammerman, *Pillars of Faith: American Congregations and Their Partners* (Berkeley and Los Angeles: University of California Press, 2005), 151.

5. Several excellent studies describe the essential ingredients of effective interfaith coalitions; among others, see Grace Yukich and Ruth Braunstein, "Encounters at the Religious Edge: Variation in Religious Expression across Interfaith Advocacy and Social Movement Settings," *Journal for the Scientific Study of Religion* 53, 4 (December 2014), 791–807; Ram C. Cnaan, Stephanie C. Boddie, Charlene C. McGrew, and Jennifer J. Kang, *The Other Philadelphia Story: How Local Congregations Support Quality of Life in Urban America* (Philadelphia: University of Pennsylvania Press, 2006), 197–216; Kate McCarthy, *Interfaith Encounters in America* (New Brunswick, NJ: Rutgers University Press, 2007), 84–125; and David T. Buckley, *Faithful to Secularism: The Religious Politics of Democracy in Ireland, Senegal, and the Philippines* (New York: Columbia University Press, 2016), 9–41.

6. Grace Yukich, *One Family under God: Immigration Politics and Progressive Religion in America* (New York: NYU Press, 2013) is an excellent study showing how spiritual practice interweaves with advocacy for social justice; another is Braunstein, *Prophets and Patriots*; and on the relationship of spiritual practice and concerns about power, see especially Nancy Tatom Ammerman, *Studying Lived Religion: Contexts and Practices* (New York: NYU Press, 2021).

7. There is an extensive literature on systemic racism, but an especially helpful source is Joe R. Feagin, *Systemic Racism: A Theory of Oppression* (New York: Routledge, 2006); and as an influential source, Eduardo Bonilla-Silva, "Rethinking Racism: Toward a Structural Interpretation," *American Sociological Review* 62, 3 (June 1997), 465–80; it is also helpful to consider systemic racism through the lens provided by Charles Tilly, *Durable Inequality* (Berkeley and Los Angeles: University of California Press, 1998).

8. Monica McDermott, *Whiteness in America* (Cambridge, UK: Polity Press, 2020) and Monica McDermott and Frank L. Samson, "White Racial and Ethnic Identity in the United States," *Annual Review of Sociology* 31 (2005), 245–61.

9. Ijeoma Oluo, *So You Want to Talk about Race* (New York: Seal Press, 2019), especially pages 53–69, provides an excellent discussion of practical steps for checking one's privilege,

whether it be White privilege or socioeconomic privilege; Brianne Hastie and David Rimmington, "'200 Years of White Affirmative Action': White Privilege Discourse in Discussions of Racial Inequality," *Discourse and Society* 25, 2 (2014), 186–204, offers a case study of how respondents use arguments about privilege in online discussions.

10. Stuart Buck, *Acting White: The Ironic Legacy of Desegregation* (New Haven, CT: Yale University Press, 2010).

11. This is not to suggest of course that tight and declining budgets were unimportant; see for example comments from Methodist leaders in Steven M. Tipton, *Public Pulpits: Methodists and Mainline Churches in the Moral Argument of Public Life* (Chicago: University of Chicago Press, 2008).

12. Partnering with institutions from other sectors, such as schools, nonprofit associations, unions, and neighborhood associations was also a significant feature of the institution-building organizations studied in Brad R. Fulton and Richard L. Wood, "Interfaith Community Organizing: Emerging Theological and Organizational Challenges," *International Journal of Public Theology* 6 (2012), 398–420; additionally, the data demonstrated the net contribution of religious congregations and religious culture to these organizations; see Brad R. Fulton and Richard L. Wood, "Civil Society Organizations and the Enduring Role of Religion in Promoting Democratic Engagement," *Voluntas* 29 (2018), 1068–79.

Chapter One: Fair and Affordable Housing

1. Fairfax County Office of Research and Statistics, *1988 Fairfax County Profile* (Fairfax City, VA: Fairfax County Board of Supervisors, 1988); Monroe W. Karmin, "Forced Integration? Not in Fairfax," *Wall Street Journal*, September 29, 1971; Ina Lee Selden, "Gerald W. Hopkins: Finding Houses for Fairfax's Needy," *Washington Post*, May 17, 1979.

2. US Department of Commerce, Bureau of the Census, *Statistical Abstract of the United States: 1976* (Washington, DC: Government Printing Office, 1976), 16, 746, 749; Charles M. Lamb, *Housing Segregation in Suburban America since 1960: Presidential and Judicial Politics* (New York: Cambridge University Press, 2005); Edward G. Goetz, *The One-Way Street of Integration: Fair Housing and the Pursuit of Racial Justice in American Cities* (Ithaca, NY: Cornell University Press, 2018).

3. "Church Backs Public Housing," *Baltimore Sun*, June 10, 1950; "Detroit Given 15 in Public Housing," *Michigan Chronicle*, March 18, 1950; "Protestants Seek New Housing Law," *New York Times*, January 29, 1959; Betty Driscoll Mayo, "Clergymen Alerted on Public Housing," *Christian Science Monitor*, December 7, 1954.

4. R. Allen Hays, *The Federal Government and Urban Housing*, 3rd ed. (Albany: State University of New York Press, 2012), 139–63.

5. "Racism and the Church," *Chicago Defender*, May 13, 1967.

6. Gary Washburn, "Worshipers 'Confess' Housing Segregation," *Chicago Tribune*, February 1, 1973.

7. Bruce Kalk, "Interview with J. Randolph Taylor," Southern Oral History Program Collection, 1985, online at docsouth.unc.edu.

8. Henry Clark, "Churchmen and Residential Desegregation," *Review of Religious Research* 5, 3 (Spring 1964), 157–64; Paul L. Montgomery, "Town's Churches Taking New Role," *New York*

Times, February 1, 1964; Jerry Demuth, "Chicago Housing Integration Gains Sharply, Study Finds," *Atlanta Constitution*, January 16, 1966;

Harold E. Quinley, "The Dilemma of an Activist Church: Protestant Religion in the Sixties and Seventies," *Journal for the Scientific Study of Religion* 13, 1 (March 1974), 1–21; liberal clergy in the study were identified from responses to questions about the Bible, God, salvation, and other beliefs; clergy so classified included 77 percent of United Church of Christ pastors, 70 percent of Methodists, 48 percent of Presbyterians, and 44 percent of Episcopalians; additional details are included in Harold E. Quinley, *The Prophetic Clergy: Social Activism among Protestant Ministers* (New York: Wiley, 1974), 114–15.

9. "United Church of Christ to Build Housing," *Chicago Tribune*, July 5, 1965; Frederic B. Bill, "Group Hints Project Interest," *Baltimore Sun*, August 10, 1967; "Churches Participate in Non-Profit Housing," *New York Amsterdam News*, August 14, 1971.

10. Ted Lacey, "Church Group Plans Project," *Chicago Defender*, April 22, 1970; "Church Backs $15 Million Housing Project," *Chicago Defender*, June 30, 1969; Jack Eisen, "Two Housing Projects Approved," *Washington Post*, March 25, 1969.

11. "Church Fights Racism, But," *Chicago Defender*, November 17, 1973, based on a report conducted by the Community Renewal Society.

12. Ralph K. Skinner, "Church Groups Build High-Rise Housing," *Christian Science Monitor*, April 10, 1970; "Housing for Elderly Plan," *Chicago Tribune*, March 2, 1969; George Cornell, "US Churches Help Build Housing for Poor as a Way to Serve Christ," *Boston Globe*, August 28, 1971.

13. Michael Regan, "Church-Backed Housing Plan to Face Strong Opposition," *Hartford Courant*, February 6, 1972; James Nelson Coleman, "Does Public Housing Bring Blacks?" *Call and Post*, February 10, 1973.

14. US Congress, *Oversight on Housing and Urban Development Programs: Hearings before the Subcommittee on Housing and Urban Affairs of the US Senate Committee on Banking, Housing, and Urban Affairs* (Washington, DC: Government Printing Office, 1973), 937.

15. Ibid., 939.

16. Carol Honsa, "Rent Supplements Available," *Washington Post*, February 17, 1967; Laurence Meyer, "New Wrinkle in Rent Picture," *Washington Post*, August 11, 1969.

17. Douglas Watson, "Baber Project Is Disappointing," *Washington Post*, June 5, 1970; Leonard Downie Jr., "FHA Helps Developers Strike It Rich," *Washington Post*, July 21, 1970; Priscilla S. Meyer, "Housing the Poor," *Wall Street Journal*, July 21, 1971.

18. Jerry DeMuth, "Church Entry into Housing Studied," *National Catholic Reporter*, April 9, 1971.

19. US Department of Housing and Urban Development, *Housing in the Seventies: A Report of the National Housing Policy Review* (Washington, DC: Government Printing Office, 1974).

20. Goetz, *One-Way Street of Integration*, 20–25.

21. William G. Connolly, "New Housing Law Gets Mixed Reviews," *New York Times*, September 8, 1974.

22. US Commission on Civil Rights, *Equal Opportunity in Suburbia* (Washington, DC: Government Printing Office, 1974), 54–55.

23. Laurie Osborn, Peter Stine, and Almus Thorpe, "In Memory: John L. Quigley Jr. '63," Amherst College, amherst.edu.

24. Judson W. Calkins, "Arouses Churches on Blight," *St. Louis Post-Dispatch*, January 29, 1969.

25. Church to Lend $200,000 for Low-Income Housing," *St. Louis Post-Dispatch*, June 23, 1969; L. F. Palmer Jr., "Will Seize Churches, Black Unit Boasts," *Pittsburgh Press*, April 28, 1969; "Militant Begging, Rustin Says," *Atlanta Constitution*, May 9, 1969; David Holmstrom, "Reparations Demand Jolts US Clergy," *Christian Science Monitor*, May 10, 1969; Dan L. Thrapp, "Presbyterians Agree to Study Forman Demands," *Los Angeles Times*, May 17, 1969; Robert Adams, "Blacks Visit Church, Demand $50,000,000," *St. Louis Post-Dispatch*, May 26, 1969; W. Sherman Skinner, "Present Trends in American Protestantism," *Journal of the Department of History* 16, 8 (December 1935), 356–72; James R. Blackwood, "Arthur Compton's Atomic Venture," *American Presbyterians* 66, 3 (Fall 1988), 177–93; W. Sherman Skinner, "More Democracy," *Presbyterian Outlook*, 150, 43 (November 25, 1968), 8; "Presbytery Names Special Unit to Study Race, War, Poverty," *Chicago Defender*, July 3, 1965; W. Sherman Skinner, "The Shape of the Church," *Presbyterian Outlook*, 151, 14 (April 7, 1969), 8–9; Barbara Dianne Savage, *Your Spirits Walk Beside Us: The Politics of Black Religion* (Cambridge, MA: Harvard University Press, 2008), 271, notes that Forman's demand was initially meant to include Black churches as well but Black leaders resisted that part.

26. "Church-Sponsored Housing Project Is Under Attack," *St. Louis Post-Dispatch*, April 8, 1970.

27. "Suburban Housing for the Poor," *St. Louis Post-Dispatch*, August 4, 1970.

28. "Inter-Church Group Endorses Apartment Project in Black Jack," *St. Louis Post-Dispatch*, July 22, 1970.

29. Peter Braestrup, "HUD Asks Suit against Racial Zoning," *Washington Post*, November 11, 1970.

30. "Black Jack Developers Assail Housing Policy," *St. Louis Post-Dispatch*, December 21, 1970; B. Drummond Ayres Jr., "Bulldozers Turn Up Soil and Ill Will in a Suburb of St. Louis," *New York Times*, January 18, 1971.

31. Lamb, *Housing Segregation in Suburban America*, 99–104.

32. *United States v. City of Black Jack, Missouri*, 372 F. Supp. 319 (E.D. Mo. 1974); *United States of America, Appellant-appellee v. City of Black Jack, Missouri, Appellee-appellant*, 508 F.2d 1179 (8th Cir. 1975).

33. Kimberly Ferrari, "The State of Disparate Impact under the Fair Housing Act: Interpreting Robust Causality after Inclusive Communities," *Journal of Affordable Housing and Community Development* 29, 2 (2020), 327–60.

Chapter Two: Community Development

1. "Reagan, in South Bronx, Says Carter Broke Vow," *New York Times*, August 6, 1980.

2. Charles L. Edson, "Affordable Housing—An Intimate History," *Journal of Affordable Housing and Community Development Law* 20, 2 (Winter 2011), 193–213.

3. Ira S. Lowry, "Low-Income Housing: A Strategy Shift," *Los Angeles Times*, December 16, 1981.

4. Edson, "Affordable Housing."

5. Lee Hockstader, "Area Said to Face Severe Shortage of Low-Income Housing," *Washington Post*, July 6, 1985; Tony Lee and Sue Taoka, "Community Groups Propose Measures to Save Low-Income Housing Units," *International Examiner*, November 7, 1984; Louise Axelson, "Bristol Housing Decried," *Hartford Courant*, November 24, 1983.

6. John Doyle, Lee A. Daniels, "About Real Estate," *New York Times*, July 30, 1982; Dick Ryan, "Black Baptist Church Donates $100,000 to Nehemiah Housing Plan," *National Catholic Reporter*, September 28, 1984; "Affordable Housing Grows in Brooklyn," *Hartford Courant*, September 29, 1985; Timothy Alden Ross, *The Impact of Community Organizing on East Brooklyn, 1978–1995* (College Park, MD: PhD Dissertation, University of Maryland, 1996); Dennis Deslippe, "'As in a Civics Text Come to Life': The East Brooklyn's Congregations' Nehemiah Housing Plan and 'Citizens Power' in the 1980s," *Journal of Urban History* 45, 5, (2019), 1030–49.

7. Elizabeth O'Connor, *The New Community* (New York: Harper and Row, 1976); "Good Housing from Slum Housing," *Washington Post*, February 16, 1977.

8. Jane Seaberry, "New Rouse Firm to Aid Low-Income Housing," *Washington Post*, April 8, 1981; Howard Gillette Jr., "Assessing James Rouse's Role in American City Planning," *Journal of the American Planning Association* 65, 2 (Spring 1999), 150–67.

9. Ellen W. Lazar and Michael S. Levine, "Community-Based Housing Development: The Emergence of Nonprofits, Enterprise, and LISC," *ABA Journal of Affordable Housing and Community Development Law* 2, 2 (Winter 1993), 6–9, 17.

10. Patricia Lefevere, "Interfaith Efforts Fight Yonkers Housing Battles," *National Catholic Reporter*, December 9, 1988; Xavier de Souza Briggs, Joe T. Darden, and Angela Aidala, "In the Wake of Desegregation: Early Impacts of Scattered-Site Public Housing on Neighborhoods in Yonkers, New York," *Journal of the American Planning Association* 65, 1 (Winter 1999), 27–49, concluded from an examination of housing values and an attitude survey that the affordable housing program had been implemented effectively and with relatively high satisfaction from White and Black residents, although the study did not address the possible impact of the interfaith coalition's efforts.

11. Stanley Ziemba, "First Subsidized Housing Planned for Wilmette," *Chicago Tribune*, March 4, 1976; Stevenson O. Swanson, "'Interfaith' Works in Open Housing," *Chicago Tribune*, February 4, 1982; Howard Witt, "Economics, Fear Leave Integration Untested on North Shore," *Chicago Tribune*, December 2, 1984.

12. Mark McIntyre and Joye Brown, "Homes for Poor Elusive on LI," *Newsday*, September 25, 1983.

13. Joseph Sullivan, "Jersey Ruling Aids Housing for Poor," *New York Times*, January 21, 1983; Doreen Carvajal, "Panel Ponders Low-Income Housing Future," *Philadelphia Inquirer*, February 3, 1985.

14. Tom McCabe, "Reagan's Budget Cuts Challenge the Church," *Christianity Today*, October 2, 1981.

15. Hays, *The Federal Government and Urban Housing*, 231, 281–82.

16. Mark Chaves and William Tsitsos, "Congregations and Social Services: What They Do, How They Do It, and with Whom," *Nonprofit and Voluntary Sector Quarterly* 30, 4 (December 2001), 660–83, provides evidence from the National Congregations Study and discusses

other studies describing the extent of collaboration between congregations, secular nonprofits, and government in social service provision, although not specifically with reference to affordable housing construction.

17. Charles J. Orlebeke, "The Evolution of Low-Income Housing Policy, 1949 to 1999," *Housing Policy Debate* 11, 2 (2000), 489–520, quotes on pages 513–15.

18. Corianne Payton Scally, Amanda Gold, and Nicole DuBois, *The Low-Income Housing Tax Credit: How It Works and Who It Serves* (Washington, DC: Urban Institute, 2018).

19. Larry Foundation, Peter Tufano, and Patricia H. Walker, "Collaborating with Congregations," *Harvard Business Review* 77, 4 (1999), 57–66.

20. Allon Yaroni, *The Low Income Housing Tax Credit Program: Issues of Allocations and Locations* (New York: PhD Dissertation, New York University, 2010).

21. Brian Goldstein, "Abyssinian Development Corporation," in *Affordable Housing in New York: The People, Places, and Policies That Transformed a City*, edited by Nicholas Dagen Bloom and Matthew Gordon Lasner (Princeton, NJ: Princeton University Press, 2015), 270.

22. These numbers reflect IRS reported data for nonprofit organizations classified under National Taxonomy of Exempt Entities (NTEE) codes L20 and L21; National Center for Charitable Statistics, nccs.urban.org.

23. John W. Johnson biographical sketch included in "New UL Executive Meets Community," *New York Amsterdam News*, March 21, 1970, and "John W. Johnson Obituary (1929–2019), online at andersonragsdalemortuary.com; Reverend Kermit White quoted in John C. Waugh, "San Diego's Ghetto Seethes," *Christian Science Monitor*, April 10, 1968; additional information, indicating that in 2021 San Diego Interfaith Housing Foundation owned and managed more than $30 million in property and operated on an annual budget of approximately $2 million, according to IRS 990 forms from Guidestar.org.

24. RCHP Affordable Housing Corporation, online at rchp-ahc.org.

25. Janette Rodrigues, "Coalition Seeks Housing Solutions," *Daily Press* [Newport News, Virginia], October 4, 1993.

26. Shawn G. Kennedy, "Delay on Tax-Credit Measure Stalls Projects to House Poor," *New York Times*, February 8, 1993, discusses the problem uncertainty about federal funding caused an affordable housing project in East Harlem initiated by Our Lady of Mount Carmel Church.

27. David A. Vise, "A Rising New Force in DC Wins First Lady's Attention," *Washington Post*, December 22, 1996; Michael Powell, "Interfaith Group Struggles to Keep Housing Dream Alive," *Washington Post*, March 14, 1997; Michael Powell, "Interfaith Church Group Wins Fight to Build on District-Owned Land," *Washington Post*, March 15, 1997; Robert E. Pierre, "Work Begins on Affordable Homes," *Washington Post*, December 1, 2000; John T. Bullock, *Build to Win: Community Organizing, Power, and Participation in Local Governance* (College Park, MD: PhD Dissertation, University of Maryland, 2009), 162–66; Kelly Christine Hill, *Affordable Housing and Governance in Cities* (Atlanta: PhD Dissertation, Emory University, 2009), 174–75; "Striving for Affordable Housing," Washington Interfaith Network, 2019, online at windc-iaf.org.

28. Jane Adler, "Faith, Hope, and Equity Builder Builds Affordable Housing," *Chicago Tribune*, November 29, 1997.

29. Jerome P. Baggett, *Habitat for Humanity: Building Private Homes, Building Public Religion* (Philadelphia: Temple University Press, 2001).

30. Robert Wuthnow, *Loose Connections: Joining Together in America's Fragmented Communities* (Cambridge, MA: Harvard University Press, 1998), 211–12.

31. Jody Veenker, "Business Funnels Profits to Churches," *Christianity Today*, October 25, 1999; "Church Group Joins Mortgage Firm to Bring Affordable Homes," *Miami Times*, July 4, 1996; "An Update of the Efforts of the Revelation Corporation," *Sacramento Observer*, August 26, 1998; Craig Pittman, "Questions about Lyons Cast Doubt on Buyer's Club," *Tampa Bay Times*, October 1, 2005.

32. Kendall M. Thu, Mark Schuller, Tiara Huggins, and Valarie Redmond, "'Being Heard, Not Only Seen': Intersections of Tea Partyism, Racism, and Classism in a Low-Income Housing Struggle in Dekalb, Illinois," *Human Organization* 76, 4 (2017), 348–57, is a valuable ethnographic study illustrating the various discourses involved in an affordable housing debate.

33. Sue E. S. Crawford, *Clergy at Work in the Secular City* (Bloomington, IN: PhD Dissertation, Indiana University, 1995), 79–80.

34. Henry Y. White, *Project Nehemiah: Preparing a Black Urban Church to Engage in Community Revitalization Through Housing Renovation* (Dayton, OH: DMin Dissertation, United Theological Seminary, 1997).

35. Henry G. Cisneros, "Higher Ground: Faith Communities and Community Building," *Cityscape* (December 1996), 71–84.

36. George M. Anderson, "Housing and the Poor: An Interview with Andrew Cuomo," *America*, May 30, 1998.

37. "Center Launches Justice Conference Series," *Building Communities Together* [HUD newsletter] 1, 11 (October 1999), 1; "What's New in HUD Policy?" *Building Communities Together* [HUD newsletter] 2, 6 (June 2000), 1; Joseph R. Hacala, "Faith-Based Community Development: Past, Present, Future," *America* 1984, 14 (April 2001), 15–17; Isaac Kramnick and R. Laurence Moore, "Can the Churches Save the Cities? Faith-Based Services and the Constitution," *American Prospect* 35 (1997), 47–53.

38. Andrew Cuomo, "Remarks to the Community and Faith-Based Organizations Conference," September 25, 2000, online at archives.hud.gov.

39. "Congregations Building CommUNITY Kickoff," *PR Newswire*, February 29, 2000.

40. Avis C. Vidal, *Faith-Based Organizations in Community Development* (Washington, DC: Urban Institute, 2001); Sue Anne Pressley, "Faith-Based Groups under Fresh Scrutiny," *Washington Post*, February 11, 2001.

41. Mel Martinez, "Remarks at the Faith-Based and Community Initiative Conference," December 12, 2002, online at archives.hud.gov.

42. Mel Martinez, "5 Steps to Becoming a HUD-Approved Housing Counseling Agency," Center for Faith-Based and Community Initiatives, 2003, online at archives.hud.gov; Mel Martinez, "10 Things Your Faith Community Can Do to Encourage Homeownership," Center for Faith-Based and Community Initiatives, 2003, online at archives.hud.gov; Ted Cornwell, "HUD Turns to Faith-Based Counseling," *Mortgage Servicing News* 9, 1 (2005), 1, 20; "Martinez Launches 'Reaching the Dream' Faith-Based Homeownership Initiative," *Atlanta Inquirer*, September 13, 2003.

43. Steve Dubb, "Interview of Steven McCullogh," Democracy Collaborative, September 2009, online at community-wealth.org.

44. "Faith-Based Groups Prosper under Bush," *Voice of Reason* 2 (2004), 11; *Reaching New Heights: Trends and Achievements of Community-Based Development Organizations* (Washington, DC: National Congress for Community Economic Development, 2005), online at community -wealth.org; Roland V. Anglin, ed., *Building the Organizations That Build Communities: Strengthening the Capacity of Faith- and Community-Based Development Organizations* (Washington, DC: US Department of Housing and Urban Development, 2004).

45. Ram Cnaan, *The Other Philadelphia Story: How Local Congregations Support Quality of Life in Urban America* (Philadelphia: University of Pennsylvania Press, 2006), 84.

46. Maria Torres, *Faith-Based Participation in Housing: A Literature Review* (Cambridge, MA: Hauser Center for Non-Profit Organizations, Harvard University, 2005); see also Mark Chaves, "Religious Congregations and Welfare Reform: Who Will Take Advantage of Charitable Choice?" *American Sociological Review* 64 (1999), 836–46.

47. Steve Brandt, "Affordable Housing Gains Prove Elusive," *Star Tribune*, April 22, 2003.

48. Andrea Rubin, "Clergy to Take Part in Fair-Housing Fight," *Journal News* [White Plains, NY], April 18, 2003; Richard Lawson, "Churches Pitch In on Affordable Housing," *Tennessean*, July 15, 2003; La Risa Lynch, "Faith-Based Housing Group Works to Replenish Neighborhood Housing Stock," *Chicago Citizen*, September 20, 2006.

49. Mary A. Ward, *A Mission for Justice: The History of the First African American Catholic Church in Newark, New Jersey* (Knoxville: University of Tennessee Press, 2002), 85; Edward C. Burks, "Racial Separation Wide in City," *New York Times*, February 20, 1972; additional background on the circumstances in Newark giving rise to NCC is included in Richard L. Madden, "Police Criticized in Newark Riots," *New York Times*, March 3, 1968; Paul D. Colford, "New Co-ops Spruce Up Riot Zone in Newark," *New York Times*, March 14, 1976; Ellen Rand, "New Jersey Housing: Balance Sheet on Inner-City Project," *New York Times*, November 12, 1978; Alfonso A. Narvaez, "Newark Housing Dream Coming True," *New York Times*, August 11, 1979.

50. Michael Stern, "Dissident Priests Aided in Newark," *New York Times*, January 14, 1969.

51. William J. Linder, "Faith as the Foundation for the New Community Corporation," in *Sacred Places, Civic Purposes: Should Government Help Faith-Based Charity?* edited by E. J. Dionne Jr. and Ming Hsu Chen (Washington, DC: Brookings Institution Press, 2001), 155–57; and Heidi Rolland Unruh and Ronald J. Sider, *Saving Souls, Serving Society: Understanding the Faith Factor in Church-Based Social Ministry* (New York: Oxford University Press, 2005), 83, who write: "NCC affirms that God's power works through those who struggle prophetically for justice in accordance with God's revealed design."

52. "New Community," Understanding: The Communication Media for Operation Understanding, June 1973, online at riseupnewark.com.

53. Don Drumm, "Conscience in the Lily-White Suburbs," *Courier-News* [Plainfield, NJ], August 22, 1969; George H. Favre, "Suburbs Remember," *Christian Science Monitor*, April 10, 1970.

54. Douglas S. Massey, Jacob S. Rugh, Justin P. Stell, and Len Albright, "Riding the Stagecoach to Hell: A Qualitative Analysis of Racial Discrimination in Mortgage Lending," *City Community* 15, 2 (2016), 118–36, cite examples of Wells Fargo targeting Black preachers who the company's agents thought could persuade unwitting borrowers to take out loans at predatory rates.

55. Thomas Silverstein and Diane Glauber, "Leveraging the Besieged Assessment of Fair Housing Process to Create Common Ground among Fair Housing Advocates and Community Developers," *Journal of Affordable Housing and Community Development Law* 27, 1 (2018), 33–43.

56. Jake Blumgart, "Fair Housing at 50," *Planning* 84, 4 (April 2018), 17–23; Mid-America Regional Council, *Fair Housing Assessment* (2018), online at marc.org.

57. "A Seat at the Table," *PolicyLink*, October 13, 2016, online at policylink.org; Sara Patenaude, "How Ben Carson's New Housing Rule Would Deepen Racial Segregation," *Washington Post*, January 13, 2020.

58. "Presbyterian Church Issues Public Comment on HUD Proposed Rule," *Targeted News Service*, March 21, 2020.

59. "Evangelical Lutheran Church Comments on HUD Implementation of Fair Housing Act Disparate Impact Standard," *Targeted News Service*, October 8, 2019.

60. "Conference of Catholic Bishops, Catholic Charities Issue Joint Public Comment on HUD Proposed Rule," *Targeted News Service*, March 19, 2020.

61. "Religious Action Center of Reform Judaism Issues Public Comment on HUD Proposed Rule," *Targeted News Service*, March 24, 2020.

62. "Leading Civil Rights Groups Commend President Biden's Executive Action to Advance Fair Housing," *Targeted News Service*, January 27, 2021.

63. Deslippe, "As in a Civics Text Come to Life."

64. Mark Chaves and Alison J. Eagle, "Congregations and Social Services: An Update from the Third Wave of the National Congregations Study," *Religions* 7, 5 (2016), 55–64, provides data from the 2012 National Congregations Study demonstrating congregations' commitment to helping the poor—for example, with 83 percent of congregations involved in social service programs of one kind or another, including 18 percent engaged in "building or repairing homes"; however, the authors caution that social service programs often consist of relatively small numbers of volunteers and in the case of housing may mean helping with a Habitat for Humanity project; they write that most congregations' social service activity is peripheral to their main activities and "is focused on meeting short-term, immediate needs, especially the need for food" (p. 64).

65. Gillette, "Assessing James Rouse's Role," 160–61.

66. Paul Lichterman, *Elusive Togetherness: Church Groups Trying to Bridge America's Divisions* (Princeton, NJ: Princeton University Press, 2005).

67. McGuire Woods Consulting, *Zoning and Segregation in Virginia*, 2021, online at nvaha.org.

Chapter Three: Busing and Affirmative Action

1. Frye Gaillard, *The Dream Long Deferred* (Chapel Hill: University of North Carolina Press, 1988), 18–36; a more recent perspective on the case is included in Michael J. Graetz and Linda Greenhouse, *The Burger Court and the Rise of the Judicial Right* (New York: Simon and Schuster, 2016), 83–87.

2. Bart Barnes, "Charlotte 'Survives' Busing," *Washington Post*, November 19, 1972; "Mecklenburg Calls for Compliance with School Desegregation Orders," *Presbyterian Outlook*,

August 10, 1970; Weldon Wallace, "Fast-Growing Baptists Reaffirm Basic Tenets," *Baltimore Sun*, November 30, 1972; Frye Gaillard, "Charlotte's Road to Busing," *Christianity and Crisis* 33 (October 29, 1973), 216–19.

3. Judge James B. McMillan, quoted in Stephen Samuel Smith, *Boom for Whom? Education, Desegregation, and Development in Charlotte* (Albany: State University of New York Press, 2004), 60.

4. *Swann v. Charlotte-Mecklenburg Bd. of Educ.*, 402 US 1 (1971).

5. E. C. McNair, "Mothers Fearful," *Charlotte Observer*, March 8, 1970.

6. Mrs. Roy F. Fowler Jr., "My Child First," *Charlotte Observer*, February 18, 1970.

7. Rev. Preston Pendergrass, "Fear of Competition behind Issue," *Charlotte Observer*, February 19, 1970.

8. Louis Harris, "Increasing Controversy Hardens Opinions against Racial Busing," *Chicago Tribune*, April 10, 1972.

9. Reverend Leon Riddick, quoted in Hannar Miller, "Ministers Denounce Bombings, KKK," *Charlotte Observer*, December 1, 1965.

10. Alfred Alexander quoted in Lee A. Daniels, "In Defense of Busing," *New York Times*, April 17, 1983.

11. Reverend John K. Ferree quoted in Sam R. Covington, "Curb Anger, Minister to Tell School Parents," *Charlotte Observer*, August 29, 1970.

12. Frye Gaillard and Polly Paddock, "Out of Court and into the Future—with Hope," *Charlotte Observer*, July 12, 1975.

13. Total enrollment in the Charlotte Mecklenburg school district was 83,555 in 1969 and 77,167 in 1974. Polly Paddock, "Busing Spurs Growth in Private Schools," *Charlotte Observer*, October 6, 1974; J. Dennis Lord, "School Busing and White Abandonment of Public Schools," *Southeastern Geographer* 15, 2 (November 1975), 81–92; Bart Barnes, "Charlotte Learns to Live with Busing," *Washington Post*, September 3, 1975; B. Brummond Ayres Jr., "Cross Town Busing, Begun in '71, Is Working Well in Charlotte," *New York Times*, July 17, 1975.

14. Polly Paddock, "Busing Spurs Growth in Private Schools."

15. Charles L. Glenn, "Curriculum Vitae," School of Education, Boston University, 2011; J. Anthony Lukas, *Common Ground: A Turbulent Decade in the Lives of Three American Families* (New York: Knopf, 1985), 239; Ronald P. Formisano, *Boston against Busing: Race, Class, and Ethnicity in the 1960s and 1970s* (Chapel Hill: University of North Carolina Press, 1991), 48, noting Glenn's community activism during his freshman year at Harvard, writes, "Well before other white middle-class youths discovered the black poor and civil rights in the 1960s, Glenn was doing the Lord's work in urban ghettos."

16. Lukas, *Common Ground*, 241; "In the News: Charles Glenn," *Bay State Banner*, November 4, 1971.

17. For a detailed account of the busing-related violence, see Jack Tager, *Boston Riots: Three Centuries of Social Violence* (Boston: Northeastern University Press, 2019), 188–227.

18. In a 1973 interview, Glenn said inner-city volunteer work as an undergraduate persuaded him that "the clergy were the only people living and sharing their lives with people in the city," Nina McCain, "Equal Education the Goal of This Academic Minister," *Boston Globe*, January 7, 1973; Glenn would subsequently write and lecture extensively about faith-based

education, racial and religious injustice, and pluralism. In 2019, he recalled having been officially removed from the Episcopal priesthood in 1992, at which time he described himself as a Calvinist who had joined an Anglican parish, Charles L. Glenn, "My Excommunication," *First Things* (November 2019), firstthings.com.

19. Rick Casey, "Boston Bus Order Splits Catholics," *National Catholic Reporter*, February 21, 1975; a study conducted in 1975 concluded that Catholic clergy in Boston were less involved in social activism than Protestant clergy but the study's lack of rigorous sampling necessitates caution about this conclusion; Charles B. Thomas Jr., "Clergy in Racial Controversy: A Replication of the Campbell and Pettigrew Study," *Review of Religious Research* 26, 4 (June 1985), 379–90.

20. Casey, "Boston Bus Order Splits Catholics."

21. Gary McMillan, "Busing Supporters Say 'Quality Education' Is the Chief Objective," *Boston Globe*, October 20, 1974.

22. Lauren Tess Bundy, *The Schools Are Killing Our Kids: The African American Fight for Self-Determination in the Boston Public Schools, 1949–1985* (College Park: PhD Dissertation, University of Maryland, 2014).

23. Bundy, *The Schools Are Killing Our Kids*, 101; "Statement of Reverend James Breeden," June 17, 1963, repository.library.northeastern.edu.; Breeden left Boston in 1965 to serve for two years with the National Council of Churches and two years with the Massachusetts Council of Churches, earned a doctorate in education, and returned to Boston in 1975, working with the city's council monitoring school desegregation.

24. Ron Hutson, "School Desegregation in Boston and the Emerging Black Leadership," *Boston Globe*, November 17, 1974.

25. Ann LaGrelius Siqueland et al., *Desegregation: What's Best for All of Our Children?* (Seattle: Church Council of Greater Seattle, 1978); Ann LaGrelius Siqueland, *Without a Court Order: The Desegregation of Seattle's Schools* (Seattle: Madrona, 1981); Gary Iwamoto, "School District Defends Desegregation," *International Examiner* [Seattle]), March 31, 1979; *Washington v. Seattle Sch. Dist. No. 1*, 458 U.S. 457 (1982).

26. One of the longest running busing controversies was in Prince George's County, Maryland, where a coalition of churches called the Interfaith Action Communities played a role in supporting desegregation; Lisa Frazier, "Final Accord Reached on Ending Prince George's Busing," *Washington Post*, March 20, 1998.

27. David Firestone, "Churches and Race Relations Critics Say Organized Religion Not Doing Enough to Ease Tensions," *Newsday*, June 7, 1990, identifies Boston, Chicago, and Minneapolis among cities in which religious groups played a positive role; Harriet Elaine Glosson Adair, *Trends in School Desegregation: An Historical Case Study of Desegregation in Dayton, Ohio; Denver, Colorado; Los Angeles, California; and Seattle, Washington, 1954–1985* (Provo, UT: Brigham Young University, PhD Dissertation, 1986), credits church groups with important roles in Dayton and Seattle.

28. In 1977, approximately 12 percent of all students enrolled in grades nursery through twelfth were in private schools, of which an estimated 89 percent were church-related; Gil B. Lloyd, "The Impact of the *Brown* Decision on Religion during the Past Twenty-Five Years," *Negro Educational Review* 30, 2 (1979), 136–96.

29. For example, National Council of Churches, *School Desegregation: Community Prepara-tion and the Role of the Churches* (New York: National Council of Churches, 1977); *Education and Inclusion: A Report on the Church's Ministry in School Desegregation and Bilingual/Bicultural Education* (Philadelphia: United Presbyterian Church in the USA, 1977); *School Desegregation: Statement and Supporting Documents* (Indianapolis: Indiana Interreligious Commission on Human Equality, 1977).

30. Editors, "Affirmative Action and the DeFunis Case," *Christian Century*, May 8, 1974; Rabbi Irwin M. Blank, "Towards a New Black-Jewish Coalition," *Jewish Advocate*, December 12, 1974.

31. Sharae Wheeler, "*DeFunis v. Odegaard*: Another Kind of 'Jewish Problem,'" Seattle Civil Rights and Labor History Project, University of Washington, 2008, depts.washington.edu/civilr /DeFunis.htm.

32. Some support was also registered by the Synagogue Council of America; see "Synagogue Council Is Urged to Oppose Quotas," *New York Times*, September 10, 1972; Steven Frank, "After 'DeFunis': Affirmative Action and the Jewish Community," Synagogue Council of America, September 30, 1974.

33. Quoted in William Raspberry, "Fighting Campus Discrimination," *Washington Post*, March 15, 1974.

34. Jim Rensen, "Blacks and Jews: Rebuilding a Bridge," *Jewish Exponent*, June 27, 1975.

35. Stanley Mosk quoted in Murray Olderman, "Skin Pigmentation Should Not Determine Fate," *Reno Evening Gazette*, October 22, 1977.

36. *Regents of Univ. of California v. Bakke*, 438 U.S. 265 (1978).

37. "Brief of American Jewish Committee, American Jewish Congress, et al.," US Supreme Court, No. 76–811, 1977; "Jewish Group Urges Renewal of Civil Rights Coalition," *Atlanta Daily World*, July 23, 1978.

38. Russell E. Richey, Kenneth E. Rowe, and Jean Miller Schmidt, *The Methodist Experience in America: A History*, vol. 1 (Nashville, TN: Abingdon Press, 2010), chapter 14.

39. "Church Must Continue Support of Affirmative Action Regardless of Outcome of Bakke Case," *Philadelphia Tribune*, March 28, 1978.

40. "Rip Bakke, Revolt!" *Michigan Chronicle*, September 9, 1978; "United Church of Christ Opposes Bakke," *Philadelphia Tribune*, April 18, 1978; "Ministers Hold Vigil to Seek Carter's Support in Affirmative Action Case," *Atlanta Daily World*, September 15, 1977; "Church, Civic Groups Plan National Meet on Bakke Case," *Atlanta Daily World*, October 18, 1977.

41. On Ingram and the Shrine of the Black Madonna, see "Oral History Interview with Reverend Dan Aldridge," June 22, 2016, detroit1967.detroithistorical.org.; on Reverend Albert B. Cleage Jr., see Angela D. Dillard, "Religion and Radicalism: The Reverend Albert B. Cleage Jr. and the Rise of Black Christian Nationalism in Detroit," in *Freedom North: Black Freedom Struggles Outside the South, 1940–1980*, edited by Jeanne Theoharis and Komozi Woodward (New York: Palgrave, 2003), 153–75.

42. Jim Ingram, "Affirmative Action—Religious Style," *Michigan Chronicle*, August 19, 1978.

43. Ibid.

44. Ibid.

45. William J. Bennett and Terry Eastland, "Why Bakke Won't End Reverse Discrimination," *Commentary*, September 1, 1978; William J. Bennett and Terry Eastland, *Counting by Race:*

Equality from the Founding Fathers to Bakke and Weber (New York: Basic Books, 1979); William J. Bennett and Terry Eastland, "The 'New Right' Christians," *Wall Street Journal*, September 17, 1980.

46. Louis Kohlmeier, "Supreme Court Has Exorcised Church Freedom," *Courier-Post* [Cherry Hill, NJ), June 28, 1976.

47. *Bob Jones Univ. v. United States*, 461 U.S. 574 (1983).

48. Charles W. Schoenherr, "A Self-Study on the Impact of Federal Programs on the Sterling College Campus," 1977, eric.ed.gov; "Equal Opportunity Employment of Methodist Church Questioned," *Atlanta Daily World*, July 31, 1977.

49. James L. Franklin, "Affirmative Action Given Affirmation," *Boston Globe*, May 4, 1989.

50. William C. Spohn, "Negative Action in California: A Gospel Perspective," *America*, February 22, 1997.

51. Paul Nowell, "Judge Halts Racial Busing in His Ruling," *Associated Press*, September 11, 1999.

52. Roslyn Arlin Mickelson, "Subverting Swann: First- and Second-Generation Segregation in the Charlotte-Mecklenburg Schools," *American Educational Research Journal* 38, 2 (Summer 2001), 215–52; see also Stephen B. Billings, David J. Deming, and Jonah E. Rockoff, "School Segregation, Educational Attainment and Crime: Evidence from the End of Busing in Charlotte-Mecklenburg," *NBER Working Papers*, October 2012, who conclude that the end of busing widened racial inequality.

53. "Brief *Amici Curiae* of the American Jewish Committee, Central Conference of American Rabbis, Hadassah, et al.," US Supreme Court, 2003.

54. David Crumm, "Spiritual Leaders Rally for Affirmative Action," *Detroit Free Press*, September 13, 2006.

55. *Fisher v. University of Texas at Austin*, 579 US Supreme Court (2016).

56. "Brief of *Amici Curiae* the American Jewish Committee, Central Conference of American Rabbis, and Union for Reform Judaism in Support of Respondents," US Supreme Court, 2012, quote on page 14.

57. "Brief of *Amici Curiae* Religious Organizations and Campus Ministries," US Supreme Court, 2012, quotes on pages 14 and 15.

58. M. Kelly Carr, *The Rhetorical Invention of Diversity: Supreme Court Opinions, Public Arguments, and Affirmative Action* (East Lansing: Michigan State University Press, 2018) offers a valuable overview of the language shift away from race and toward individuality and diversity.

59. For example, see Ayana Jones, "A Call to Action: Churches Helped Mobilize Marchers," *Philadelphia Tribune*, August 26, 2003.

Chapter Four: Racial Reckoning

1. Jesse Jackson quoted in "Excerpts of Speeches," *Washington Post*, August 28, 1983.

2. Robert L. Johnston, "Church on Racism?" *National Catholic Reporter*, September 26, 1975; "Church Urged: 'Challenge the System of Racism,'" *Atlanta Daily World*, March 19, 1982.

3. "Church and Race Councils Plan to Celebrate Reunion," *Presbyterian Outlook*, January 17, 1983; Jackie Ross, "Despite Lively Topics, Synod Delegates Foresee Little Dissension," *Hartford*

Courant, June 20, 1981; James Lyke, "The Pastoral of US Roman Catholic Bishops on Racism," *Call and Post* [Cleveland], May 10, 1980.

4. James L. Franklin, "The Battle against Racism," *Boston Globe,* March 24, 1980.

5. "Synagogues Ask Reagan to Move on Black Deaths," *New York Jewish Week,* March 1, 1981; Scott Austin and May Lee, "Blacks View Reagan's Term with Fear, Some Optimism," *Los Angeles Times,* December 8, 1980; Frank P.L. Somerville, "Reagan Immigration Policy Sharply Criticized," *Baltimore Sun,* January 31, 1982.

6. Charles E. Cobb, "Racism: Sin Not Skin?" *Afro-American,* October 29, 1983; Ronald Reagan, "Remarks at the Annual Meeting of the American Bar Association in Atlanta, Georgia, August 1, 1983," reaganlibrary.gov.

7. Catherine Meeks, "Rage and Reconciliation," *Sojourners* (June 1981), 17.

8. On desegregation in Detroit, see Charles T. Clotfelter, "The Detroit Decision and 'White Flight,'" *Journal of Legal Studies* 5, 1 (January 1976), 99–112.

9. "Pontiac Bombing Charged to Klan," *New York Times,* September 10, 1971; Wayne King, "White Supremacists Voice Support of Farrakhan," *New York Times,* October 12, 1985.

10. Sources for the Livingston County story include Jim Totten, "Battling a Legacy," *Livingston County Daily Press & Argus,* November 7, 2008; Brenda J. Gilchrist, "Trading Pulpits," *Detroit Free Press,* October 20, 1992; Associated Press, "Livingston Group Wants to Make Minorities Welcome," *Lansing State Journal,* February 11, 1993; Christopher Behnan, "Pastor Witness to Decades of Change," *Livingston County Daily & Argus,* June 3, 2011; and Hawke Fracassa and Steve Pardo, "Assault Case Produces Plea Deal," *Detroit News,* February 7, 2002.

11. "Ministerial Courtesy," *Congregationalist and Christian World* [Boston], February 3, 1906.

12. "Chicagoan Urges White and Negro Pulpit Exchange," *Pittsburgh Courier,* January 16, 1926.

13. Reverend Caleb W. Johnson, "The Whites Can't Take It," *Afro-American* [Baltimore, MD], March 17, 1934.

14. Associated Press, "Selling the Message of Brotherhood Seems to Be Missing in Many Black and White Churches," *Grand Rapids Press,* October 26, 1991.

15. "Promoting Race Relations," *Cincinnati Post,* April 13, 1996.

16. Reverend Jean Robinson-Casey quoted in Hamil R. Harris, "Churches Unite in Worship," *Washington Post,* November 11, 1999.

17. Marco Bazan, "A Call for Racial Reconciliation," *Austin American Statesman,* June 26, 1996.

18. Judith Cebula, "Igniting the Fire of Hope," *Indianapolis Star,* June 22, 1996.

19. Eric Frazier, "Southern Baptists Repent," *Post and Courier* [Charleston, SC], June 21, 1995; Pentecostal Partners, "Racial Reconciliation Manifesto (1994)," *Pneuma Review,* May 12, 2000, which pledged, among other things, "We will seek partnerships and exchange pulpits with persons of a different hue."

20. Reverend Curtis Herron, quoted in David Peterson, "Sunday-Morning Race Barriers Breaking Down," *Star Tribune,* November 1, 1995.

21. "1,200 Worshippers at Philly's First Interracial Church," *Afro-American,* October 26, 1935.

22. Ram Cnaan, *The Other Philadelphia Story: How Local Congregations Support Quality of Life in Urban America* (Philadelphia: University of Pennsylvania Press, 2006), 111.

23. "Interracial Church in Charlotte Uses Christianity in Daily Living," *New Journal and Guide* [Norfolk, VA], January 28, 1950.

24. C. Kirk Hadaway, David G. Hackett, and James Fogle Miller, "The Most Segregated Institution: Correlates of Interracial Church Participation," *Review of Religious Research* 25, 3 (March 1984), 204–19.

25. "Interracial Photo Causes Baptists to Ban Book," *Sunday School Quarterly*, November 6, 1971.

26. Christopher Lasch, *The Culture of Narcissism: American Life in an Age of Diminishing Expectations* (New York: Norton, 1979), and Robert N. Bellah, Steven M. Tipton, William M. Sullivan, Richard Madsen, and Ann Swidler, *Habits of the Heart: Individualism and Commitment in American Life* (Berkeley and Los Angeles: University of California Press, 1985).

27. For example, James H. Davis and Woodie W. White, *Racial Transition in the Church* (Nashville, TN: Parthenon Press, 1980).

28. Robert E. Jones, *The Ministry of Racial Reconciliation at the Congregational Level* (Dayton, OH: United Theological Seminary, DMin Dissertation, 1994).

29. For example, James H. Parker, "The Integration of Negroes and Whites in an Integrated Church Setting," *Social Forces* 46, 3 (March 1968), 359–66.

30. The Lakeview Presbyterian Church information is from an unpublished DMin Dissertation by Reverend Earl Smith, a summary of which is available on the church's website, lakeviewpresbyterianchurch.org, and from Elizabeth Whitney, "Church Integration: How It Stands," *Tampa Bay Times*, June 26, 1965; Mary Ann Simmons, "The Churches in a Changing Neighborhood," *Tampa Bay Times*, March 16, 1968; "Negro Teacher Transfers Are Decried," *St. Petersburg Times*, July 10, 1969; David Plott, "Religion by Race," *St. Petersburg Times*, August 16, 1986; Thomas J. Billitteri, "A Call for Harmony," *St. Petersburg Times*, March 14, 1992; Craig Basse and Monica Davey, "Activist Robert Gemmer," *St. Petersburg Times*, December 23, 1992; Reverend Elligan left Lakeview in 1970 for a pastorate at the New Covenant Presbyterian Church in Miami, Florida, a congregation formed in 1965 with a vision of becoming an interracial church.

31. Lisa Stoffels, "Tiny Church Makes a Big Contribution," *St. Petersburg Times*, May 22, 1993; Robert Trigaux, "Activists Hit Banks with Statistics," *St. Petersburg Times*, January 4, 1994; Anne Lindberg, "Board Changes Student Code," *St. Petersburg Times*, June 28, 1995; Nicole Piscopo, "Church Prides Itself on Long Tradition of Interracial Harmony," *St. Petersburg Times*, June 29, 1996; Waveney Ann Moore, "Tiny Church Gets a Gift of Money," *St. Petersburg Times*, March 12, 2000.

32. Mark Chaves, *National Congregations Study: Data File and Codebook* (Tucson: University of Arizona, Department of Sociology, 1998); Michael O. Emerson and Karen Chai Kim, "Multiracial Congregations: An Analysis of Their Development and a Typology," *Journal for the Scientific Study of Religion* 42, 2 (June 2003), 217–27.

33. Emerson and Kim, "Multiracial Congregations"; George Yancey and Michael Emerson, "Integrated Sundays: An Exploratory Study into the Formation of Multiracial Churches," *Sociological Focus* 36, 2 (May 2003), 111–26; and Michael O. Emerson, *People of the Dream: Multiracial Congregations in the United States* (Princeton, NJ: Princeton University Press, 2006).

34. Kevin D. Dougherty and Kimberly R. Huyser, "Racially Diverse Congregations: Organizational Identity and the Accommodation of Differences," *Journal for the Scientific Study of Religion* 47, 1 (March 2008), 23–44.

35. Heather Susan Entrekin, *Community through Divergence: Metaphors of a Multiracial Church* (Lawrence: University of Kansas, PhD Dissertation, 1999), quotes on page 105; see also Jacqueline Lewis, *The Power of Stories: A Guide for Leading Multiracial and Multicultural Congregations* (Nashville, TN: Abingdon, 2008).

36. Korie L. Edwards, Brad Christerson, and Michael O. Emerson, "Race, Religious Organizations, and Integration," *Annual Review of Sociology* 39 (2013), 211–28.

37. Emerson, *People of the Dream*, and Gerardo Marti, "The Religious Racial Integration of African Americans into Diverse Churches," *Journal for the Scientific Study of Religion* 49, 2 (June 2010), 201–17.

38. Examples of these challenges are discussed in Jessica M. Barron and Rhys H. Williams, *The Urban Church Imagined: Religion, Race, and Authenticity in the City* (New York: NYU Press, 2017); Jessica M. Barron, "Managed Diversity: Race, Place, and an Urban Church," *Sociology of Religion* 77, 1 (Spring 2016), 18–36; Melissa Wilde and Lindsay Glassman, "How Complex Religion Can Improve Our Understanding of American Politics," *Annual Review of Sociology* 42 (2016), 407–25; Richard N. Pitt, "Fear of a Black Pulpit? Real Racial Transcendence versus Cultural Assimilation in Multiracial Churches," *Journal for the Scientific Study of Religion* 49, 2 (June 2010), 218–23; and the essays in Grace Yukich and Penny Edgell, editors, *Religion Is Raced: Understanding American Religion in the Twenty-First Century* (New York: NYU Press, 2020).

39. A wealth of thoughtful, empirically based reflection about the possibilities and challenges of racial reconciliation in multiracial congregations can be found in Curtiss Paul DeYoung, Michael O. Emerson, George Yancey, and Karen Chai Kim, *United by Faith: The Multiracial Congregation as an Answer to the Problem of Race* (New York: Oxford University Press, 2003).

40. Reverend Lee Brown quoted in David Waters, "Memphis Clergy Discuss Ways to Reconcile Races," *Scripps Howard Service*, September 23, 1993.

Chapter Five: Criminal Justice

1. US Congress, "Hate Crime Statistics Act: Hearing before the Subcommittee on Criminal Justice of the Committee on the Judiciary, House of Representatives," March 21, 1985 (Washington, DC: Government Printing Office, 1985).

2. "NCC Board to Take Up Domestic Racial Justice," *Atlanta Daily World*, November 8, 1979.

3. National Council of Churches Governing Board, "Challenges to the Injustices of the Criminal Justice System," November 10, 1979, nationalcouncilofchurches.us.

4. May Jane Cornell, "Outrageous Love: Criminal Justice Sunday," *Presbyterian Outlook* 164, 6 (February 8, 1982), 4, excerpts from a sermon delivered at Columbia Presbyterian Church, Decatur, Georgia.

5. Allan C. Brownfeld, "The National Council of Churches: Advocate for the World's Militant Left," *Human Events* 41, 6 (February 7, 1981), 121–28.

6. United Church of Christ, *Minutes of the Seventh General Synod* (1969), 87.

7. George M. Collins, "UCC Synod Approves Black Unit," *Boston Globe*, July 1, 1969; "Thirteenth March Ends Peacefully," *St. Petersburg Times*, July 7, 1968; United Church of Christ, *Minutes of the Seventh General Synod* (1969), 78; United Church of Christ, *Minutes of the Fourth General Synod* (1963), 41.

8. "Racial Justice Commission Pressures for Penal Reform," *Atlanta Daily World*, October 15, 1970.

9. "United Church to Aid NC Church," *Bay State Banner*, April 1, 1971.

10. On Chavis at the University of North Carolina, Charlotte, see "Uplifting, Uniting, and Empowering the Black Community at UNC Charlotte: The Origins and Legacy of the Black Student Union," *US Fed News Service*, February 23, 2021.

11. For details of the events leading up to and during the violence, see Kenneth Robert Janken, *The Wilmington Ten: Violence, Injustice, and the Rise of Black Politics in the 1970s* (Chapel Hill: University of North Carolina Press, 2015).

12. United Church of Christ, *Minutes of the Ninth General Synod* (1973), 57; United Church of Christ, *Minutes of the Tenth General Synod* (1975), 35; on Northern Congregational churches' early denunciation of slavery and pre–Civil War Black participation in Southern Christian Church congregations, see United Church of Christ, *A Short Course in the History of the United Church of Christ* (Cleveland, OH: Pilgrim Press, 2017), and Barbara Brown Zikmund, ed., *Hidden Histories in the United Church of Christ* (Cleveland, OH: Pilgrim Press, 2007).

13. Ben Chavis, "The Wilmington Ten: Prisoners of Conscience," in *It Did Happen Here: Recollections of Political Repression in America*, edited by Bud Schultz and Ruth Schultz (Berkeley and Los Angeles: University of California Press, 1989), 195–211; Angela Y. Davis, "The Struggle of Ben Chavis and the Wilmington 10," *Black Scholar* 6, 7 (April 1975), 26–31, quote on page 27; Signe Waller, *Love and Revolution: A Political Memoir* (Lanham, MD: Rowman and Littlefield, 2002), 125–32; "Thirteenth March Ends Peacefully," *St. Petersburg Times*, July 7, 1968; "Tense NC City after Sniping," *New York Amsterdam News*, February 13, 1971; "United Church to Aid NC Church," *Bay State Banner*, April 1, 1971; "Gregory Church Is Target of Violence," *Call and Post* [Cleveland], April 17, 1971; "2 Young Felons Plan to Testify in Riot Trial of Black Minister," *New York Times*, September 25, 1972; "Convicted Black Showed 2 Images," *New York Times*, October 23, 1972; Linn Washington, "President Carter Ignores Plea of Wilmington 10," *Philadelphia Tribune*, May 14, 1977; "Issues at Synod Not Covered," *Muncie Star*, July 9, 1977; Pamela Smith, "It Cost Wilmington 10 $2M, 10 Years to Get Justice," *Philadelphia Tribune*, December 12, 1980.

14. Brian Kates, "We Haven't Kicked the Klan," *Daily News*, February 11, 1979.

15. Maximillian Longley, "Greensboro Shootings," North Carolina History Project, undated, northcarolinahistory.org.

16. Waller, *Love and Revolution*, 250–59, 305–10; Kirk Loggins and Susan Thomas, "Klan Activity Accompanied by Surge of Criminal Acts," *Fort Myers News-Press*, March 2, 1980.

17. Janken, *Wilmington Ten*, 107–9.

18. Sandy Wittkop, "Anti-Klan Conference Scheduled," *Daily World*, November 9, 1979; Rosemary Yardley, "The Communists and the Ku Klux Klan," *Newsday*, November 13, 1979; Mark I. Pinsky, "Left Gathers in Shadow of Death," *Boston Globe*, December 7, 1980; "Anti-Klan Network Doesn't Fight Fascism," *Workers Vanguard*, January 30, 1981.

19. "Council of Churches Condemns the Klan," *New Journal and Guide*, November 16, 1979; David Treadwell, "Massive Attacks Mounted to Combat Revival of Klan," *Los Angeles Times*, December 8, 1980; Michel McQueen, "Network Takes Aim at KKK," *Washington Post*, February 5, 1981; Billie Cheney Speed, "Church Attacks the Klan," *Atlanta Constitution*,

June 21, 1981; Stephanie Sevick, "Klan Leader Arrested at Anti-Klan Meeting," *Hartford Courant*, September 27, 1981.

20. US Commission on Civil Rights, *Intimidation and Violence: Racial and Religious Bigotry in America* (Washington, DC: Government Printing Office, 1983).

21. See for example, Gertrude Selznick and Stephen Steinberg, *The Tenacity of Prejudice* (New York: Harper and Row, 1969); and Charles Y. Glock, Jane Piliavin, Metta Spencer, and Robert Wuthnow, *Adolescent Prejudice* (New York: Harper and Row, 1975).

22. Susan Howard, "Ministers Condemn Racial Incident," *Atlanta Constitution*, January 17, 1984; Julia Dolan, "Was It Even Passing Through or Something Dark Within?" *Los Angeles Times*, March 27, 1988; the identity of the perpetrators remained unknown.

23. US Commission on Civil Rights, *Intimidation and Violence: Racial and Religious Bigotry in America* (Washington, DC: Government Printing Office, 1990), 28.

24. Laurie Olson, "Church Deacon Charges Police Brutality," *Skanner* [Portland, OR], July 23, 1980.

25. Laura R. Woliver, "A Measure of Justice: Police Conduct and Black Civil Rights, the Coalition for Justice for Ernest Lacy," *Western Political Quarterly* 43, 2 (June 1, 1990), 415–36; Nathaniel Sheppard Jr., "5 Policemen Face Charges in Arrested Man's Death," *New York Times*, October 15, 1981; Tim Cuprisin, "Lacy's Legacy: Death Left a Lasting Impact," *Milwaukee Journal*, July 14, 1991.

26. Sam Roberts, "Police Brutality Charged at Forum," *New York Times*, September 20, 1983; Richard Levine and Alan Finder, "The Mayor Finally Has His Say on Police Brutality," *New York Times*, December 4, 1983.

27. Neal Gendler, "Church Council Working to Strengthen Its Ties to Black Congregations," *Star Tribune*, February 26, 1989.

28. Lowell Lawson and Tomas C. Mijares, "Recruiting and Training a Police Chaplain Corps," *Police Chief* 52, 6 (June 1985), 68–70; Pat Galbincea, "12 Members of Clergy Sworn in by Mayor as Police Chaplains," *Plain Dealer*, July 27, 1990; Robin Warshaw, "God on the Beat," *Philadelphia Daily News*, January 26, 1984, a report in which it was estimated that there were some five hundred police chaplains nationwide.

29. Darlene Ricker, "Behind the Silence," *ABA Journal* 77, 7 (July 1991), 44–49.

30. Virgie W. Murray, "Parishioners Seek Comfort in Various Churches," *Los Angeles Sentinel*, May 7, 1992; Beth S. Bergman and Charlotte M. Hartwell, "Rebuilding Los Angeles—One Year Later: The Bitter Aftermath and Lessons Learned," *ABA Journal of Affordable Housing and Community Development Law* 2, 3 (Spring 1993), 11–13; Steven B. Sample, "USC and the Rebuilding of Los Angeles," *Change* 25, 4 (July/August 1993), 48–55.

31. Darrell Turner, "Clerics Respond to Rioting," *Washington Post*, May 2, 1992; see also Benjamin F. Chavis Jr., "Reflections from Los Angeles," *Los Angeles Sentinel*, May 28, 1992.

32. Lynda Richardson, "Church of Christ Urges Action against Racism," *Washington Post*, 12, 1991; Michael Walton, "UCC Church Urges Members to Lead Fight against Racism," *Call and Post*, May 30, 1991.

33. "Suit Says Police Single Out Blacks for Traffic Stops," *Morning Call* [Allentown, PA], November 18, 1992; Reid Kanaley, "Tinicum Police Violating Rights of Minority Drivers, Lawsuit Says," *Philadelphia Inquirer*, November 18, 1992.

34. Jody Benjamin, "Traffic Stops and Race: A Turnpike Case Tests the Issue Anew," *Philadelphia Inquirer*, August 3, 1994; Nicholas Wishart, "Ex-Trooper Links Traffic Stops to Race," *Philadelphia Inquirer*, December 21, 1994; Nicholas Wishart, "Statistics Support Racial Profiling on Turnpike, Lawyers Say," *Philadelphia Inquirer*, July 12, 1995.

35. Robert D. McFadden, "Police Singled Out Black Drivers in Drug Crackdown," *New York Times*, March 10, 1996; Linn Washington Jr., "Bill Proposed to Deter Race-Based Drug Searches," *Philadelphia Tribune*, August 6, 1996.

36. John Kifner and David M. Herszenhorn, "Racial 'Profiling' at Crux of Inquiry into Shooting by Troopers," *New York Times*, May 8, 1998.

37. Deepti Hajela, "Racial Profiling Protested at Shooting Site," *Philadelphia Tribune*, May 19, 1998; Rick Sarlat, "Clergy in NJ Press Officials on Racial Profiling," *Philadelphia Tribune*, June 2, 1998.

38. "Morris Clergy Pen Open Letter on Shooting of Stanton Crew," *Daily Record* [Morristown, NJ], June 25, 1999.

39. "Timeline of NJ State Police Struggles with Racial Discrimination," NJ.com, January 20, 2014.

40. Lauren E. Glaze, "Correctional Populations in the United States, 2010," US Department of Justice, Office of Justice Programs, December 2011, bjs.ojp.gov.

41. Becky Pettit and Bruce Western, "Mass Imprisonment and the Life Course: Race and Class Inequality in US Incarceration," *American Sociological Review* 69, 2 (April 2004), 151–69; Christopher Wildeman and Emily A. Wang, "Mass Incarceration, Public Health, and Widening Inequality in the USA," *Lancet* 389, 10077 (April 8, 2017), 1464–74.

42. United Church of Christ, *Minutes of the Ninth General Synod* (1973), 80; Alice Murray, "Episcopalians Study Penal Reform," *Atlanta Constitution*, September 30, 1974.

43. Ronald J. Ostrow, "William Barr: A 'Caretaker' Attorney General Proves Agenda-Setting Conservative," *Los Angeles Times*, June 22, 1992; H. R. Harris, "Ministers Meet on Reducing Number of Black Males in Jail," *Washington Post*, June 13, 1992; "Church Commission Raises Hell over Thomas' Opinion," *Los Angeles Sentinel*, March 26, 1992.

44. Derrick Henry, "Interfaith Program Helps Inmates," *Atlanta Journal-Constitution*, October 30, 1999; Mark Oppenheimer, "With Prison Ministry, Colson Linked Religion and Reform," *New York Times*, April 27, 2012; on the church–state issues, see Winnifred Fallers Sullivan, *Prison Religion: Faith-Based Reform and the Constitution* (Princeton, NJ: Princeton University Press, 2009).

45. Manning Marable, "Racism, Prison and the Future of Black America," *New Pittsburgh Courier*, October 14, 2000.

46. Bruce Dixon, "Mass Incarceration Is an Abomination," *Black Commentator*, July 21, 2005.

47. Advisory Committee on Social Witness Policy, *Resolution Calling for the Abolition of For-Profit Private Prisons* (Louisville, KY: Presbyterian Church [USA], 2003), pcusa.org; "Criminal Justice and Prison Reform," Unitarian Universalist Association (2005), uua.org.

48. Connie Schultz, "A Collaboration of Congregations," *Plain Dealer*, June 8, 2011; Phillip Morris, "Kasich Starting to Win Converts," *Plain Dealer*, July 18, 2012.

49. Michelle Alexander, *The New Jim Crow: Mass Incarceration in the Age of Colorblindness* (New York: New Press, 2010); the study guide was produced and distributed by the Samuel

DeWitt Proctor Conference; the Virginia Interfaith Center collected and updated many of the faith communities' statements about criminal justice, virginiafaithcenter.org; see also Frank Butler, *God's Gonna Trouble the Waters: Social Ethics, Religious Organizations, and Crime Policy* (Philadelphia: PhD Dissertation, Temple University, 2005).

50. J. E. Espino, "Group Forms to Oppose Two Interfaith Organizations," *Post-Crescent* [Appleton, WI], February 20, 2010.

Chapter Six: Politics of Hope

1. Clarence Page, "Bush's 'Values' Got More Black Voters in His Camp than in 2000," *Chicago Tribune*, November 7, 2004.

2. "Religion and the Presidential Vote," Pew Research Center, December 6, 2004, pewresearch.org. And from an analysis of General Social Survey data, Andrew M. Greeley and Michael Hout, *The Truth about Conservative Christians: What They Think and What They Believe* (Chicago: University of Chicago Press, 2006), 39–68.

3. Howard Dean quoted in Tony Carnes, "Dean Vows to Reach Evangelicals as Democratic Leader," *Christianity Today*, February 14, 2005; Rolando Garcia, "Man of Faith Kerry Hopes to Close the Religion Gap," *National Post*, August 9, 2004; Amy Sullivan quoted in Jim Vandehei, "Kerry Keeps His Faith in Reserve," *Washington Post*, July 16, 2004; and more fully, Amy Sullivan, *The Party Faithful: How and Why Democrats Are Closing the God Gap* (New York: Scribner, 2008).

4. Dan Gilgoff, "'Religious' Voters Get Political Overtures," *Houston Chronicle*, October 27, 2007; Martin Kasindorf, "Some Democrats Go Online to Click with Religious Voters," *USA Today*, September 5, 2006.

5. Leah Daughtry, "Remarks as Prepared for Delivery," *US Newswire*, August 25, 2008; Daniel Bergner, "Can Leah Daughtry Bring Faith to the Party?" *New York Times Magazine* (July 20, 2008), 24–29.

6. On the Matthew 25 Network, see Matthew25.org; see also Bill Berkowitz, "US Left-Leaning Religious Groups Back Obama's Campaign," *Global Information Network*, August 5, 2008.

7. "Church Speech by Obama Gets IRS Scrutiny," All Things Considered, February 27, 2008; the portion of Reverend Wright's sermon the media replayed thousands of times was "The government gives them [African Americans] the drugs, builds bigger prisons, passes a three-strike [felony] law and then wants us to sing 'God Bless America.' No, no, no, Goddamn America, that's in the Bible for killing innocent people. Goddamn America for treating our citizens as less than human. Goddamn America for as long as she acts like she is God and she is supreme." Obama's relationship with Reverend Wright is described extensively in Clarence E. Walker and Gregory D. Smithers, *The Preacher and the Politician: Jeremiah Wright, Barack Obama, and Race in America* (Charlottesville: University of Virginia Press, 2009), who stress how Wright's calling out of racism threatened the notion among many White Americans that the United States was a postracial society; see also Carl A. Grant and Shelby J. Grant, *The Moment: Barack Obama, Jeremiah Wright, and the Firestorm at Trinity United Church of Christ* (New York: Rowman & Littlefield, 2013).

8. Rev. Dr. Yvonne Delk quoted in "Interview with the Council of Elders," *New Conversations* 19, 3 (1999), 23.

9. William Fisher, "Theologians Decry Media Frenzy over Obama's Pastor," *Global Information Network*, April 3, 2008; "UCC Head Denounced Political 'Attacks' on Obama's Church," *Religious News Service*, January 15, 2008.

10. Jim Wallis, "Healing the Wounds of Race," *Sojourners Magazine* 37, 5 (May 2008), 5; Pastor Lance Watson, quoted in "Many Can 'Relate' to Rev. Wright's Words," *Tennessee Tribune*, March 20, 2008.

11. Barbara Dianne Savage, *Your Spirits Walk beside Us: The Politics of Black Religion* (Cambridge, MA: Harvard University Press, 2008), 278.

12. Barack Obama, "Text of Obama's Speech: A More Perfect Union," *Wall Street Journal*, March 18, 2008; the variation in responses among scholars examining details of the text is evident in Ebony Utley and Amy L. Heyse, "Barack Obama's (Im)Perfect Union: An Analysis of the Strategic Successes and Failures in His Speech on Race," *Western Journal of Black Studies* 33, 3 (Fall 2009), 153–63; David A. Frank, "The Prophetic Voice and the Face of the Other in Barack Obama's 'A More Perfect Union' Address, March 18, 2008," *Rhetoric and Public Affairs* 12, 2 (Summer 2009), 167–94.

13. Manya A. Brachear, "'Sacred' Discourse on Race Sought," *Chicago Tribune*, April 4, 2008; Ed Laiscell, "Conversation on Race Continues among Churches," *Washington Informer*, November 20, 2008; "W. Evan Golder, "What Makes a Conversation 'Sacred'?" *United Church News* 24, 3 (June/July 2008), A8–A9.

14. "National Unity Calls by US Churches after Obama Victory," *Presbyterian Outlook* 190, 40 (December 1, 2008), 8; Allen G. Breed, "Churches across US Reflect on Election," *Associated Press*, November 10, 2008; "How the Faithful Voted," Pew Forum, November 10, 2008, pewforum.org.

15. Joshua Dubois, "President's Advisory Council on Faith-Based and Neighborhood Partnerships Deliberates Recommendations," White House, November 16, 2009, obamawhitehouse .archives.gov; "President Obama's Advisory Council on Faith-Based and Neighborhood Partnerships," Pew Research Center, September 9, 2009.

16. David Yonke, "Local Clergy Full of Hope as Obama Era Commences," *Blade* [Toledo, OH], January 19, 2009; "Dallas-Area Pastors Deliver Messages of Hope about Obama Inauguration," *McClatchy—Tribune Business News*, January 19, 2009.

17. Leslie Boyd, "Clergy Members Call for Racial Justice," *Asheville Citizen*, July 10, 2009; the law was repealed in 2013 but the repeal was found unconstitutional in 2020.

18. Barack Obama, "Remarks by the President in Remembrance of Dr. Martin Luther King, Jr.," delivered at Vermont Avenue Baptist Church, Washington, DC, January 17, 2010, obamawhitehouse.archives.gov. This was one of many occasions in which Obama referred to Joshua's leadership; Savage, *Your Spirits Walk beside Us*, 276.

19. Debbie Gruenstein Bocian, Wei Li, and Keith S. Ernst, "Foreclosures by Race and Ethnicity: The Demographics of a Crisis," Center for Responsible Lending, June 18, 2010, responsiblelending.org; Rakesh Kochhar, Ana Gonzalez-Barrera, and Daniel Dockterman, "Through Boom and Bust: Minorities, Immigrants and Homeownership," Pew Hispanic Center, May 12, 2009, pewhispanic.org.

20. "Faith Leaders from across US Come to DC to Pray in Front of Treasure Department for a Real Solution to Foreclosure Crisis," *US Newswire*, November 12, 2008; Laura Crimaldi, "Clergy to Feds: Help Curb Foreclosures," *Boston Herald*, November 18, 2008; "Foreclosure Victims, Clergy on Cross-Country 'Recovery Express' Bus Caravan," *US Newswire*, March 9, 2009.

21. President's Advisory Council on Faith-Based and Neighborhood Partnerships, *A New Era of Partnerships: Report of Recommendations to the President*, March 2010, obamawhitehouse .archives.gov.

22. "Brown, Cordray Discuss the Economy, Housing, and Education with African American Clergy Leaders in Columbus," *Congressional Documents and Publications*, October 28, 2010; Brown, who had won 56 percent of the vote in the 2006 senate race, was a focus of Republican opposition that would narrow his victory to 50.7 percent in 2012 and was keenly aware of Black voters' crucial role in Ohio elections.

23. Leonard N. Fleming, "Bing Unveils Faith-Based Task Force," *Detroit News*, July 24, 2009; "City, County, Clergy Wrap Up Successful Demolition Campaign," *Michigan Chronicle*, July 28, 2010; Leah Harris, "Rebuilding Detroit," *Michigan Chronicle*, August 28, 2002; Nancy Kaffer, "Stretched Agency Gears Up to Handle $47 Million to Battle Blight," *Crain's Detroit Business* 25, 12 (March 23, 2009), 17; Corry Buckwalter Berkooz, "Repurposing Detroit," *Planning* 76, 9 (November 2010), 26–31.

24. Robert Boczkiewicz, "Building Affordable Housing a Work of Mercy," *National Catholic Reporter*, January 19, 1990; "Mercy Housing's Midwest Operations Merge with Lakefront Supportive Housing," *PR Newswire*, January 31, 2006; Norman Carroll, Molly Burke, and Mark Carroll, "A Case of Social Entrepreneurship: Tackling Homelessness," *Journal of Business Case Studies* 6, 5 (September/October 2010), 83–95; Robert Sharoff, "Home of Chicago Rail Cars Set to Undergo Renovation," *New York Times*, March 21, 2012.

25. Mary Anderson Cooper, "Statement to the Health Care Task Force," March 23, 1993, Clinton Presidential Records, FOIA ID 3925, clinton.presidentiallibraries.us.

26. Beatrix Hoffman, "Health Care Reform and Social Movements in the United States," *American Journal of Public Health* 93, 1 (January 2003), 78–85.

27. Stephanie Guerilus, "Pastor Enlists Churches to Back Health-Care Plan," *Philadelphia Tribune*, February 24, 2008; David Briggs, "Faith Leaders Make Health Care for All a Moral Imperative," *Plain Dealer*, June 14, 2008; "With UCC's Support, Interfaith Advocates Insist Universal Health Care Is Critical," *United Church News* 24, 4 (August/September 2008), A11.

28. Susan Campbell, "Clergy Unite on Health Care," *Hartford Courant*, January 27, 2009; Micki Carter and Jeff Woodard, "Single-Payer Health Care Gets Nod and a March from UCC Assembly," *United Church News* 25, 4 (September/October 2009), A6.

29. Anne Farris Rosen and Scott Clement, "Religious Groups Weigh In on Health Care Reform," Pew Research Center, October 8, 2009, pewforum.org; on PICO's role, see Richard L. Wood and Brad L. Fulton, *A Shared Future: Faith-Based Organizing for Racial Equity and Ethical Democracy* (Chicago: University of Chicago Press, 2015), 102–16.

30. John Dart, "Churches Weigh In on Health-Care Reform," *Christian Century* 127, 8 (April 20, 2010), 14.

31. Rosen and Clement, "Religious Groups Weigh In."

32. Bruce Nolan, "Clergy United to Urge: 'Thou Shalt Be Civil,'" *Christian Century* 127, 2 (January 26, 2010), 15; raw denunciations of Obamacare appeared with some frequency in *Human Events*, "Hannity," the *Washington Examiner*, and media with similar audiences.

33. Jim Towey, "Pastors for ObamaCare?" *Wall Street Journal*, September 25, 2010; Thomas C. Buchmueller, Zachary M. Levinson, and Barbara L. Wolfe, "Effect of the Affordable Care Act on Racial and Ethnic Disparities in Health Insurance Coverage," *American Journal of Public Health* 106, 8 (August 2016), 1416–21.

34. R. Khari Brown, "Racial Differences in Congregation-Based Political Activism," *Social Forces* 84, 3 (March 2006), 1581–1604; and on Black congregations' orientation toward social justice, R. Khari Brown, "Racial/Ethnic Differences in the Political Behavior of American Religious Congregations," *Sociological Spectrum* 29, 2 (March 2009), 227–48; the role of congregations' income and overall services and outreach activities as a positive relationship with voter registration is emphasized in Paul A. Djupe and Jacob R. Neiheisel, "Political Mobilization in American Congregations: A Religious Economies Perspective," *Politics and Religion* 12, 1 (March 2019), 123–52.

35. George L. Denny, "In My Opinion Stop Those Voter Registration Drives," *Atlanta Journal Constitution*, October 9, 1996.

36. Neil A. Lewis, "Civil Rights Mission Reshaped for Religious Focus," *New York Times*, June 17, 2007; National Council of Churches, "Resolution to Reaffirm Commitment to Voting Rights Act," November 9, 2005, nationalcouncilofchurches.us.

37. Melde Rutledge, "Thousands in NC March for Change," *Chicago Citizen*, February 21, 2007; Jesse James DeConto, "Massing for Schools, Peace," *News & Observer* [Raleigh, NC], February 11, 2007.

38. Titan Barksdale, "NAACP Can Fight Voting District Suit," *McClatchy-Tribune Business News*, January 16, 2008; Kristin Collins, "'Historic Thousands' March to Legislature," *McClatchy-Tribune Business News*, February 10, 2008; Tital Barksdale, "NAACP Lodges Call Complaint," *McClatchy-Tribune Business News*, May 4, 2008; Cash Michaels, "NAACP Pres. Jealous Endorses NC's 'Millions Voting March,'" *New York Amsterdam News*, October 9, 2008.

39. Brandon Lowrey, "Black Churches Use King's Legacy in Voter Drive Politics," *Daily News* [Los Angeles, CA], January 15, 2008; Ryan S. Clark, "Getting Out the Devout," *Beaumont Enterprise*, October 23, 2008; "High Marks for the Campaign," Pew Research Center, November 13, 2008.

40. Wendy R. Weiser, "The State of Voting in 2014," Brennan Center for Justice, June 17, 2014, brennancenter.org.

41. Olympia Meola, "Black Pastors Criticize Governor," *Richmond Times*, April 16, 2010.

42. "Brief of the Leadership Conference on Civil and Human Rights and the Leadership Conference Education Fund et al. as *Amici Curiae* in Support of Appellees," US Supreme Court, *Shelby v. Holder*, February 1, 2013.

43. William H. Frey, "Minority Turnout Determined the 2012 Election," *Brookings Report*, May 10, 2013, brookings.edu.

44. George Reed, "Resources for Voting Rights Sunday," Raleigh Report, March 12, 2013, nc-churches.org; "Sacred Conversation on Race: The Journey Continues," United Church of Christ Factsheet, Fall 2012, uccfiles.com; Aleta Payne, "Our Responsibility to Vote," NC Council of

Churches, October 25, 2012; Jerry L. Van Marter, "More than 80 Religious Groups for Passage of Voting Rights Amendment Act of 2014," June 4, 2014, pcusa.org; Mara Sawdy and Nora Leccese, *We Shall Not Be Moved: Advocacy in the New Age of Voter Suppression* (Louisville, KY: Office of Public Witness, Presbyterian Church USA, 2016); deliberate efforts to suppress Black voting by eliminating Sunday voting are described in US House of Representatives, Subcommittee on Elections, *Report on Voting Rights and Election Administration in the United States of America* (2019), 51, 132.

45. Michael Eric Dyson quoted in David A. Love, "The Progressive Interview: Michael Eric Dyson," *Progressive* 78, 10 (October 2014), 34–38, quote on page 37; Benjamin F. Chavis Jr., "Race Realities Persist in America," *Washington Informer*, November 24, 2011; and for an example of how race was skirted in discussions of diversity in three multiracial communities that had strongly supported Obama, see Meghan A. Burke, "Diversity and Its Discontents: Ambivalence in Neighborhood Policy and Racial Attitudes in the Obama Era," *Journal of Race and Policy* 6, 1 (May 2010), 80–94.

46. Michael Roman-John Koscielniak, *Ground Forces: Dirt, Demolition, and the Geography of Decline in Detroit, Michigan* (Ann Arbor: University of Michigan, PhD Dissertation, 2020).

Chapter Seven: Black Lives Matter

1. McKay Coppins, "The Christians Who Loved Trump's Stunt," *Atlantic*, June 2, 2020; Astead W. Herndon and Dionne Searcey, "How Trump and the Black Lives Matter Movement Changed White Voters' Minds," *New York Times*, June 27, 2020; Mia Jankowicz, "Trump's Evangelical Base Is Ecstatic over His Bible Photo Op, Which Many Other Christian Leaders Have Condemned," *Insider*, June 4, 2020.

2. "White Clergy and Leaders from across Faith Traditions United to Denounce White Supremacy, Debut Public Declaration against Anti-Racism," *Targeted News Service*, June 9, 2020; Jeff Barker, "Baltimore Faith Communities Rally for Black Lives Matter Movement and Call It a Beginning," *Baltimore Sun*, August 29, 2020; Jessica Lerner, "Enfield Police Chief Prays with Protesters," *TCA Regional News*, June 5, 2020.

3. Details of the events surrounding the investigation of Trayvon Martin's death are from concurrent articles in the *Orlando Sentinel* and *Florida Today*; Darryl E. Owens, "Here's Why People Are So Angry over Trayvon's Death," *Orlando Sentinel*, March 17, 2012; and Anthony Man, "Frederica Wilson Brings Trayvon Martin Case to Congress," *South Florida Sun-Sentinel*, March 20, 2012.

4. Charles M. Blow, "The Curious Case of Trayvon Martin," *New York Times*, March 17, 2012.

5. Eddie S. Glaude Jr., "Religion and Violence in Black and White," in *From Jeremiad to Jihad: Religion, Violence, and America*, edited by John D. Carlson and Jonathan H. Ebel (Berkeley and Los Angeles: University of California Press, 2012), 128–42, quote on page 130.

6. "The National Black Church Initiative Says to George Zimmerman That It Was Not God's Will to Kill Trayvon Martin," *Chicago Defender*, July 25, 2012.

7. Rev. Mark S. Hanson quoted in "ELCA Leaders Respond to the Death of Trayvon Martin," *Targeted News Service*, March 27, 2012; Jeff Kunerth, "Pastor Talks of His Journey of Understanding in Trayvon Martin Case," *Orlando Sentinel*, April 21, 2012; M. Linda Jaramillo, "Racial Profiling Has Mortal Consequences," *Sacramento Observer*, April 26, 2012.

8. "Church Condemns Zimmerman's Claim It's God's Will to Kill Trayvon," *New York Beacon*, July 26, 2012; Heidi Hall, "SBC's Richard Land Stands by Trayvon Martin Comments," *Tennessean*, April 4, 2012; David Gibson, "Land Says Obama Used Martin Case for Politics," *Christian Century* 129, 9 (May 2, 2012), 17–18.

9. Rev. Harry Rucker quoted in "Sanford Pastors Aim for Unity Amid Crisis," *Orlando Sentinel*, April 25, 2012.

10. Jeff Kunerth, "After Trayvon Was Shot, Mediator Made Sure Calm Prevailed," *Orlando Sentinel*, October 2, 2012; Jeff Weiner, "Orlando Faith Leaders: Improving Race Relations Means Building Relationships," *TCA Regional News*, June 4, 2015. Thomas Battles earned national recognition for his work in the aftermath of Trayvon Martin's death. The local group, Sanford Pastors Connecting, continued to hold monthly meetings, monitored the George Zimmerman trial, helped keep the peace when Zimmerman was acquitted, and served briefly as a model for other groups of clergy and community leaders in the region before disbanding in 2015.

11. "Protesters Rally across US after Zimmerman Acquitted," *Telegraph* [London], July 15, 2013.

12. Lizette Alvarez, "A Florida Law Gets Scrutiny after a Killing," *New York Times*, March 21, 2012; Joe Balazzolo and Rob Barry, "More Killings Called Self-Defense," *Wall Street Journal*, March 31, 2012; and on the legal arguments, Joshua K. Roberts, "Deadly Force and the Right of Self-Defense Stand Your Ground Laws," *Forensic Examiner* 22, 1 (Winter 2012), 89–92.

13. David Montgomery, "Greater St. Mark Family Church among Those Offering 'Safe Place' in Ferguson," *Washington Post*, November 23, 2014; "Ferguson Pastor Reacts to Grand Jury Decision," *All Things Considered*, November 24, 2014.

14. George Wayne Smith, "Blood Cries Out from the Ground: Reflections on Ferguson," *Anglican Theological Review* 97, 2 (Spring 2015), 255–63; Lilly Fowler, "Churches to Serve as Safe Spaces after Ferguson Grand Jury News," *St. Louis Post-Dispatch*, December 1, 2014. Tyler R. Chance, *The Church and Michael Brown: The Influence of Christianity on Racialized Political Attitudes in Ferguson, Missouri* (St. Louis: University of Missouri St. Louis, PhD Dissertation, 2021), 144–45, notes that greater distance from the location where Brown was killed appeared to have mixed results, either "insulating congregations from the unrest" or "freeing them to take action without as much risk of congregational or community backlash."

15. Osagyefo Uhuru Sekou, *God, Gays, and Guns: Essays on Religion and the Future of Democracy* (St. Louis, MO: Chalice Press, 2012); Yuri Han, "Putting His Faith in Ferguson," *Chicago Reporter* (Summer/Fall 2015), 14–15; Jeremy C. Fox, "Prayers for Peace Taking Wing," *Boston Globe*, August 18, 2014; Colin Campbell, "Church's Prayers for Ferguson," *Baltimore Sun*, August 18, 2014.

16. Matt Pearce, "An Oasis of Calm near Tense Ferguson," *Chicago Tribune*, November 24, 2014; Lilly Fowler, "On Easter, Four Pastors Reflect on Rebirth in Ferguson," *St. Louis Post-Dispatch*, April 5, 2015.

17. Frank Edwards, Michael H. Esposito, and Hedwig Lee, "Risk of Police-Involved Death by Race/Ethnicity and Place, United States, 2012–18," *American Journal of Public Health* 108, 9 (September 2018), 1241–78; Gabriel L. Schwartz and Jaquelyn L Jahn, "Mapping Fatal Police Violence across US Metropolitan Areas: Overall Rates and Racial/Ethnic Inequities, 2013–2017," *PLoS One* 15, 6 (June 2020), e0229686; T. K. Barger, "'Black Lives Matter' Focus of Churches

on Sunday," *TCA Regional News* [Chicago], December 12, 2014; "Local Churches Joined Pastor Jamal Bryant and Others in the National #BLACKLIVESMATTER Solidarity Movement," *Speakin' Out News* [Huntsville, AL], December 17, 2014.

18. Barbara Ransby, *Making All Black Lives Matter: Reimagining Freedom in the Twenty-First Century* (Berkeley and Los Angeles: University of California Press, 2018); Keeanga-Yamahtta Taylor, *From #BlackLivesMatter to Black Liberation* (Chicago: Haymarket, 2016); Anthea Butler, "Black Lives Matter," *Christian Century* 133, 6 (March 16, 2016), 24–47, 29–31.

19. Mark Oppenheimer, "A Debate over Black Lives Matter," *New York Times*, January 23, 2016.

20. Lawrence T. Brown, "The Movement for Black Lives v. the Black Church," *Kalfou* 4, 1 (Spring 2017), 7–17; similar conclusions were drawn in research described in Korie L. Edwards and Michelle Oyakawa, *Smart Suits, Tattered Boots: Black Ministers Mobilizing the Black Church in the Twenty-First Century* (New York: NYU Press, 2022).

21. "How Donald Trump Feels about Black Lives Matter," *Jacksonville Free Press*, September 24, 2015.

22. Barbara Marshall, "Vandal Fails to Sway Pastor," *Palm Beach Post*, September 7, 2015; Perry Stein, "The Bethesda Church Whose 'Black Lives Matter' Signs Were Vandalized Has a New Way to Spread Its Message," *Washington Post*, October 7, 2015; James Joiner, "Church Gets Violent Threats over 'Black Lives Matter' Sign," *Daily Beast*, September 11, 2015.

23. Cora Jackson-Fossett, "LA Clergy Demand Apology from Black Lives Matter," *Los Angeles Sentinel*, October 29, 2015; Angel Jennings, "Some Clergy Keep Black Lives Matter at a Distance," *Los Angeles Times*, August 29, 2016.

24. Beatrice Dupuy, "Clergy Take Their Place in Protests," *Star Tribune*, December 15, 2015.

25. Luke Broadwater, "Police Brace for March," *Baltimore Sun*, April 25, 2015; Jonathan Pitts, "Voices of Local Pastors Shape Calls for Justice," *Baltimore Sun*, April 25, 2015; Rachel Weiner, "Maryland Senators Introduce Post-Freddie Gray Legislation," *Washington Post*, June 15, 2015; Jennifer E. Cobbina, *Hands Up, Don't Shoot: Why the Protests in Ferguson and Baltimore Matter, and How They Changed America* (New York: NYU Press, 2019), 72–102.

26. Celeste Kennel-Shank, "Clergy on the Front Lines in Charlottesville," *Christian Century* 134, 19 (September 13, 2017), 12–13.

27. Jack Jenkins, "Faith-Based Protesters Flock to Washington to Counter White Supremacists," *Salt Lake Tribune*, August 13, 2018.

28. Elijah Anderson, "Emmett and Trayvon," *Washington Monthly* 45, 1/2 (January/February 2013), 31–33.

29. John D. Delehanty, "Prophets of Resistance: Social Justice Activists Contesting Comfortable Church Culture," *Sociology of Religion* 77, 1 (Spring 2016), 37–58, quote on page 51.

30. David Anderson, "Episcopal Bishops Condemn Racism in Letter," *Washington Post*, May 7, 1994.

31. Garrett Naiman, *Plugging into Movement Work: White Racial Justice Action in the Era of Colorblind Racism* (San Francisco: University of San Francisco, PhD Dissertation, 2016), 204, 207.

32. Jim Wallis, *America's Original Sin: Racism, White Privilege, and the Bridge to a New America* (Ada, MI: Brazos Press, 2016); Jeff Kunerth, "Pastors Work to Advance Racial Understanding,"

Orlando Sentinel, April 27, 2015; T. K. Barger, "United Church of Christ Pastor Attempts to Bridge Race Divide," *TCA Regional News* [Chicago], November 5, 2016, who notes how Dorhauer's work has been informed by his study of UCC history; and "White Privilege in the United States," *Book of Resolutions* (Nashville, TN: United Methodist Publishing House, 2016), Resolution #3376.

33. Christopher Keating, "Privilege? Nah. Not Me," *St. Louis Post-Dispatch*, May 12, 2018.

34. Reverend Traci Blackmon quoted in John Eligon, "Where Today's Black Church Leaders Stand on Activism," *New York Times*, April 3, 2018.

35. Miguel De La Torre quoted in "Southern Baptist Churches Try to Diversify," *Indianapolis Recorder*, March 6, 2015.

36. Cheryl Townsend Gilkes, "Lift Every Voice? White Domination Still Matters, Even in Sacred Space: A Sociologist's Reflection on 'Sounding Black, Acting White,'" in *Sounding Together: Collaborative Perspectives on US Music in the 21st Century*, edited by Charles Hiroshi Garrett and Carol J. Oja (Ann Arbor: University of Michigan Press, 2021), 138–44, quote on page 142.

37. For the contrast between racial reconciliation and racial reckoning, repentance, and restitution, see Audra L. Savage, "Aunt Jemima's Resignation Letter," *Columbia Law Review* 121, 7 (November 2021), 186–219.

38. William H. Brackney, *Historical Dictionary of the Baptists* (Lanham, MD: Scarecrow Press, 2020), 429; Deborah Yaffe, "Seminary Pledges to Set Aside $27.6 Million as Reparations for Its Ties to Slavery," *Princeton Alumni Weekly*, November 13, 2019; Rachel L. Swarns, "Is Georgetown's $400,000-a-Year Plan to Aid Slave Descendants Enough?" *New York Times*, October 30, 2019.

39. Raphael G. Warnock, *The Divided Mind of the Black Church: Theology, Piety, and Public Witness* (New York: NYU Press, 2014), 175.

40. Among other examples of anti-racism study guides, see Presbyterian Church USA, *Facing Racism: A Vision of the Intercultural Community Antiracism Study Guides* (Louisville, KY: Presbyterian Church USA, 2016) and United Church of Christ, *White Privilege: Let's Talk* (Cleveland, OH: United Church of Christ, 2016); there were also guides for clergy, for example, John Cleghorn, *Resurrecting Church: Where Justice and Diversity Meet Radical Welcome and Healing Hope* (Minneapolis, MN: Fortress Press, 2021) and Karen A. McClintock, *Trauma-Informed Pastoral Care: How to Respond When Things Fall Apart* (Minneapolis, MN: Fortress Press, 2022).

41. Maggie Potapchuk, "Assessment Report of the Synod Anti-Racism Teams in the Evangelical Lutheran Church in America," MP Associates, Inc., 2008, offers insights into how the ELCA anti-racism effort that preceded many of the other denominations' initiatives was organized.

42. Mark Pattison, "Bishops Overwhelmingly Approve Pastoral against Racism," *National Catholic Reporter*, November 14, 2018; Bishop Michael Curry quoted in Vickie Oliphant, "Michael Curry Royal Wedding Sermon," *Express* (London), May 20, 2018.

43. "Feds Deliberately Targeted BLM Protesters to Disrupt the Movement, a Report Says," NPR, August 20, 2021; Philip Gorski, "White Christian Nationalism: The Deep Story behind the Capital Insurrection," ABC Religion and Ethics, January 13, 2021, abc.net.au. And for an in-depth analysis of the ethno-nationalism behind the insurrection, see especially

Philip S. Gorski and Samuel L. Perry, *The Flag and the Cross: White Christian Nationalism and the Threat to American Democracy* (New York: Oxford University Press, 2022).

44. Robin DiAngelo, *White Fragility: Why It's So Hard for White People to Talk about Racism* (Boston: Beacon Press, 2018), and Robin DiAngelo, *Nice Racism: How Progressive White People Perpetuate Racial Harm* (Boston: Beacon Press, 2021).

45. George Schroeder, "Seminary Presidents Reaffirm BFM, Declare CRT Incompatible," *Baptist Press*, November 30, 2020; D. A. Horton, "Voices with Ed Stetzer: A Missiological Assessment of Critical Race Theory," *Church Leaders*, September 23, 2021; Morgan Lee, "Critical Race Theory: What Christians Need to Know," *Christianity Today*, July 2, 2021.

Conclusion

1. Although progressive faith communities' activism was long overshadowed in the media by the Religious Right and although scholarly attention has focused considerably more on evangelical Protestantism than any other sector of American religion, there have been a number of valuable contributions in recent years to the study of progressive faith-based social activism, among which several volumes that offer excellent overviews and case studies include Ruth Braunstein, Todd Nicholas Fuist, and Rhys H. Williams, eds., *Religion and Progressive Activism: New Stories about Faith and Politics* (New York: NYU Press, 2017); Grace Yukich and Penny Edgell, eds., *Religion Is Raced: Understanding American Religion in the Twenty-First Century* (New York: NYU Press, 2020); Jason S. Lantzer, *Mainline Christianity: The Past and Future of America's Majority Faith* (New York: NYU Press, 2012); and Darren Dochuk, ed., *Religion and Politics beyond the Culture Wars: New Directions in a Divided America* (Notre Dame, IN: University of Notre Dame Press, 2021).

2. See Paul Spickler, *Reclaiming Individualism: Perspectives on Public Policy* (Bristol, UK: Bristol University Press, 2013), for a succinct discussion of the varieties of individualism; a valuable treatment of individualism in relation to racial inequality is Nancy DiTomaso, *The American Non-Dilemma: Racial Inequality without Racism* (New York: Russell Sage Foundation, 2013), who, like other scholars, emphasizes the extent to which racial inequality is rooted in attitudes about people working or not working hard and being responsible for their own difficulties in life. For those interested in an illuminating discussion of religion's role in this kind of individualism, see Christopher D. Jones and Conor M. Kelly, "Sloth: America's Ironic Structural Vice," *Journal of the Society of Christian Ethics* 37, 2 (Fall/Winter 2017), 117–34.

3. Michael O. Emerson and Christian Smith, *Divided by Faith: Evangelical Religion and the Problem of Race in America* (New York: Oxford University Press, 2000), and Paul Lichterman, *Elusive Togetherness: Church Groups Trying to Bridge America's Divisions* (Princeton, NJ: Princeton University Press, 2005), are two quite different studies that emphasize the role of individualized religious beliefs in impeding racial justice, drawing these insights from research among evangelical Protestants but in ways that pertain more broadly to US Christianity; and on individualism in progressive faith communities, see Wade Clark Roof, *Spiritual Marketplace* (Princeton, NJ: Princeton University Press, 1998), and Rhys H. Williams, "The Languages of the Public Sphere: Religious Pluralism, Institutional Logics, and Civil Society," *Annals of the American Academy of Political and Social Sciences* 612 (2007), 42–61. A focus-group study of pastors and congregations

challenged the prevailing wisdom about individualism, though, by showing that individual-level explanations of racial differences were seen as the products of structural constraints; Daniel Bolger and Elaine Howard Ecklund, "Seeing Is Achieving: Religion, Embodiment, and Explanations of Racial Inequality in STEM," *Ethnic and Racial Studies* 45, 1 (January 2022), 3–21; perhaps suggesting that clergy could find more effective ways about discussing the connections between individual and structural differences.

4. See John D. Delehanty, "Prophets of Resistance: Social Justice Activists Contesting Comfortable Church Culture," *Sociology of Religion* 77, 1 (Spring 2016), 37–58, who characterizes this kind of individualism as "cultural orientations that stem from deeply rooted ideas about what religious commitments are, how religion should be practiced in local communities, and the broader role of religious culture in American civic and political life," and which require the formation of an alternative discourse of public religion.

5. Eduardo Bonilla-Silva, *Racism without Racists: Color-Blind Racism and the Persistence of Racial Inequality in the United States* (Lanham, MD: Rowman and Littlefield, 2019); for an insightful discussion of colorblindness as a narrative about America, see Ruth Braunstein, "The 'Right' History: Religion, Race, and Nostalgic Stories of Christian America," *Religions* 12 (2021), 1–21.

6. Jacqueline Yi, Nathan R. Todd, and Yara Mekawi, "Racial Colorblindness and Confidence in and Likelihood of Action to Address Prejudice," *American Journal of Community Psychology* 65, 3–4 (June 2020), 407–22. Colorblindness was measured by a battery of questions assessing students' unawareness of racial privilege, institutional discrimination, and racial issues. The students who scored higher on colorblindness showed less empathy toward other racial groups. They also were less likely to say that they would act against prejudice. The results, the authors suggested, reinforced the idea that an awareness of racial inequality is necessary before people are likely to do much to address it.

7. Studies of post-colorblind initiatives suggest they may be easier to implement in new congregations than in established congregations and that a congregation's desire to grow can be an incentive for a program that aligns the congregation more closely with the racial and ethnic demographics of its community. Another takeaway is that post-colorblind initiatives are improved by the presence of a Black or Hispanic staff person—if that person is not treated merely as a token of inclusion; Christopher W. Munn, "Finding a Seat at the Table: How Race Shapes Access to Social Capital," *Sociology of Religion* 80, 4 (2019), 435–55; Carolyn Smith Goings, *Racial Integration in One Cumberland Presbyterian Congregation: Intentionality and Reflection in Small Group* (Los Angeles: Antioch University, PhD Dissertation, 2016).

8. Michelle Boorstein, Julie Zauzmer, and DeNeen L. Brown, "On the Anniversary of Martin Luther King Jr.'s Death, Faith Groups Rally to Combat Systemic Racism," *Washington Post*, April 4, 2018.

9. Thomas H. Lee, *Towards Color Brave Multiculturalism at Grace Chapel: Considering the Progress of the Multicultural Initiative* (La Mirada, CA: Biola University, DMin Dissertation, 2021); additional examples are discussed in Sarah Shin, *Beyond Colorblind: Redeeming Our Ethnic Journey* (Downers Grove, IL: IVP Books, 2017).

10. See, for example, William Donohue, "Meet the New Racists," *Eurasia Review*, July 6, 2021; Benjamin Wallace-Wells, "How a Conservative Activist Invented the Conflict over Critical Race

Theory," *New Yorker*, June 18, 2021; David Theo Goldberg, "The War on Critical Race Theory," *Boston Review*, May 7, 2021.

11. Erica Jane Dollhopf, *The Causes and Consequences of Formalization and Professionalization in the US Advocacy Sector, 1960–2009* (State College: Pennsylvania State University, PhD Dissertation, 2016).

12. Edward C. Polson and Rachel Gillespie, "The Bridging Activity of Multiracial Congregations," *Religions* 10 (2019), 1–14, identifies external ties with interracial and other service programs as an additional contribution of multiracial congregations.

13. Douglas S. Massey, "Segregation and Violent Crime in Urban America," pp. 317–44 in *Problem of the Century: Racial Stratification in the United States*, edited by Elijah Anderson and Douglas S. Massey (New York: Russell Sage Foundation, 2001), 341; see also Michael T. Light and Julia T. Thomas, "Segregation and Violence Reconsidered: Do Whites Benefit from Residential Segregation?" *American Sociological Review* 84, 4 (2019), 690–725, and on the implications of housing policy, Edward G. Goetz, *The One-Way Street of Integration: Fair Housing and the Pursuit of Racial Justice in American Cities* (Ithaca, NY: Cornell University Press, 2018).

14. David E. Kresta, *Can Churches Change a Neighborhood? A Census Tract, Multilevel Analysis of Churches and Neighborhood Change* (Portland, OR: Portland State University, 2019); Junia Howell and Michael O. Emerson, "Preserving Racial Hierarchy amidst Changing Racial Demographics: How Neighborhood Racial Preferences Are Changing while Maintaining Segregation," *Ethnic and Racial Studies* 41, 15 (2018), 2770–89.

15. Ingrid Ellen, "Welcome Neighbors? New Evidence on the Possibility of Stable Racial Integration," *Brookings Report*, December 1, 1997; "'Don't Put It Here!' Does Affordable Housing Cause Nearby Property Values to Decline?" NYU Furman Center, 2008.

16. Michael Mascarenhas, Ryken Grattet, and Kathleen Mege, "Toxic Waste and Race in Twenty-First Century America: Neighborhood Poverty and Racial Composition in the Siting of Hazardous Waste Facilities," *Environment and Society* 12, 1 (September 2021), 108–26.

17. Jacob S. Rugh, "Why Black and Latino Home Ownership Matter to the Color Line and Multiracial Democracy," *Race and Social Problems* 12, 1 (March 2020), 57–76.

18. Laura R. Olson, "Mainline Protestant Washington Offices and the Political Lives of Clergy," in *The Quiet Hand of God: Faith-Based Activism and the Public Role of Mainline Protestantism*, edited by Robert Wuthnow and John H. Evans (Berkeley and Los Angeles: University of California Press, 2002), 54–79.

19. Among studies suggesting connections between participation in religious congregations and specific kinds of involvement in charitable, volunteer, and advocacy activity, see Paul A. Djupe and Laura R. Olson, "Diffusion of Environmental Concerns in Congregations across the U.S. States," *State Politics and Policy Quarterly* 10, 3 (Fall 2010), 270–301; Allison Schnable, "Religion and Giving for International Aid: Evidence from a Survey of U.S. Church Members," *Sociology of Religion* 76, 1 (Spring 2015), 72–94; and Paul A. Djupe, "The Effects of Descriptive Associational Leadership on Civic Engagement: The Case of Clergy and Gender in Protestant Denominations," *Journal for the Scientific Study of Religion* 53, 3 (September 2014), 497–514; on faith communities' ties to external organizations, see especially Ammerman, *Pillars of Faith*; on social capital in faith communities, see especially Robert D. Putnam and David E. Campbell, *American Grace: How Religion Divides and Unites Us* (New York: Simon and Schuster, 2010);

and on the related topic of philanthropic giving, a useful summary of the literature is provided in Rene Bekkers and Pamela Wiepking, "Who Gives? A Literature Review of Predictors of Charitable Giving, Part One: Religion, Education, Age and Socialization," *Voluntary Sector Review* 2, 3 (2011), 337–65.

20. Jason Roach and Jessamin Birdsall, *Healing the Divides: How Every Christian Can Advance God's Vision for Racial Unity and Justice* (Epsom, UK: Good Book Company, 2022); Donald Heinz, *Matthew 25 Christianity: Redeeming Church and Society* (Eugene, OR: Cascade Books, 2022).

21. My thoughts about disagreement among faith communities and the contribution of this disagreement to an agonistic understanding of democracy are found in Robert Wuthnow, *Why Religion Is Good for American Democracy* (Princeton, NJ: Princeton University Press, 2021).

INDEX

A NOTE ON THE TYPE

This book has been composed in Arno, an Old-style serif typeface in the
classic Venetian tradition, designed by Robert Slimbach at Adobe.